Masala Memsahib

Recipes and Stories from My Culinary Adventures in India

KAREN ANAND

First published 2022 by Macmillan
an imprint of Pan Macmillan Publishing India Private Limited
707 Kailash Building
26 K. G. Marg, New Delhi 110 001
www.panmacmillan.co.in

Pan Macmillan, The Smithson, 6 Briset Street, London EC1M 5NR
Associated companies throughout the world
www.panmacmillan.com

ISBN 978-93-90742-04-2

1 3 5 7 9 8 6 4 2

Designed by Haitenlo Semy
Printed and bound in India by Replika Press Pvt. Ltd.

AUTHOR'S NOTE

India has given me a great life full of incredible memories, laughter, learning and joy. One helluva rollercoaster ride really! It has given me people to adore and people who adore me, friends I cherish and a career I love. Most importantly, I have had the privilege of being around some of the best food in the world and have come close to the people who create it. It has been, and continues to be, one long, delicious journey of discovering and experiencing food with depth and complexity, humour and humility. India is larger than life and undergoes perpetual challenge and change. As does its food. So here is a glimpse of my adventures with the unbelievable food of this country.

EXI

Indian food is still heavily misunderstood and misrepresented. I am growing weary of the homogenized puddles of red/yellow/brown oily gravies with bits of meat or vegetables floating around in many Indian restaurants in the name of 'Indian' food. These 'curries' in no way represent the lightness and the sensitivity of home cooking.

I once told the great Indian culinary impresario, Jiggs Kalra, that, while I considered his work on traditional Indian recipes invaluable, it would take me a week to gather all the ingredients for any one! Tradition and documentation are important but let's be practical. The narrative has changed. Many old Indian recipes belong to a particular context situated at a particular time, region and season. It is virtually impossible to find some of those ingredients today.

Today, more than ever, we need to somehow find that right balance between taste, health and tradition. We need a culinary response to fast lives. Modern Indian food can be fast but it need not be junk. You just need to make informed decisions on where your produce is from, how it is farmed and for how long it is stored. In this day and age of processed food, genetically modified plants, hormone-injected meats and chemically sprayed fruits, vegetables and grains, we have to take responsibility for what we put into our bodies very seriously, no matter what we are cooking.

Was I faced with a difficult choice? Not at all! I simply didn't include such ingredients in the book. I may make a passing reference to them, but my intention is not to waste your time or energy on the impossible in the name of 'authenticity'. What I do hope all the recipes share is a genuineness and practical approach to cooking today. I have based the ingredient tables on what is available in India but have tried, wherever possible, to provide alternatives, available without too much of a hassle in major European and American cities. What has also helped the sourcing of ingredients enormously are platforms like Markets by Karen Anand – which I created nine years ago to bring together small producers of organic and natural products from across India. Many of these producers use creative and well-designed packaging and have moved into retail, online and export. Efforts and initiatives of this kind have made many ingredients I use in this book available across the country and abroad.

SOME BACKGROUND

I grew up in London in the sixties and seventies with a mother who cooked because she had to, not because she wanted to, and a father who never entered the kitchen except to eat. They argued and bickered and my mother never forgave him for bringing her to 'this cold country' but they were completely united in one thing – their love for Indian food and the fact that they missed it. My father talked endlessly of hot, crusty *brun* with lashings of malai from the top of the milk, which he used to eat at Irani cafes in Bombay then. He drooled at the mere mention of '*kheema gutli*' and 'bun chop', favourites at St Mary's, the school he went to in Byculla. St Mary's must have been one hell of a place if you can still remember what you ate there after forty years!

He talked about the salt beef his mother used to make when he was a child, and of Christmas cake and the blessed batter which had to be stirred for hours in the days before mixers, food processors and blenders. He missed kebabs and biryani and *balchao* and *bhel*. He missed what he called 'tart' – raw mangoes at the onset of summer, *imli* from the street carts parked outside the school and sour *bora* or dry *ber* – brown berries sprinkled with rock salt. He had very clear ideas about the food he liked and disliked, the nostalgia made all the more potent by the lacklustre of the English table then. He used to make sneak visits to Wembley for *chivda* and to an Indian butcher, Mr Sheikh, for Indian mutton or goat. My parents disliked British lamb which they found smelly and insipid. My father would wait patiently for my mother to run out of Basmati rice or fresh coriander so that he could drive to Southall (which was quite a long way). Groceries were an excuse to stop at the mithai shop for *chum chums*, *gulab jamuns* and chocolate *barfi*. As children, we were well acquainted with a hotchpotch of Indian flavours, but completely ignorant as to the background and history.

My mother confused our culinary heritage further. She grew up in a half-Parsi, half-Goan household in Bombay. You can imagine the chutney of cuisines and cultures there. But it was Bombay's restaurants that made her eyes sparkle. Bombellis at Breach Candy and 'Continental' food at Gourdon somewhere near Churchgate, Chinese at Nanking behind the Taj and Lobster Thermidor at The Little Hut at the top of The Ritz. She experienced Bombay in its heyday in the 1950s, walked to work from Breach Candy to Kemps Corner where she worked in a French company and had a snazzy wardrobe. Her tailor was her best friend and on an average day she looked like a Hollywood star. When she married my father, the fun continued. The cooks walked in and she never needed to step into the kitchen – not, that is, until she reached England. They were not only united in their love for the Indian table but their dislike of English food. They found it bland, boring and tasteless. They thought the British idea of a sandwich for lunch was laughable and my poor mother, who I'm convinced never really liked to cook, ended up slaving over a hot stove every day.

Consequently, we were brought up on a strange mix of European-looking dishes which tasted Indian and Indian 'curries' which began with onion, ginger-garlic and Italian tomato puree. Don't get me wrong, everything tasted good. It just all tasted the same. There was no distinction between, say the punch of a *Rogan Josh* or the subtlety of a fish *caldin*. It was mutton curry, beef curry, prawn or chicken curry. My mother rarely made fish curry in England because she said the fish had no taste. She opened packets of coconut cream with great finesse, and she soon discovered a miracle marriage-saver called 'Kashmiri masala' made by the pickle people, Pataks. This was the answer to all her problems, the cure all and the ultimate 'must' in every one of her Indian dishes, whether it was dal, vegetable or pork chops. My father learned to cook in his sixties when my mother began to spend a lot of time playing grandmother to my two boys in India, with much the same repertoire.

Hence, my early memories of Indian food were not very defined and certainly not based on any real knowledge in the intellectual sense. My mother had a great 'hand'. She made very authentic *batata vadas* and excellent *puris*. She always cooked rice in a handi with a tight-fitting lid and placed a tea towel between the lid and the utensil at the end of cooking to absorb any condensation. I have copied her. The rice always comes out perfect. She could never roll a roti to save her life. Neither can I. But she put things together in a matter of minutes and could set an extraordinary table (mainly courtesy Marks and Spencer's). That's my British Asian heritage.

After I finished school, I went to Paris for a year to ostensibly master the language. By day I attended the Sorbonne but I really woke up in the evenings and was out meeting friends every night of the week. 'Cuisine' was a heavy part of my syllabus and I had excellent teachers – a wonderful and dedicated nanny from Lyon who cooked in the style of Bocuse – classic, traditional French; a photojournalist with a penchant for quick, quality dishes which usually translated into a perfectly grilled lamb chop and a salad; and a host of student friends, all of whom had at least one speciality each. I also discovered that men cooked quite happily in France, as opposed to the men and boys I knew from the Indian subcontinent who did well to find their way to the kitchen. There was no discrimination between the sexes across the Channel and specifically in the kitchen. Men took pride in cooking and showing off about it. They chose the wine and cheese with awareness. Not surprising since their fathers had probably done the same thing. I had some of the best meals at homes of some of my male friends who opened oysters by the dozen and served perfectly chilled Muscadet along with them. Not very creative, but it took a lot of devotion to open a hundred oysters in one evening. The same bunch prepared excellent onion tart, cabbage stuffed with baby pigeon and could select magnificent cheese.

I was once asked to cook 'Indian' in Paris and concocted something which looked like koftas in a masala gravy or what my mother called 'ball curry'. I had found the famous Kashmiri masala in a grubby Indian grocer near St Denis. It met with great applause. I became a pretty good cook churning out a handful of Indian dishes, but my culinary education was from the French school of gastronomy. I learned the meaning of the word 'quality', how to shop, where to shop, how to avoid supermarkets like the plague, how to pick a perfect Brie, which dressing went with which salad and why and how to handle a leg of lamb. I learned which cut of meat to use for each dish and why the age of the animal was so important to cooking. I was taught well and I was an eager and willing student. When I returned to University in England, the country had become much more cosmopolitan and wiser in matters of food. The British began drinking wine like they were born to it and eating quiche like it was their national dish. I approached all this trendy hype with my nose firmly in the air. I was beyond all the fluff. I had lived in Paris. Nothing could better that.

It was decided by majority vote one day that each one in our flat on campus would cook for the rest of us once a week. I looked through all the fancy recipes I had accumulated and painstakingly written down only to be told that the rest of them wanted me to make a curry. 'A curry,' I thought in disgust. 'Me make curry?' I was appalled. My protests fell on deaf ears. Apparently, Coq au Vin was too elitist. Curry was fine for the proletariat. Instead of calling mother and asking for help, I rushed out and brought a book by a lady called Madhur Jaffrey. Her recipes were amazingly accurate and brought Indian cooking out of the restaurant and into the kitchen. She also gave you very convenient alternatives if you didn't have the authentic ingredients. This little paperback became my Bible for the next four years. To everyone's amazement, and mine, I turned out fabulous *koftas*, *parathas* and *baingan ka bhartas*. I learnt to follow flavours and not just instructions.

From then on, there was no looking back. I became a fiend with the frying pan. Wherever I travel, whether it is Italy or Spain, Hong Kong or Bali, food is my ambassador. It opens difficult doors and helps me make lifelong friendships. And yes, I always sneak in my *potlis* of masalas because I never know when someone is going to ask me to cook something Indian – Malvani masala from India's west coast and *Kolhapuri* masala from Maharashtra, both stone ground in small batches by hardworking ladies, *panch phoran*, the five spice blend from West Bengal, fresh curry leaves picked from the tree in my garden, washed and wrapped in kitchen paper and packed in ziplock bags, pepper from Goa and Kerala and tea from Darjeeling (that's to soothe my nerves after cooking) – all these Indian Cooking 101 essentials go into the side pockets of my suitcase. I often recreate recipes included in this book and I use my masalas both in traditional recipes and to enliven contemporary everyday cooking.

I arrived back in Bombay towards 1984 (we had emigrated in 1966) and the rest, as they say, is history. I started cooking European food and experimenting with ingredients available in India. I became known professionally as 'the Salad Queen' because of my specialty – salads. Each was a different, composite recipe gleaned from my travels, and presented in a different manner. I looked to Europe for inspiration, especially the sunny countries of the Mediterranean since that is what I knew and what I felt would work well in India. I started experimenting and learning about Indian ingredients and cooking techniques. I applied all the principles of great cooking and sourcing I had learned in France and found that they had been doing the same thing in India ... and for probably much longer. The only difference being, the French wrote everything down in detail and our culinary knowledge was, for the most part, verbal.

Cooking Indian food has been an acquired skill for me. Even though I grew up in a home fond of traditional Indian food, there were no 'grandmas' around. My first professional training was in French cooking, and I applied those skill sets to document interesting Indian recipes. This gave me the confidence to write a book for both novices and intermediary cooks who have a basic understanding of cooking and a passion for Indian food. *Masala Memsahib* is an easy guide through the flavours of India for anyone ready to experiment.

Now to explain the title of this book. 'Masala' is a term that is often used synonymously with Indian food and, by extension, popular Indian culture. When, in reality, it does not denote a generic Indian curry, rather a spice mix, a combination of spices ground together in the form of a dry powder or combined with water or vinegar to make a paste, usually destined for a particular dish. This masala, the unique combinations of spices, is the key to unlocking and demystifying the secrets of Indian cooking. Understanding the essence of each spice and the flavour it brings to a dish is key to adapting it to any ingredient. And having mastered this, even an amateur can easily play around with Indian food without being overwhelmed by daunting instructions.

'Memsahib' is a term of respect for a woman of a certain age, usually with means, in India. I use it playfully with tongue firmly in cheek referring to myself as I take you on this culinary journey.

Masala Memsahib is a collection of my favourite home-style recipes from India, steeped in tradition, some hidden secrets and some twists – they span my journeys through this vast country over the last thirty-five years. Some of the recipes that follow have been shared with me by great chefs and friends, others by homemakers, some were written on the back of a napkin, others over messaging apps and most were verbal and began with '... take some chilli powder and a handful of ... ' It was up to me to figure out the origins and name of the chilli, its potency and how much really a 'handful' weighed. For, as is with Indian cooking, '*andaaz*' or an estimation is the consistent form of measurement across the subcontinent.

This collection offers a glimpse into my personal culinary adventures in India and the chapters that follow are representative of many years of travelling for pleasure, work and shoots. I had three television series on-air in the 1990s; the one for Star TV was called *The Good Food Guide* which ran to fifty-two episodes. It was quite path breaking for its time in India and took me across the country to discover the world of both home and professional cooks. Half the time, there was no proper script so what emerged was quite real and unrehearsed – an unconscious forerunner of reality TV! In these fifty-two episodes, I ran into many many wonderful people – some great closet cooks, some great storytellers and others who introduced me to both. They are all special and they all play a significant part of my culinary education.

I start with Goa because that's the closest to my heart and heritage and the recipes are so spot on I could recreate them blindfolded! Maharashtrian food is rarely written about and, since I live here and am exposed to several communities within this state, I had to take on the challenge of writing down family recipes and nuances. With the increase in vegetarianism globally, the land of Gandhi was an obvious choice for a totally vegetarian chapter. I would like to stress here that Indian vegetarians are mainly so as a result of religion or upbringing and not so much for health reasons, so there is no holding back when it comes to fat, sugar and butter! They are not necessarily vegan. The vegan movement in India is indeed significant but relatively new. I love Kerala and travel there whenever I can. I love the integrity of the food, the purity of the landscape and the clearly defined flavours which are consistently delicious. You either love or hate Kolkata. It is falling to pieces but there is also great beauty in the city and the obsessive arguments over food are unbelievable. Lastly, a collection of special recipes and people from all over India make up the last section of the book – Memorable Meals.

While I was choosing recipes for this book, I was also curating the menu for a new Indian restaurant I was working on in London called Colonel Saab. I realize my choices overlapped. While I wanted to include only unusual recipes and go down the untrodden path of 'firsts', I had to be mindful of ingredient availability and palate. So each chapter of this book contains some familiar, some hopefully new and many definite keepers. Thanks to the pandemic, I had time to finally write this book, put together the recipes, choose my favourites and cook them all. Then thanks to Colonel Saab – the award-winning restaurant in central London for which I curated the menu – I tried and tested many of the recipes once again, some of which are on the restaurant menu. I hope to take you behind the scenes and share with you a slice of India that you may or may not have seen; a look at the way we really cook with recipes relevant to today's style of living. The idea is to give the reader an insight into the flavours of Indian cuisine through understanding the foods of different regions and how the palate differs across the subcontinent. The end result, I hope, is perfect whichever country you live in. I consider myself an accomplished cook but certainly not a chef. I don't compromise on taste and I never compromise on good quality ingredients.

So here are a hundred or so of my favourite recipes, personally experienced, eaten and enjoyed from my wanderings all over the country. It is by no means an attempt at naming the 'the best 100' or anything like that. I sincerely apologize if your favourite Indian cuisine or recipe is not included. No black daal or butter chicken in this book, I'm afraid!

farmers' market
by Karen Anand
Fly Emirates

GOA

Most people don't know that I have Goan ancestry. Though I have never lived in Goa, I have been visiting regularly for over thirty-five years. India's sunshine state has attracted wave after wave of migration, from Europeans looking for a bit of inexpensive, warm bliss, to the Indian 'literati' who seek the tranquillity to be creative. As for me, it is the Goa of great food and culinary traditions that I love to explore in a laidback setting. There is still a very fine, deep-rooted food tradition and a love for life that is second to none. Scratch the surface and you'll find it. I anticipate each visit with a yearning to eat, drink and relax – my holy trinity – and to feel blessed by the sight of Goa's rich red soil and swaying palms. Over the years, I have also discovered its backwaters, local haunts, ingredients and seasonal nuances.

The Portuguese came to India well before the British or the Mughals and left Goa as recently as 1961, after 450 years. They had a remarkable influence on this territory and introduced many ingredients now common in Indian cooking from their exploits in South and Central America, like the chilli, tomatoes, cashew, corn, potatoes and pork. The Portuguese loved the Goan mango so much that they grafted new varieties or cultivars with Portuguese names like Alfonso (after Nicolau Afonso the botanist). It was the Jesuit priests who brought with them science and botany and 'baptized' new mango species with the same missionary zeal that they displayed while converting locals to Catholicism. These new, baptized varieties were later sent to Brazil, renamed again, and then trailed through the Philippines and Mexico. The Mughal Emperor Akbar also propagated the Portuguese grafts across his orchards in Bihar, which after much refinement and through the years became the *Langra*, *Dassheri*, *Chausa* and *Totapuri* varieties common in India today.

The effect of the cultural amalgamation due to Portuguese Catholic priests sent to Goa and from Portuguese men incited by handsome rewards of lands and other benefits if they married native women, has been a unique cuisine which combined Catholic Iberian with local Hindu Saraswat. Portuguese soldiers and artisans, who married after arriving in India, were allowed to leave the royal service and settle down as citizens or traders. They were called *Casados* or married settlers. The intention was to create a community of people faithful to the Portuguese to carry on trade as well as to maintain the *Estado da India Portugesa*. It resulted in a unique Goan lifestyle and cuisine quite distinct from other parts of the country.

So what is Goan food? For the uninitiated, it usually starts at a beach shack. They offer no nuance, no subtlety and no claim to originality but they are right on the beach. Nothing beats that! Stick to a beer and watch the sunset – that's my advice. Try not to eat in one. Visit a modest local restaurant or speak to a Goan home cook and that is where you will encounter a rich culinary world – a world where Portuguese customs intermingle with local traditions, where both Portuguese dishes and (Gaud) Saraswat kitchens have secrets to share and where restaurant food catering to the tourists' palates is light years away from home-style dishes. Goan food has been documented but not always with accuracy. It isn't easy to write down a complicated recipe as somebody throws pinches of many spices into a pan spluttering with oil. Traditional dishes also require a great deal of grinding masalas to an excruciating fine paste and slow cooking. While everyone wants the definitive prawn curry recipe, it is not always possible to get it right if you live outside Goa; the chillies are different and the kokum is not as fresh. Even accomplished Goan cooks go off track in search of easier options. If you really want to attempt a traditional *vindalho* (no, not *vindaloo*), you'll find one in the pages that follow. And if you would like to create the essence of Goa but only have a few minutes, then you will want my simple recipe of prawns with kokum (also included in this section).

But first a note on ingredients. Both Catholics and Hindus in Goa use coconut in all its forms – creamy milk, grated flesh and the water for drinking – and both eat all manner of seafood and poultry. The Goan Catholic repertoire has a local soul and a Portuguese spirit. The community uses kokum and tamarind as souring agents for their seafood and vinegar made from the palm sap, called *toddy*, for pork and beef. The Hindus in Goa restrict themselves to mutton and chicken as well as seafood and vegetables, and commonly use kokum and *triphal* or *teflan* (a sour spicy local black berry) as souring agents.

When I am in Goa, the first thing I do is make a pilgrimage to Mapusa market (pronounced 'mapsa') in North Goa. I have been coming here for longer than I care to remember and most of the local vendors have remained and look the same as if they have a secret painting which is ageing somewhere à la Dorian Gray. I like to think it has something to do with the food, the lifestyle and the *feni*. Spices are a great buy here; wonderfully aromatic, punchy, locally grown black pepper, rolled cinnamon (probably from Sri Lanka), highly aromatic cardamom and Kashmiri chillies. It's not that any of these spices (except the pepper) are grown locally but they are all used in Goan dishes on a daily basis so the quality you find in Goa is superlative. I buy grayish sea salt, which is collected from the salt flats during the rains and makes all the difference to a prawn curry; kokum so fresh that your fingers turn purple when you touch it, red unpolished rice and pyramids of black coconut palm jaggery which reminds me of the treacle pudding of my childhood days in England.

The *poder* delivering Goan bread or *poiee* on a bicycle, with the quick sound of a tolling bell at the crack of dawn, is part of every Goan household's morning ritual. Wholemeal *poiee* made with bran is similar to wholemeal pitta bread. They have a large area devoted to these breads at Mapusa Market. They also sell the slightly crusty, bow-shaped white bun *cathro* and the white crusty bangle-shaped one called *cancom*. The Portuguese introduced leavened bread into Goa and subsequently the rest of the country. I also find vendors peddling their homemade tender mango pickle in brine, *miscut* – a spicy pickle made with whole tender raw mangoes, *para* – a spicy fish pickle usually made with dried, salted mackerel and a red spicy pickle with dried Bombay duck. Next, I stop at Simonia, a sweetmeat shop in the centre of the covered market, for *dodol* – a dark brown toffee-like sweet made from coconut milk and jaggery, *perada* – guava cheese, *doce de Grao* – made from lentils, sugar and coconut, *batika* – a flat coconut cake with lattice pastry and, of course, *bebinca* – a layered dessert which takes much patience and skill to produce and is made from coconut milk, sugar, egg yolks and flour.

I stock up on *feni*. I like to drink it with fresh pineapple juice or Sprite and a squeeze of lime. The locals drink it neat! This is a local distilled clear alcohol made from the heady aromatic cashew fruit or from the coconut palm. It is cheap, cheerful and available in every watering hole in Goa. Traditionally sold in large containers known as *garafaons* directly from the source, *feni* now has a Geographical Identification (GI) classification which has moved it out of the 'country liquor' category and into a new 'heritage liquor' classification which will hopefully raise the bar and the image of *feni*. The first distillation is called *uraq* and is only available in April, the second

distillation is made into *feni*. The Portuguese brought cashew trees to Goa from Brazil and planted them on hillsides to prevent erosion along the riverbanks. The cashew nut, which dangles on the outside of the fruit, served as a cash crop and the fragrant nectar of the fruit was distilled into the local brew. A true connoisseur will only drink 'cashew'. A hidden gem is a visit to the Cazulo *feni* distillery, a farm-to-table experience owned by Hansel Vaz who also owns the best-looking liquor shops in South Goa and a great bar – Tesouro by Firefly. The *feni* tour starts with a welcome drink featuring *feni*, Sprite and a pepper leaf! You take a look at the sorting, crushing and fermenting process of the cashew juice in eighty-year-old terracotta pots, with no added yeast, distilling in copper stills. The tour ends with an interactive tasting of their three *fenis* paired with a board of Goan and European delicacies. The last stage is done in their tasting room which is filled with Hansel's collection of glass *garafa* – gigantic glass bottles where they stored alcohol or wine – some of which date back to the eighteenth century and which came from Europe. Interestingly, their cashew *feni* paired exceedingly well with Goa sausage (even with the vinegar) and other spicy, savoury items and the palm *feni* went distinctively better with fruit and vegetables.

The people that feature here, my friends and family, are all very special, as are their recipes that made this section of my food adventures possible.

NAOMI AND LENNY MENEZES

Naomi and Lenny Menezes aren't your everyday Goan couple, but aspects of their lifestyle are. Widely travelled with homes across the world, they have now planted their roots, metaphorically and physically, on their glorious Goan estate – Quinta de Menezes – in the slightly off grid North Goan village of Pilerne. The thing about Goans who have travelled is that, when they come back home, they combine their love for tradition with a lighter and easier approach to everyday meals. They have shown me that it is possible to keep Goan flavours intact without the fuss of traditional methods. Lenny, after his retirement from the highest echelons of the hospitality industry (his last stint was as chairman of Hilton India), now makes sourdough bread and delights his guests with homemade pickles and fruits and vegetables from their organic backyard garden. Naomi was an absolute whizz on Whatsapp, pen and plate in hand ferreting treasured recipes out of old families and helped me to research terms and traditions. Together they were the most generous hosts who set a table that could feed the entire village. From a whole red snapper which Lenny would have gone down to the docks to choose himself, to the most divine velvety prawn curry, an invitation to dinner at Quinta de Menezes has always been a highlight of my trips to Goa. As this book goes to edit, I am saddened to share that we lost Naomi to cancer late last year.

CHEF URBANO REGO

Chef Urbano Rego has been a legendary figure at the Taj Holiday Village in Goa for as long as I can remember. Humble beyond belief, he looked after us as a family for many years and introduced me to facets of Goan cuisine to which I was clueless. A true Goan by birth and in spirit, he once took me on a tour of Mapusa Market (thankfully not on an over-crowded Friday when the market is at its robust best) to discover the treasures of the sea during the rains. It is generally advised not to touch fish in months which don't have the letter 'r' (May to August) for three main reasons: first, because fish decomposes easily and the fishing boats stay out at sea for close to three days; second, it is spawning season so we will eventually deplete their numbers and, third, it is unsafe for fishermen to venture out during the often rough Monsoon rain. This was July and the fish market was surprisingly packed with all manner of creatures that I had never seen before – *choncul* (a small variety of bhetki), *veleu* (a tiny silver fish similar to fresh anchovy), *candoeur* (a round, flat, vaguely striped blackish creature), *coro*, *shetuk*, *thomosa* (red snapper), stingray and many types of clams, crabs and mussels. From the month of May till late September, sea water and its great variety of marine life is allowed to drift into the many salt pans of Goa and fishing is restricted to ponds, rivers and the sandy shore. According to Rego, the distinct flavour of Monsoon fish comes from the salt pans. Reams have been written about Rego. He has an unbelievable 'hand', especially when it comes to traditional Goan and Portuguese Goan food. I have been known to daydream about his prawn curry, clams in coriander and steamed prawns with kokum. His guidance helped me decide when and how to retain the traditional flavours and authenticity of Goan cooking in recipes.

CAETANO D'COSTA

Caetano D'Costa worked as a cook at the old Mandovi hotel in Panjim which overlooks the Mandovi river. At one time, the hotel was the only place you could find both exceedingly good Goan Catholic and Hindu Saraswat food. It was the kind of place smart Goan families would take grandma for Sunday lunch. The dining room had a sort of faded elegance ... heavy Indo-Portuguese furniture, worn velvet upholstery and Amália Rodriguez playing softly in the background. From this setting, Caetano jumped to village life. We discovered him in the mid–1980s when he had just built an unattractive concrete structure in front of his modest home in Saligao. The kitchen was opposite the eatery and food would literally be thrown from the frying pan to the fire and in a matter of minutes be on your table with some rough and tumble cabbage salad on the side. He used to be highly embarrassed when I stood and watched his theatricals from the kitchen window. He also served home-brewed *uraq* in season and palm and cashew *feni* from the tiny bar for the princely sum of ₹2. The 7UP I had along with it was ₹7. I imagine this has gone up a bit but surely not by that much. His chicken *cafreal* is legendary, especially good after a night of partying in Goa. The chicken is marinated in a green masala overnight and then pan fried with a weight on top. This is salt of the earth Goan food at its best.

MARIE WADIA

Every family in Goa and indeed every Goan family throughout the world (you will find large pockets of them in the US, Canada, UK, East Africa and Australia) has its own prawn curry recipe. Since my family's culinary heritage was a bit of a cocktail, our recipe is tainted with a touch of Parsi and a generous sprinkling of cosmopolitan Bombay. My great aunt Marie Wadia, whose recipe I share in this section, made a mean prawn curry which I considered traditional, that is, until I went to Goa. She cooked her masala in thin coconut milk and sometimes added ground sesame seeds to thicken the curry. She also threw in okra which were meticulously picked from Bhaji Galli near Grant Road Station, each no longer than three inches in length. The prawns had to be small and white with very little or no black vein. In Goa, she would have used freshwater prawns from Goa's backwaters. In her days, pre-made coconut milk and cream were not available. You had to go through the laborious process of removing the outer husk of a dried coconut, then scrape off the brown skin and finally grate the white flesh in a grinder, continuing on to a fairly messy process of squeezing the first and second milk through a muslin cloth. Traditionally, a *villi* is used which is used to both grate coconut and clean fish. I remember trying to be clever and putting coconut bits into a mixer with hot water and running it at full speed, thinking I could simplify the

process; the lid flew off because of the pressure, leaving me to clean the snowy coconut off my kitchen walls for days. Making any curry with coconut milk was an ordeal in those days. Then came along well-packaged coconut milk in tins and tetra paks which gave perfect results everytime and didn't 'split' even if you left the stove on carelessly, as I sometimes do. It allows you to make velvety coconut curries at the drop of a hat. In villages in Goa, a coconut curry would be cooked in a heavy terracotta pot known as a *modki*, available in most Goan open markets. I still use that sometimes or cook in a stone pot from Kerala known as a *kalchetti*. This much tradition I can manage and I like to think it does make a difference to the taste.

MARIA DE LOURDES FIGUEIREDO DE ALBURQUERQUE

Maria De Lourdes is nothing short of an enigma. A force to reckon with in any of the three languages she speaks fluently, you wouldn't want to be up against her in a debate anywhere. She was a member of parliament in Portugal in the late 1960s and recounts with great honesty her meetings with the dictator Salazar. She is also the perfect hostess who carried on the tradition of grand entertaining and supporting her family mansion in Loutolim in South Goa. We were honoured to be the first people she had ever allowed to photograph her home. She comes from a family of distinguished advisors to the government and lawyers who were also great patrons of the Arts (both local and Portuguese) and fine living. Dinners in the old days would be for a minimum of sixty people and featured canapés, a soup, cold fish, a meat main course, a leg of ham from Portugal, asparagus imported from Holland and roast turkey as a centre piece. Today her teatime spread consists of *apa de camarão* (a prawn and rice cake), a few almond cakes, her famous orange roll, *empadinhas* (little pork pies), chicken tart and *rissois*. She passed away peacefully at her home aged ninety-two in 2021. Her daughter Fatima has returned from Portugal and converted the main house into a museum of sorts and the other side into a stunning heritage homestay, keeping both heritage and home intact.

DOMINIC & ROSALINA FERNANDES

Dominic and Rosalina make undoubtedly the best *Chouriço* in Goa. This is a small family business worth talking about. They do everything – from raising the pigs and brining the pork to grinding their own masala in their homemade *toddy* vinegar and hand-filling the sausages. The sausages are then slow smoked over burnt coconut shells, dried, cured and smoked again. Very few traditional food artisans still smoke Goa sausages in this way. They now have a store selling their sausages in Varca in South Goa, opposite the Church. I must admit, I miss the days of walking into their once humble home past the sausages drying over fire, greeting a smiling Rosalina wearing a bright coloured dress, making her famous masala. I would then go outside to claim my bounty from Dominic who would be wrapping my package in the local newspaper.

CORINNE MIRANDA

Corinne Miranda dreamt of having her own traditional Goan Restaurant, a dream she finally realized in 2007 when she opened her restaurant in Candolim, North Goa.

The restaurant was called Corinne's, although a more appropriate name would have been 'Flying to Feasting', since she was a stewardess with Air India for many years. Her homestyle cooking is tasty and delicious. She even makes all her own pickles and chutneys. A meal in her home is a treat beyond words.

CELIA AND RUBEN VASCO DA GAMA

I had heard about the great restoration work Celia and Ruben had been doing since 2002 to bring the Palacio do Deao (the Dean's Mansion) back to life. I had also heard about the great food they serve at lunch. For some strange reason (probably laziness), I had never visited till quite recently and was bowled over by both the setting and the exquisite food Celia cooks. The house belonged to Jose Paulo de Almeida, a priest from Braga in Portugal, who came to Goa as part of the entourage of the archbishop in the late eighteenth century. He loved the village of Quepem in South Goa and built this spacious mansion which he modestly described as a farmhouse and divided his time between the Diocese in Old Goa and his home in Quepem. Ruben and Celia came upon the house in ruins and, since Ruben had already undertaken the restoration of the Tiracol Fort in North Goa, decided to undertake restoration of this house and the beautiful gardens. In 2006, they moved in and Celia set about putting together a fabulous Portuguese Goan menu which they still serve to guests at lunch only (through prior reservations) on the enchanting terrace at the back of the mansion. Home-brewed *feni*, kokum squash, followed by a volley of deliciousness which could include fresh crab salad, *rissois de camaro*, some vegetarian dishes, including her signature pumpkin pie, whole fried sea bass, prawn curry and rice and a creme caramel with a whiff of fresh orange for dessert. This is an original farm-to-table story in such a wonderful heritage setting!

ST. FRANCIS
XAVIER

1 Crab Salad

2 Dry Prawn Relish – Kismur

3 Pallacio Do Deao Pumpkin Pie

4 Creamy Coconut Beans – Feijoada

5 Masala Fried Fish – Fish Reichado

6 Spicy Pickled Prawns – Prawn Balchao

7 Portuguese Style Prawn Patties – Rissois De Camarao

8 White Pumpkin with Shrimp – Doodhi Ros

9 Steamed Prawns with Kokum

10 Two Prawn Curries

11 Pork Belly with Cumin and Black Pepper – Pork Jeere Meere

12 Pork Cooked with Vinegar, Spices and Garlic – Pork Vindalho

13 Choriz and Bacon Pullao

14 Brinjal Pickle

15 Pancakes Stuffed with Black Jaggery and Coconut – Alle Belle

CRAB SALAD

This is Celia Vasco da Gama's deliriously delicious and extraordinarily simple crab salad. For a perfect result, your crab must be really fresh. If you are using fresh crab, buy the biggest available simply because it is quite tedious to clean small crabs. If using tinned crab, I would add more seasoning to pep it up ... think chopped green chillies, fried onion and garlic and a dash of mustard.

***Serves:* 2**

INGREDIENTS

1 heaped cup or 150 g crab meat
2 tbsp thick fresh cream
2 tbsp dry white wine
1 tbsp chopped parsley
A pinch of red chilli powder
Salt and black pepper to taste

METHOD

First cook your fresh crab in boiling salt water. The cooking time will depend on the size of your crab. A large one should take around 10 minutes. Use a pair of tongs to remove the crab from the water and leave it to cool. Break its tail flap from the underside and discard. Twist off the two claws and legs. Then, using a crab pick or a marrow spoon (basically anything long, thin and rigid), start removing the flesh. The claws will need cracking with a hammer. Try and make one large crack to avoid shattering the shell. The aim is to keep the shells intact to serve the crab. The feathery looking gills in the body of the crab, also called 'dead men's fingers', need to be thrown out.

To remove any fishy odour from the shells, add some vinegar or lemon juice to a large pot of water, enough to submerge the shells completely. Bring to the boil. Remove and leave the shells to dry completely.

If this initial preparation sounds like too much work, fresh crab meat is available, failing which the last resort is tinned crab meat.

Finally, combine the cream, white wine, salt, pepper and chilli powder into a pan and heat gently. Remove the sauce from the fire, cool to room temperature and toss into a bowl with the crab meat and some parsley. Fill the crab salad into the crab shells to serve.

DRY PRAWN RELISH

KISMUR (PRON: KISS-MOOR)

So what happens, I wondered, during the monsoon in Goa, when fisherfolk lay down their nets to rest? What happens to the great Goan lust for fish? Does the fun-and-frolic end and do all Goans go into a state of passive dormancy until marine life reappears in September? Hell no! Trust the Goans to not take this lying down. A little rain is not going to stop them from getting their daily fix. They carefully dry the fish, conjure up a whole new repertoire of dishes which feature dried fish and prawns as a base. *Kismur* is a dry prawn relish that satisfies one's desire for seafood when it is not freshly available. Most Southeast Asian countries that have a coastline possess a specialty salad or relish using dried prawns or fish. The Goan one is either made with fried onions and roasted coconut or raw onions and roasted prawns. I prefer the latter and that's the one I am sharing with you.

Serves: 4

INGREDIENTS

1 cup dried prawns (preferably with shell)
2 tsp coconut oil
1 tbsp tamarind pulp
1 tsp red chilli powder
¼ tsp turmeric powder
1 large onion, finely chopped
½ cup fresh coconut, grated (or ¼ cup desiccated)
¼ cup fresh coriander leaves
2–3 pieces of kokum (optional)
Salt to taste

METHOD

In a hot frying pan or griddle, roast the dried prawns in the coconut oil till they turn golden and crisp. Toss them into a bowl with the rest of the ingredients and mix gently. Garnish with fresh coriander leaves. Serve at once. *Kismur* works gorgeously well when served with hot steaming rice and prawn or fish curry.

PALLACIO DO DEAO PUMPKIN PIE

Celia Vasco da Gama sets a truly mindfully sourced table at their restored mansion and home, Pallacio do Deao, in South Goa. Apart from all the authentic fish and prawn dishes, I was really impressed with her vegetarian spread – something you rarely find in Goa. She does a smashing *methi bhaji* with garlic, onion and a hint of chilli; stuffed baby aubergines; a lovely fresh salad with seasonal fresh strawberries; a beetroot salad with sour cream and this marvellous dish of creamy, soft-baked pumpkin, which my husband gobbled up entirely. The Portuguese make a sweet pumpkin pie with cinnamon. This is her savoury version.

Serves: 4

INGREDIENTS

600 g red pumpkin (butternut squash), chopped
3 cloves of garlic, sliced
1 tsp oil
75 ml water
100 g mild cheddar cheese, grated
1 tbsp butter
1 boiled potato, mashed or grated
Sea salt to taste
⅛ tsp freshly ground black pepper
A pinch of grated nutmeg
3 eggs, yolks and whites separated

METHOD

In a pan, heat the oil and add the sliced cloves of garlic and fry till lightly golden. Put the water and chopped pumpkin into a saucepan, cover and cook till the pumpkin is just tender. The water will have almost disappeared. Remove the sauce pan from the stove and add some grated cheese, butter, boiled mashed potato, sea salt, freshly ground black pepper, fried garlic and nutmeg. Beat this mixture with a fork till smooth or blend with a hand blender. Keep it aside for about half an hour to allow the flavours to develop. In a separate bowl, beat the egg yolks and mix into the pumpkin mixture. Whisk the egg whites till stiff and fold into the mixture. Transfer to a baking dish and bake in a preheated oven for 20 mins at 180C. Eat warm.

CREAMY COCONUT BEANS

FEIJOADA (PRON: FAIR-JOO-AHDA)

Goa is one region in India where dal or lentils are not usually eaten, but the Goans do have *feijoada*. *Feijoada* comes from the Portuguese word *feijão*, which means beans. Feijoada is a popular slow-cooked black bean stew in Brazil and Portugal which is made tastier with salted and smoked pork and can also include 'cheaper' cuts like pig's ears, feet and tails and beef tongue. The rich, smoky stew is then served with rice, sautéed collard greens or kale, orange slices and topped with toasted cassava flour. It is comfort food for the soul. In Goa, people sometimes also throw in a piece or two of Goan sausage (*chouriço*) for flavour. This vegetarian version is prepared using coconut milk which adds a creamy texture in lieu of the pork fat.

Serves: 4

INGREDIENTS

1 cup black beans or kidney beans
2 tbsp oil
2 onions, finely chopped
4 cloves of garlic, crushed coarsely
4 bay leaves, crushed
4 cloves, crushed
4 cups vegetable stock or water
2 medium tomatoes, peeled and grated
1 tsp mild red chilli powder
½ cup coconut milk
Salt to taste

METHOD

Soak the black beans overnight in water. Wash them in several changes of water and soak in fresh water overnight or for at least 4–6 hours. The beans will swell to double their size. In a pressure cooker, heat the oil and fry the onions and garlic till they turn golden. Add the crushed bay leaves and cloves. Drain the beans of their water and wash again in fresh water once. Add the beans and 4 cups of vegetable stock to the onion and garlic and cook until the beans are soft. This should take around 10–12 minutes in a pressure cooker and at least 35 minutes in an open pan. Once the beans are cooked, add the tomatoes and chilli powder and stir well on a low flame for about 10–12 minutes. Add the coconut milk and salt to taste. Simmer on a low flame until the gravy thickens. Serve your creamy coconut beans with rice.

MASALA FRIED FISH

FISH REICHADO (PRON: RAY-SHAD)

Florentine has been running for over twenty-five years. With its limited menu and homestyle way of functioning, this little eatery in Saligao serves some of the best and the most reasonably priced Goan food in North Goa today. Run by the young, ever-smiling Florencio Caetano, Florentine is a family business worth talking about. With very little catering background – Caithan, as he is called – dressed always in shorts, t-shirt and flip flops, makes a sublimely gentle pomfret *reichado* and a chicken *cafreal* which he is renowned for. It's a wonder anybody can find this tavern, which is down the alley next to Cottage Industries in Saligaon, on the Candolim–Panjim Road. I was introduced to it one late monsoon evening by Lance Lobo of Captain Lobo's Hideaway. After an evening of heady bar hopping, we badly needed food and, since it was off-season, most restaurants had shut early or altogether. 'You'll get the best chicken *cafreal* in town here,' boasted Lance. Unfortunately, by the time we staggered in, Caithan was closing for the day, but, after some reasonable groveling, he generously gave us one of the *cafreals* he had saved for his own family dinner. Hot, pan-fried and heavy with green masala, the chicken hit the spot. We returned to Florentine's on several occasions and in several different seasons, to find the quality of the chicken and everything else on the menu as magnificent as the first time. But here is Florentine's *reichado*, which I honestly love more than the *cafreal*.

Serves: 4

INGREDIENTS

For the main dish

4 mackerel or 2 medium-sized pomfret or 1 large red snapper, whole and gutted
1 tsp salt, juice of 1 lime
4 tbsp *reichado* masala
Oil, for shallow frying

For the *reichado* masala

8 Kashmiri dried red chillies, seeds removed
½ tsp cumin seeds
½ tsp cloves
1 tsp black peppercorns
6 cloves of garlic
¼ tsp turmeric powder
1½ inch fresh ginger, peeled and coarsely chopped
1 tsp salt
½ cup vinegar (preferably *toddy*)
½ cup vegetable oil

METHOD

Combine all ingredients for the Reichado masala in a mixer/grinder/blender and grind to a fine paste.

Clean and wash the fish well and make a slit along both sides of the backbone, almost across the fish. Rub some salt and lime juice all over the fish, leave for 15 minutes, drain and pat dry.

In a pan, heat 2 tbsp of oil and cook the spice paste over a gentle heat until it is no longer raw – until the oil separates. This will take 3–5 minutes. Remove from the heat and let it cool to room temperature. You can store this paste in the fridge for a week or in the freezer for months. Rub the fish all over and inside with the spice paste or, like Caithan, stuff the masala into the fish. In case the fish is large, tie it together with string. Heat the remaining oil in a frying pan and shallow fry the prepped fish over medium heat. Turn and cook the fish twice till it turns golden. Serve hot straight from the pan.

Tip: *If you are not used to frying and flipping fish, please toss the fish in some plain flour before frying and use a nonstick pan.*

SPICY PICKLED PRAWNS

PRAWN BALCHÃO (PRON: BAAL-CHOW)

Traditionally, *balchao* is a tangy prawn pickle. This is my grandmother Angelica D'Lima's recipe which my mother had to 'coax' out of the old lady's long-serving maid and confidante. Her *balchão* was legendary in the village of Aldona where she lived but she shared the recipe with no one.

Serves: 6

INGREDIENTS

1 kg raw medium white prawns, cleaned and deveined (about 40 pieces)
2 tbsp salt
4 cups oil
6 inches ginger, chopped
2 medium onions, finely chopped
25 cloves garlic, chopped
½ cup sugar
1 cup natural vinegar (toddy/ coconut/malt)
2 tbsp dried prawns, roasted and powdered
4-6 green chillies, slit vertically

For the masala
(ground to a fine paste)
30 dry red Kashmiri chillies (washed well)
1 tsp cumin seeds
2 tsp turmeric powder
1 tsp whole black pepper
*1 cup *toddy* or malt vinegar

METHOD

Mix the prawns with the salt and keep aside for 20 minutes. This will draw out any excess water. Drain and pat dry. Heat half the oil and fry the prawns for 3–4 minutes only. Keep aside. Heat the remaining oil in a big cooking pot. Fry onions, ginger and garlic until golden. Add masala paste and fry for a further 10–15 minutes on low heat until the masala is cooked and comes away from the edges. Add fried prawns, sugar, dried powdered prawns and the vinegar. Stir and add slit green chillies. Cook for around 7–10 minutes. Cool.

Traditionally, this recipe uses small prawns but I often make this with large ones and serve it warm as a main course.

PORTUGUESE STYLE PRAWN PATTIES

RISSOIS DE CAMARÃO (PRON: RISHOY-EES)

Many moons ago, there was a Park Hyatt in Goa. The then general manager, Paul McNally, was keen to incorporate the best of 'local' to integrate with the local community. He even named their bar 'The Miranda Bar' after Goa's famous cartoonist Mario Miranda whose ancestral house was nearby. The Hyatt kitchens weren't open yet and his yearning for local food was satisfied by his driver's wife's exceptional cooking. The lady in question was called Sarita, a home cook till then. He decided to dedicate a space to a fine-dining Goan restaurant but couldn't find a chef who produced anything close to Sarita's cooking. He finally offered Sarita the job and decided to name the restaurant after her. Today, the restaurant is called 'Tempero' and has been taken over by the ITC group. I can't imagine if back then Sarita understood the enormity of this responsibility. She and I became friends. Her 'hand' was exceptional and she found it tough to explain the idiosyncrasies that come with homestyle dishes to the male hotel chefs. We worked on several recipes together, but I couldn't get enough of her little half-moon Portuguese pasties, *rissois*. You rarely find *rissois* in restaurants today because they are such a faff to get right. Sarita's are the best with a crispy pastry and unctuous creamy prawn filling.

Serves: 4

INGREDIENTS

½ cup water
50 g butter
½ tsp salt
75 g flour
1 onion, chopped
100 g small fresh prawns, shelled, cleaned, deveined and chopped
5 tbsp thick fresh cream
¼ cup milk
1 egg, beaten
½ cup breadcrumbs
Oil for deep frying

METHOD

For the dough

In a saucepan, add the water and bring to boil. Remove the pan from the heat and add butter, salt and the flour. Stir well until you get a smooth dough. In case the dough is still wet, put it back on a low heat for just a minute to cook it properly. Once cooked, roll out the dough quite thin, about ⅛ inch, while it's still warm.

For the filling

Heat a little oil in a pan and add chopped onion. Fry till translucent. Add the cleaned prawns to the pan and fry for 2 minutes. Reduce the heat and add the milk and cream. Cook until the sauce turns thick and creamy. Remove the pan from the heat and set it aside till it completely cools down.

For the assembly

To prepare the *rissois*, cut out circles from the rolled dough, each about 2-inches in diameter, usinga cutter or pressing down a small glass. Place a tablespoon of the prawn filling on each circle, fold in half (crescent shape) and seal the edges by pinching them. Dip the raw *rissois* in beaten egg and then roll in breadcrumbs. Heat oil in a pan and deep fry the parcels till golden. Place the *rissois* on paper towels to drain out the extra oil and serve hot.

WHITE PUMPKIN WITH SHRIMP

DOODHI ROS (PRON: DOODHEE-ROSS)

This unusual vegetable dish epitomizes the best of Goan homestyle cooking. My grandmother used to make it with dried or fresh prawns. Goans are not overly fond of vegetables, although every home garden tends to grow baby aubergines, red amaranth leaves, fat orange pumpkins, chilli plants and a maze of creepers with long white pumpkin or gourd. Even small plots will have coconut trees planted to ensure the supply of fresh coconuts for the year and a *bimbli* bush – an ingredient used for souring seafood curries. When we travelled to Goa with some vegetarians, twenty years ago, we had a hard time finding anything halfway decent for them to eat. Today you'll find a huge variety of vegetables in the markets which supply the many new European- and Asian-style restaurants that have cropped up in the state. Most homestyle vegetables are still simply prepared, stir-fried with a little chilli, garlic and sometimes onion and will almost always be tossed with some grated coconut or tiny dried prawns 'for flavour' as my grandmother would say!

Serves: 4

INGREDIENTS

For the paste

1 cup fresh coconut, grated
1 tsp cumin seeds
4 cloves of garlic
½ inch piece of ginger
1 tsp coriander seeds
½ tsp turmeric powder
3 whole green chillies
1 tsp tamarind pulp

For the main dish

2 tbsp dry shrimps (peeled)
4 tbsp oil
2 onions, chopped
1 tomato, chopped
2½ cups white pumpkin (bottle gourd), peeled and cut into 1½ inch cubes
Salt to taste

METHOD

In a mixer/grinder/blender, add all the ingredients for the paste along with a cup of warm water and grind to a fine paste. Pass this paste through a fine sieve or a muslin cloth to extract the juice. Discard the remaining coconut spice paste. We now have our coconut masala.

Soak the dry shrimps in water for 10 minutes and then drain. Heat the oil in a pan and fry the onions till they turn golden. Add the chopped tomato and cook till it softens. Add the cubes of white pumpkin and the dry shrimps and cook for a further 5 minutes, partially covered, on a low heat. Add the extracted coconut masala to the vegetable-shrimp mix and bring it to just under a boil. Simmer for 10 minutes till the gravy thickens. Add salt to taste. Serve hot with Goan bread or rice.

STEAMED PRAWNS WITH KOKUM

Goa, for me, means indulging in at least one great meal by Chef Rego at the Taj Holiday Village. I once told Rego, after a week of total gluttony in Goa, that I needed something simple and fresh from the sea – inspired by Goa but without all that masala. He came up with this dish which he said was often made at his home on the island of Deewar. He tossed fresh jumbo prawns with their shell into a *modki* or terracotta pot with a few ingredients. The result was divine – light and flavourful with the aroma of the sea and the lasting memory of Goa. It was the kind of dish that makes you want to pull out the antique china and invite everybody over.

***Serves:** 4–6*

INGREDIENTS

1 kg large fresh white prawns, with shell (about 20 pieces)
2 onions, sliced roughly
2 dried red chillies, torn by hand
3 green chilies, slit
5–6 pieces of kokum
1 tsp sea salt
7–8 cloves of garlic, crushed
2 tbsp olive oil

METHOD

Thoroughly wash your fresh white prawns. Cut down the back of the prawn shell with a scissor to devein, if necessary (*white prawns from ponds and rivers generally have little or no vein to speak of*). Pat them dry and place them in a clay pot. Throw in the roughly chopped onions, the red and green chillies, kokum, sea salt and crushed garlic, and cover the pot with a tight lid. Keep on low heat for about 8–10 minutes. Remove the lid and drizzle olive oil on the cooked prawns. Serve hot out of the pot.

***Tip:** If you don't have a clay pot, you could choose to use any heavy-bottomed pan with a tight lid. The quality and variety of prawns differs from country to country. If you feel the prawns are sticking to the bottom of the pot, feel free to splash upto half a glass of dry white wine.*

TWO PRAWN CURRIES

The quintessential dish of the Goan table must be prawn curry. Every family in Goa has its own version of this famous dish. Slight differences in recipe distinguish whether the cook is from the north or south of Goa, whether Hindu or Christian, Brahmin or not. It is all revealed through one simple curry! Some households add grated coconut to the spice paste as a thickener; others fry the masala in oil before adding the coconut milk. I share with you my family recipe which is by no means traditional, but the result is a delicious, delicate curry with no oil. My great aunt **Marie Wadia**, who shared this with me, lived in Bombay. She added *bhendi* or okra which adds texture to the dish and probably because of the sour note in the curry by way of kokum or tamarind, the okra doesn't become slimy. There is nothing worse than snotty, slimy okra, trust me.

My old friend **Naomi Menezes**, who retired in Goa and spent a considerable amount of time getting to the bottom of things, enlightened me on what a 'real' Goan prawn curry should taste like. In her version, the deep orange/red masala paste is ground on a stone slab, a sort of flat mortar and pestle called *sil batta*. If the paste is to be refrigerated and used every day for say a week, you grind it with a little vinegar. If it is to be used right away, then you grind it with water. The paste must be absolutely smooth with no bits at all. You then fry a little onion till it turns translucent (not brown) and cook the paste with it on a very low flame. Once the masala is cooked (a few minutes at the most), you throw in the prawns, green chillies and the coconut milk and then add some tamarind for sourness. According to Naomi, fresh tamarind pulp is used with prawns or delicate fish like pomfret and the exceedingly sour black kokum is used to sour oily fish like mackerel. Local Goan families will also sour seafood with a fresh gherkin look alike called *bimbli* which grows wild in many gardens in Goa. In the mango season, they use raw mango as a souring agent. Incidentally, vinegar in Goa (toddy or malt vinegar) is generally only used with meat and never with seafood. Since Naomi passed away before I could lay my hands on her recipe, I share with you **Catherine D'Mello**'s. My son spent many a summer at her house with her grandson Karl and swears it is the best prawn curry he has had (outside our home of course!).

This reestablishes for me the essential difference between home and restaurant cooking. Home cooking is born of love, generosity and warmth. Even if the domestic cook, who relies on memory and not a written recipe, can't produce the same thing every time, it really doesn't matter. Restaurant cooking counts precision, consistency and expertise among its virtues, not to mention the ability to accurately replicate the dish. If you visit Goa, you will notice a sizeable difference between a prawn curry prepared in a restaurant and one made at home. In fact, I've had curries made with powdered or canned coconut milk in hotel restaurants surrounded by a mass of coconut trees. The excuse given is that 'there's nobody to go up the tree anymore'.

One thing that unites all these recipes, whether from a Goan from Boston or Bombay, London or Lisbon, is that only the fiercely red but deceptively mild Kashmiri chilli is used in the spice paste. Kashmiri chilli is a mildly spicy, highly flavourful, dried red chilli grown in Karnataka. It has little to do with Kashmir today. (*The original Kashmiri chilli is still grown in Noor Bagh and Pampore in Kashmir but the harvest is too small to send outside the state. The new Kashmiri chilli is a hybrid and the biggest producer of this strain, interestingly, is Karnataka*). There is a similar chilli in this region called *Bedige* or *Byadgi* chilli (pronounced: bed-gi). If you can't find Kashmiri chilli, this is a worthy substitute with a similar flavour sans the vibrant red colour. Whole Kashmiri red chillies, when made into a paste, produces a riot of red coloured sauce with a much milder heat than you would expect. In Goan markets, you do find other varieties of dried red chilli sold in small quantities from local, small holdings. I often buy these for fun and use them in a steamed prawn with kokum recipe or toss them with mushrooms and garlic just to test their intensity and flavour.

Prawn or fish curry is traditionally eaten with unpolished, short grain red rice. My highly anglicized

Bombay Goan father preferred long grain basmati so I never tasted the real deal until I came to India on holiday when I was sixteen. That is when I first relished my maternal grandmother's prawn curry. She lived in an old house in the stunning village of Aldona. The curry she made with coconuts from her garden and freshwater white prawns, which were still wiggling when they arrived at the kitchen door, is a memory I will cherish forever. She cooked the curry in an earthenware pot ever so gently over coconut husk and wood fire and served it with mountains of steaming red rice. She never wrote anything down and died before my interest in food took a professional turn. What I do share in this book though is her infallible recipe for prawn balchao, which can be made as a pickle or a glamorous main course with large shrimp or crayfish.

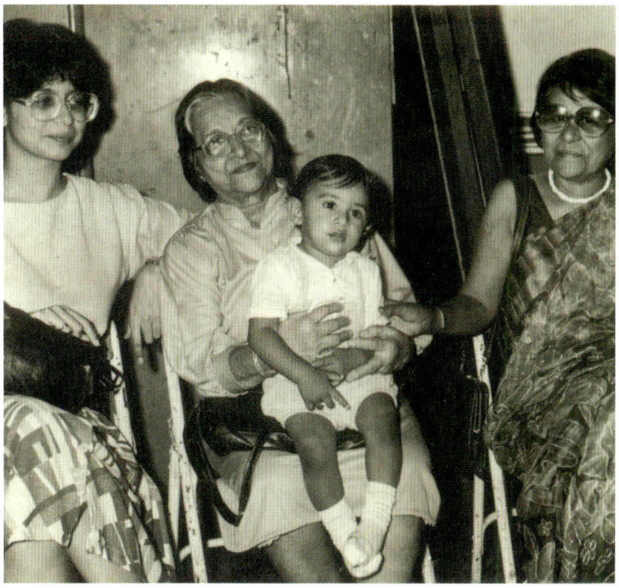

AUNTY MARIE'S PRAWN CURRY WITH OKRA

Serves: 4

INGREDIENTS

For the spice paste

12 dry Kashmiri red chillies
1 tsp black peppercorns
1 tsp cumin seeds
¼ tsp turmeric powder
10 cloves of garlic
1-inch piece of fresh ginger
Salt to taste

For the prawn curry

1 cup thin coconut milk
1 cup thick coconut milk
500 g small/medium-sized raw prawns, peeled and deveined
200 g small okra, topped and tailed with one vertical slit
4–5 pieces of kokum
Salt to taste

METHOD

Combine all ingredients for the spice paste in a mixer/grinder/blender and grind with a little water. Put the spice paste into a heavy-bottomed pan and combine it with the thin coconut milk. Cook on a very low heat and slowly stir until the masala cooks. This will take about 7–10 minutes and the colour will change from orange to a deep red colour. Add the thick coconut milk a little at a time, while stirring continuously, until it is all incorporated. Throw in the kokum and simmer. Add the prawns and okra just before serving and cook on a low heat, for about 5–7 minutes, till just done. Add salt to taste. Serve hot with steamed rice. The same masala can be used for fish curry (no need to use the okra). Sprinkle the fish with some salt and drain of any excess water before adding to the curry. Throw in some slit green chillies towards the end of cooking. Serve hot with unpolished red rice.

Note: *If you are using canned or tetra pack coconut milk, add 2:1 ratio coconut milk to water for thin coconut milk.*

CATHERINE D'MELLO'S PRAWN CURRY

Catherine D'Mello is the archetype Goan grandmother with children and grandchildren who congregate at her family home in Moira with all their friends every vacation. Like a lot of Goans, she lays a splendid table and produces not only traditional favourites like prawn or fish curry ('there would be a riot if that wasn't on the table,' she exclaims), but also her own twists and turns on *bhendi, baingan* and beef. Her food style is robust, full-flavoured and, more than anything else, she seems to love feeding family, friends and most of all her grandchildren. Her version of the prawn curry is a family recipe which 'stretches' to serve many because grated coconut is added to the spice paste for bulk. You will sometimes see beach shacks serving up a curry with bits of tomato, fried onion and green chillies. That's not wrong either. Catherine doesn't like the idea of 'bits' in her curry and grinds the whole lot up into a silky-smooth paste which produces a fiery red but not overly pungent result.

Serves: 6–7

INGREDIENTS

For the paste
½ coconut, grated (about 200 g)
8 Kashmiri chillies
2 green chillies
1 tbsp coriander seeds
1 tsp cumin seeds
8–10 peppercorns
1 tsp turmeric powder
1 tomato, medium sized
1 onion, medium sized
8 cloves of garlic

For the prawn curry
1 kg medium sized prawns (weight after peeling and deveining)
1 tsp salt
3 tbsp oil
1 tbsp tamarind paste
Salt to taste

METHOD

Finely grind the ingredients for the masala paste.

Toss the prawns with a teaspoon of salt and keep aside. Drain any excess water off before adding the prawns to the curry.

Heat the oil in a pan and fry the ground spice paste for a few minutes on low heat till the oil separates and the masala leaves the side of the pan. Add two cups of water to the cooked paste to make a curry. Bring this to a boil and add tamarind paste and prawns. Reduce the heat and stir the mix till the prawns are just cooked, about 7 minutes should be sufficient. Add salt to taste.

Note: *There are three schools of thought on prawn and fish curries. You either grind the coconut with the spices and then add water. This gives you a thickish curry and is often the preferred recipe for large families. The second way and the one that a lot of purists still prefer is that you follow this method and then remove the spiced coconut milk through a muslin cloth to obtain a thick spiced milk. The third and probably the most practical approach (the one I use) is that you grind the masala (without the grated coconut), cook it in a little bit of water or oil and add readymade coconut milk. Whichever way, the spice paste must be ground really fine with no bits. In India and the East, our mixers come with a small grinder attachment specifically designed for chutneys and spice pastes. In the West, you'll need to use a coffee grinder or a wet grinder like a Bullet, specifically designed for this purpose. A food processor or a stick blender won't do the job.*

PORK BELLY WITH CUMIN AND BLACK PEPPER

PORK JEERE MEERE (PRON: JEE-REE MEE-REE)

This is the kind of dish that people go gaga over. The sometimes-overwhelming reaction is completely disproportionate to the effort involved, which is minimal. I must thank Corinne Miranda for this recipe for homestyle pork belly stew. It certainly is a house favourite!

Serves: 6

INGREDIENTS

1 kg pork belly
2 tsp salt

For the masala
2 tsp cumin seeds
3 tbsp black peppercorns

3-4 pieces kokum
4 Kashmiri chillies, broken

METHOD

Cut the pork belly into 1-inch pieces. Grind the ingredients for the masala to a coarse powder. Marinate the pork pieces with half the salt and the cumin-pepper masala for an hour or so. Take a large pan (nonstick works well) and fry the pork on a low heat till the fat renders. You do not need to add any oil. After around 30 minutes, throw in the kokum and red chillies and the remaining salt. Cover with a tight lid and continue cooking on a low heat till the pork softens. This may take around an hour. Serve hot with rice or bread.

Tip: *In Goan households today, it is not uncommon to hear the whistles of the pressure cooker (especially used for pork). People simply don't have the time to slow cook this dish. If you do, I will strongly recommend it. It adds a different dimension and depth of flavour. You can leave it alone on a low heat for an hour without the risk of burning in a Le Creuset casserole or a terracotta pot. If you use pork leg or loin instead of belly, you may need to add a cup or more of water to cook.*

PORK COOKED WITH VINEGAR, SPICES AND GARLIC

PORK VINDALHO (PRON: VEENDALOO)

The word *vindalho* comes from the Portuguese word *vinho* for wine and *alho* for garlic. It is probably the most misunderstood Indian curry in the world. In fact, most people (even in India!) don't know that the dish comes from Goa. What you often find in restaurants in India and abroad is a generic red hotchpotch with no defining flavour called *vindaloo* (pron: veendaloo). Victor Braganza was the manager at Bombay's only lifestyle store from the 1960s all the way through to the late 1990s, Contemporary Arts & Crafts on Nepean Sea Road. It was my husband Yadu's family business. He ran the store for ten years and loitered there as a boy for many years before that. That is incidentally also where I first met him. We haggled over ceramic platters and Victor played both cupid and councillor. I was quite amazed at Yadu's love for spicy, vinegary Goan dishes and soon found out why. Like the film *Lunchbox* where the *dabba* finds its way to a wrong recipient, Victor would on many occasions share (i.e. give) his delicious homecooked Goan lunchbox, made daily by his wife Alba, with Yadu. This went on for many years and became part of Yadu's culinary memory. This is Alba's vindalho. Authentic and simple – home cooking at its best.

Serves: 6

INGREDIENTS

For the main dish

1 kg pork with a little fat, cut into 1-inch chunks
¼ cup oil
2 medium onions, chopped
2 cups water
2 tsp salt

For the paste

1 tbsp ginger, chopped
2 tbsp garlic, chopped
25 Kashmiri red chillies
2 cups vinegar (toddy or coconut vinegar or apple cider)
1 tsp turmeric powder
2-inch piece of cinnamon stick
1 tsp cloves
1 tbsp black peppercorns
5 pieces green cardamom, skins removed
1 tsp cumin seeds

METHOD

Wash the red chillies and soak them in vinegar for 30 minutes. Grind this red chilli-vinegar combination to a fine paste. Combine this with the rest of the spices and grind to a fine paste. Marinate the chunks of pork with the finely ground spice paste and half the salt for at least 3 hours. Heat the oil in a pan and fry the chopped onions till golden brown. Add the marinated meat and cook on medium heat till the oil separates. This will take at least 20 minutes. If the masala starts to stick, add a splash of warm water and continue to stir. Add a further 3–4 cups water and lightly cover and cook the pork on low heat till the meat turns tender. This may take up to an hour. Serve hot with rice or pau.

Note: *In Goa, housewives often replace half the vinegar in the recipe with the local hooch, feni. Many people today prefer to speed things up in a pressure cooker, but I haven't yet mastered that skill. I prefer to cook the pork gently in a heavy stone or terracotta pot or a Le Creuset casserole. Vindalho keeps in the fridge for days since it is almost pickled.*

Tip: *In India, pork, like most other meats, takes ages to cook. Whereas, abroad, butchers hang their meat which allows the enzymes in the meat to work on the fibres of the muscles, rendering them softer and more elastic, which ultimately leads to the meat becoming relaxed and tender. The meat doesn't decompose because of the low temperature in the cool rooms, a luxury that we in India don't have. Young meat, that is wet and underhung, carries too much water in it, which ends up in your pan during cooking. The result of cooking this normally can be dry, tough meat. So, while our meats are absolutely fresh, they need to be tenderized and the best way of imbuing the meat with flavour and tenderness is marinating and slow cooking it.*

CHORIZ AND BACON PULLAO

A dish close to my heart, and easily found in any Goan household, is the *pullao* – served towards the end of the meal after the snacks and prawns and fish and pork. It is usually yellow from the inclusion of turmeric, which the Goans refer to as 'saffron'. Light and fluffy, the *pullao* is made with basmati, not Goan red rice. The use of basmati also implies a certain status. It may have peas and prawns but it always has a piece of *choriz, chouriço* or Goan sausage which significantly elevates the flavour and sets it apart from other rice dishes. This is a recipe from O Pedro in Mumbai. They make a fabulously delicious version, complete with a fried egg on top – unputdownabale after the first mouthful!

Serves: 6

INGREDIENTS

2 cups basmati rice
¼ cup bacon fat
1 piece of cinnamon stick
2 pieces of cloves
2 cups chopped onions
3 spring onions, white and green, thinly sliced
2 cups diced tomatoes
1 bay leaf
400 g Goan choriz, cooked in 4 cups of water for 30 minutes
200 g bacon bits (*lardon*), cooked till the fat renders
5 cups chicken stock
Salt to taste
Coconut vinegar to taste (about 1 tbsp)
2 eggs, fried

METHOD

In a large bowl, place the rice with cold water. Swish the grains around gently with your hand, and then pour out the water. Wash the rice about three more times in this way, until the washing water loses its murkiness and runs clear. Drain the water from the rice using a sieve and transfer into a container.
In the meantime, heat the bacon fat in a large wide pot over moderate heat until warmed through. Add the cinnamon and cloves and cook for about 1 minute, or until the spices are fragrant. Add the onion, spring onions (only the white part) and cook on a low heat for about 10–15 minutes, stirring continuously, until softened. Make sure that the onions don't turn golden. Now add the bay leaves and tomatoes to the pot and heat through. Season, cool and reserve.

In a separate pot, bring the stock to a boil over medium heat. To this, add the rendered bacon, the cooked Goan chorizo and the onion-tomato mixture, while stirring continuously. Cook this over moderate heat. Sprinkle in the washed rice and the greens of the spring onions. Season with salt and coconut vinegar. Reduce the flame to low, cover the pot and cook for another 15–20 minutes or until the rice is perfectly cooked.

To serve, top the rice with fried eggs and serve with a side salad of tomatoes and cucumber.

Tip: *Goa sausage is not easy to find outside Goa. You can substitute with spicy Spanish chorizo (not the salami) or Italian sausage from Calabria. You may have to add a generous amount of chilli flakes and hot paprika to make up for the lack of spice.*
Note: *The best choriz sausages I have found in Goa come from Dominic & Rosalina Fernandes near Margao. Today, they have a shop on the Margao Road opposite the church in Varca. In the old days, you had to go to their ramshackle old house behind a football field guided by the oinking of the pigs. This is where I witnessed, on many occasions, Rosalina grinding the masala in her Sumeet mixer. The sausages are then smoked over burnt coconut shells, dried, cured and smoked again. It is an arduous 3–5 day process. Very few traditional food artisans still smoke Goa sausage in this way.*

BRINJAL PICKLE

My great aunt's brinjal (aubergine) pickle is as traditional as it gets and represents a snapshot of Goan flavours. She loved me and so patiently showed me how to make it step by step. When we had the Deli at Contemporary Arts & Crafts on Nepean Sea Road in Bombay in the 1990s, I made and bottled it in lovely little jars with handmade paper covers as part of our range of preserves, pickles, sauces and chutneys. It sold like hot cakes. We don't make it commercially any more so here it is for you to try.

INGREDIENTS

For the pickle

1 kg large brinjal (aubergine), cut into 1-inch cubes
2 tbsp salt
1 cup sugar
300 ml vegetable oil
50 g ginger cut into juliennes
50 g garlic cut into juliennes
20 curry leaves

For the paste

1 tsp fenugreek seeds
1 tsp mustard seeds
1 tsp cumin seeds
2 tsp turmeric
50 g Kashmiri chillies, soaked in warm water for an hour, drained
200 g garlic
100 g ginger
500 ml malt vinegar

METHOD

Combine the spices with the malt vinegar and grind to a paste. Sprinkle salt on the brinjal and leave for an hour. Squeeze the excess water out by pressing the cubes with your hands or a kitchen towel. Mix the brinjal cubes, the spice paste, sugar and oil thoroughly in a bowl and transfer to a heavy-bottomed vessel. Heat till the oil simmers. Add the ginger and garlic juliennes and curry leaves, then simmer (uncovered) till the brinjal cubes are just cooked but not mushy – this should take about 10 minutes. Remove the cooked pickle from the heat. You can fill the pickle into clean jars either while it is still hot or wait for it to cool down to room temperature. Hot filling is preferable!

PANCAKES STUFFED WITH BLACK JAGGERY & COCONUT

ALLE BELLE (PRON: AALLAY BELLAY)

Goa is packed with trendy folk from Bombay and Delhi, old hippies and pot-bellied British tourists in season. Scratch a little deeper and you always find a Goa of easy charm: men sitting on their porches in shorts and *banyans*, their *feni* -blossomed cheeks shining in the evening sun; women in floral frocks with plastic baskets, bringing home fish for lunch. Life at an enviably slow pace. This for me is the heart of Goa.

I met a charming young man, Neville Proença, many years ago when he worked at the Taj Holiday Village. After thirteen years, he took the brave decision to build a boutique hotel, Pousada Tauma, named after his father, who left him some land a few steps from the busy Calangute shopping hub. The hotel has played host to all the who's who in India and boasts a discerning foreign clientele too. Neville, devilishly good-looking and fit, presides over his twelve garden suites, all surrounding a luxurious pool, and tropical flora and fauna that is as calming as it is green and lush. There's no Chinese, Italian or Thai food here. Neville, a true blue Goan, takes pride in serving only Goan food. Their take on Alle Belle, pancakes or pan rolls as they are called in Goa, stuffed with grated coconut and jaggery, is sublime. To that wicked concoction, they add an unctuous black jaggery and coconut sauce which takes the simple stuffed pancake to another level.

Serves: 6

INGREDIENTS

For the pancakes

½ cup cornflour
1 cup milk
½ cup all-purpose flour (maida)
1 egg
½ tsp salt
1 tsp sugar
1 tsp oil

For the filling

150 g black jaggery, grated
½ coconut, grated
½ cup golden raisins, soaked for a few minutes (optional)

For the sauce

1 cup thick coconut milk
1 cup black jaggery, grated

METHOD

In a big bowl, combine all ingredients for the pancakes to form a batter of a thin pouring consistency. Keep aside for 20 minutes. Heat a nonstick pan and grease the surface with a little oil. Gently wipe it off a using a piece of tissue or a basting brush. Pour a ladleful of the batter and manoeuvre the pan such that the batter spreads over the whole surface as thinly as possible (somewhat like a French crêpe). Cook until the batter turns firm. Flip the pancake and cook for another 30 seconds. Remove from the pan and allow to cool. For the next few pancakes, reduce the heat to medium. The batter should give you 6 thin pancakes.

Once the pancakes are ready, crumble and combine the jaggery with a little warm water in a bowl. Add the grated fresh coconut and raisins to make a firm mixture for filling the pancakes.

Lastly, heat some coconut milk and jaggery on a low flame until the jaggery melts to give you a thick sauce. Strain using a sieve and let the sauce cool down to room temperature.

For the assembly

Lay a pancake flat on a dinner plate. Put 2 heaped tablespoons of filling.

Fold over the pancake, tucking in the sides first so that the filling doesn't escape. Pour the sauce on the outside in a circle around the pancake. Serve warm with vanilla ice cream.

Note: *A variation Naomi Menezes prepares and serves at teatime includes a tablespoon each of slivered almonds and broken cashew nuts, lightly fried in a tiny bit of butter or ghee which she mixes with the coconut jaggery stuffing. She sometimes also adds one heaped tablespoon or more of lightly roasted white sesame seeds to the stuffing.*

Tip: *This is a slightly unorthodox recipe for pancake batter using a mix of all-purpose flour (maida) and cornflour which gives a thinner pancake with a less 'eggy' smell that one might sometimes find in a regular pancake batter.*

GUJARAT CHAND COMMITTE

GUJARAT

My husband, who is half Maharashtrian and half Gujarati, has family that originally come from Surat, considered the home of fine cuisine in Gujarat. I have learnt a great deal from them including ingredients, dishes and recipes but more importantly the finer nuances of which vegetable to serve with which dal and for which meal. His family is Vaishnav, so they are completely vegetarian. Traditionally, there would have been no onion or garlic in their food, though now younger members of the family eat eggs and all manner of non-vegetarian dishes but usually not at home. As a result, this chapter consists of completely vegetarian recipes. Many are by default also vegan. A traditional Gujarati meal comprising *dal, bhaat, roti, shaak* (lentils, rice, chapati and vegetable) is always vegetarian with a large variety of vegetables, grains, pulses and pickles eaten in *katoris* (small bowls) on a *thali*. Flavours run from sweet, sour, spicy, salty and bitter with a lot of heady umami running through because of the combination of spices. Asafoetida, fenugreek and mustard oil make up the holy trinity of a Gujarati *chownk* or tempering. Gujaratis are notorious for being thrifty with an acute sense of business, a keen nose for money and being wise with their purchases.

Gujarat, formed only in 1960, is on the northwest coastline of India. Western Gujarat or Saurashtra (Jamnagar and Rajkot) is dry with little fresh produce. The food is spicy due to its reliance on red chillies and oils for flavour; this is a region famous for pickles and chutneys. Central Gujarat, Ahmedabad and Baroda, are known for their grains. Since grains form such a large part of their kitchen, these are usually bought and stored in large quantities for the year. Even when they move to other cities outside the state, the habit of storing grains remains. Millets, barley and wheat are used every day and snacks involving them have become an art form across the subcontinent. The famous snack *chevdo* or beaten rice is fried and mixed with salt, spices, almonds, raisins and peanuts. This is part of what is known as *nashto*, snacks or nibbles and Gujaratis are known for their constant snacking, wherever they are in the world, whether its San Francisco or Surat. Delicate, silken 'pasta' rolls made from a cooked chickpea flour batter (*khandvi*), a savoury baked 'cake' made with a mixed batter of pulses and vegetables (*handvo*) and fried chickpea and onion fritters (*bhajiyas*) are all *farsan* ... yes, more snacks.

For the purpose of understanding the cuisine, it is practical to look at communities rather than cities in Gujarat. Let's start with Surat in the south. Although the Diamond exchange of India is in Bombay, the cutting and polishing is done in Surat. *Surtis* (people from Surat) are traditionally traders, steeped in the business of diamonds, finance and share markets. The land is fertile and green with plenty of rainfall and, coupled with their prosperity, food in Surat tends to be elegant, varied and full of green vegetables. In addition to a thali filled with several *katoris* of vegetables, *kadhi* and dal, there will be one or more sweet dishes (always served with the meal, not afterwards), yoghurt, chutneys and pickles. Some of their vegetables, like fresh fenugreek with banana

or the legume *val* or even a simple cauliflower are cut and cooked with almost mathematical precision and attention to detail. Nothing is sloppy or last-minute and the presentation is always of utmost importance. The Patel community is traditionally a rich farming community with acres of cash crops around the town of Anand between Baroda and Kheda. Their food is rustic with garlic and onion and plenty of millets, and they love heightened flavours and tastes. Saurashtra, which borders with Rajasthan, thrives on desert food with plenty of oil and chilli, dried vegetables and pulses. Kutch is an area of frugality and a lot of dairy (butter, ghee, buttermilk and yoghurt) is eaten at every meal along with pulses and grains but fewer vegetables. Dishes like *undhiyo*, a winter vegetable stew of sorts, and *dal dhokhli*, sweet dal with dumplings, are made by all communities but each will have their own version.

Mangoes are much loved all over India and, as soon as spring ripens into summer (end-April to early-May on the west coast of India), we start dreaming about this fruit. It becomes obsessive. Gujaratis don't waste a bit. They make a unique soupy *kadhi* using the mango pulp left on the seed and skins of the ripe juicy mango after they have squeezed out the pulp for '*aamras*', a sort of mango puree eaten with a *Gujju* meal. This could be Alphonso (called *happoos* locally) or *pairi* or a variety called *kesar* but any sweet mango will do. I don't make *aamras* but we do eat mangoes, peeled, cubed and chilled and, therefore, have lots of leftover seeds with a fair bit of juicy flesh on them. I boil the seeds for two minutes with a little water and no longer, since that will ruin the gorgeous orange colour. I then leave the saucepan of seeds to cool and remove the pulp by taking the seed one at a time in my hand and squeezing out the flesh from around it. Sounds disgusting but it is quite therapeutic, I assure you. Think of yourself as a child playing in a sandbox!

What defines Gujarati cuisine for me is not only the vast array of dishes but the amazing aesthetics which some families bring to the table and the sheer elegance of simple meals, adding touches like flowers, fragrances and textiles. The merchants of Ahmedabad – the Sarabai, Mangaldas and Hutheesing families – have done much to take Gujarati food to another level. They were all originally Jains from Osian in the Marwar district of Rajasthan. The Hutheesings moved to the port city of Khambat in Gujarat to trade with the British (mainly opium, it is thought) under the Mughal governor. They amassed huge fortunes and through generations diversified into textiles and other businesses. The Sarabais are an Ahmedabad institution. The family is responsible for many industries as well as the famous Calico Museum. I was invited many years ago to Anand Sarabai's mother's house for lunch. The house was designed by the French architect Le Corbusier with exposed brick work and fabulous open spaces. What I remember most was the exquisite lunch served on silver thalis, the meticulous service done by local boys in starched white pajamas and shirts, the humility and grace and the scent of jasmine in the air.

Lastly, the Mangaldas family, where the tradition of hospitality has been continued by Abhay Mangaldas, who has transformed the family mansion in the heart of Ahmedabad to a stunning boutique hotel, House of Mangaldas or House of MG. He has now added three more residences in the same inimitable style. I have known Abhay for over twenty-five years and admire his passion and drive. The property celebrates local craftsmanship and cuisine and embodies responsible tourism, offering Gujarati hospitality with immense style and comfort as their motto states, 'We have consciously tried to maintain this ethos by building an ecosystem around food, textiles, appealing building structure, décor, paintings and even building a cosmetics brand.' Mahatma Gandhi was a guest at this property on his return from South Africa in 1915, which even back then was staffed by locals from the neighbouring villages.

Here are some of my friends and family who made this collection of recipes possible.

FALGUNI GOKHALE NÉE PATEL

Falguni Gokhale née Patel is a close friend, graphic designer and painter – a Gujarati version of the Brooklyn bohemian. Like many creative people, she takes time off to cook and turns and twists traditional recipes to suit her moods (there are many!) and time frame. Her recipes of *dhebra*, *marchu nu shaak* and *handvo* are practical, quick and easy – anyone, anywhere in the world can make them – and I am grateful to her for sharing them.

MALA SINHA SANKALIA

My husband's paternal family, the Sankalias, are considered a progressive Surti family that moved to Bombay from Surat at the turn of the century. The recipe for *undhiyo* is his grandmother's, shared with me by his cousin Mala Sinha Sankalia. At Mala's ecofriendly home, exquisitely designed by her and her designer husband Pradeep, it isn't unusual to have a family gathering of twenty people or more. In winter, lunch starts with a beer and the first course of *undhiyo*, which is kept hot over a wood fire. More beer, and you go back for another helping as you dig deeper to uncover more vegetables. She serves *bhajiyas* with beer and there will be *kadhi*, *pooris* and rice and then *jalebi* for dessert (I have never seen anything like the Gujju lust for sweet) but, in the old days, undhiyo would be the only dish served; it was the centre piece. Mala is one of the country's foremost textile designers specializing in block printing and exquisite hand embroidery. Together with Pradeep, she owns and runs a well-known textile brand called Bodhi. The whole Sankalia family is obsessed with good food and Mala takes pride in continuing many family traditions, especially the culinary ones.

HEENA SURAIYA

Heena Suraiya is originally a Gujarati from Kutch who grew up in Bombay, then post marriage moved to Kolkata. Many of the original recipes she learnt from her mother and from the household in Kutch were simply not possible to make in West Bengal. The vegetables, the flour, even the sugar were different as she found out as a young bride in Kolkata. Her recipe for *methi thepla* bends the rules a little to create an equally delicious roti with a slightly crispy finish; a sort of marriage between a *thepla* and a north Indian *chilla* with aspirations to become a paratha. I have to thank Heena for her dedication on every step of each recipe she shared, including a trick to make *khandvi* and an irresistible *dal dhokli* – dishes I simply devour at her home. Her recipes will also be useful for people living outside Gujarat who struggle with the ingredients yet want to replicate Gujarati flavours in their cooking.

AVON

1 Crispy Onion Fritters – Kanda Bhajiya

2 Chickpea Pasta Rolls – Khandvi

3 Corn in a Creamy Sauce – Makai Nu Shaak

4 Sweet and Sour Mango Curry – Fajeto

5 Lentil Stew with Flat Dumplings – Dal Dhokli

6 Fried Chilli Peppers – Marchu Nu Shaak

7 Winter Vegetable Stew – Undhiyo

8 Millet Puris – Dhebra

9 Steamed Rice Pancakes in Banana Leaves – Panki

10 Savoury Lentil Cake – Handvo

11 Homestyle Rice Khichidi – Kanki Bhaat

12 Two Versions of Fenugreek Rotis – Methi Thepla

13 Mango Chutney – Chhundo

14 Sweet Yoghurt – Shrikhand

15 Chickpea Flour Sweet Treat – Besan Ka Laddoo

CRISPY ONION FRITTERS

KANDA BHAJIYA (PRON: KAANDHA BHUJEEYA)

Bhajiyas are usually sold on carts near railway stations or outside offices. You will invariably have a tea stall next to it. *Bhajiyas* are India's all-time favourite teatime snack and something that everyone looks forward to, especially during the monsoon. Although they are made throughout the country, the *kanda bhajiya* in Maharashtra and Gujarat seem to have less batter and are crispier than their counterparts elsewhere in the country. Every time I'm at a train station, the irresistible aroma of hot fried onion fritters being dished out in newspaper is overwhelming. I used to resist on the grounds of hygiene, but I find – as I get older – I throw caution to the wind and happily succumb to a plate whenever I travel to Gujarat. I have never got sick from eating hot *bhajiya*. I'm not sure whether my immunity has become stronger with age or if I was being unnecessarily paranoid earlier. *Bhajiyas* are usually fried fresh and, once they're over, that's it. Any remaining batter is thrown out or fried for the owner and his friends.

Sohan Bhandari and his team at the restaurant Colonel Saab in London make the best *bhajiyas* ever, with onion, rocket leaves, kale and baby spinach. Crispy beyond belief, I can eat bowlfuls. Here's the recipe.

Serves: 4

INGREDIENTS

3 medium-sized onions, thinly sliced
2 green chillies, finely chopped
½ tsp salt
1 tsp red chilli powder
1 tsp carom seeds, crushed
1 tsp cumin seeds, crushed
1 tsp coriander seeds, crushed
1 cup chickpea flour
½ cup cornflour
Oil for deep frying

For the garnish

A generous pinch of raw mango powder or chaat masala or a South Indian *podi*.

METHOD

In a large bowl, mix the onions with all ingredients except the chickpea flour and cornflour. Set aside for 10 minutes to draw out the water.

Meanwhile, heat oil in a kadhai or deep fryer on a medium flame. Mix the two flours, add to the onions and toss gently. The mixture should be slightly wet and the flour should stick to the onion but not look like a thick batter. This needs to rest for a couple of minutes. Drop spoonfuls of the mixture in batches into the hot oil and fry till golden brown. Remove and drain on paper towels. Garnish with a sprinkling of raw mango powder (*amchur*) or chaat masala or some *podi* if you're going for a South Indian flavour profile. Peanut and curry leaf podi are excellent tossed with the *bhajiya* just as they come out of the hot oil.

CHICKPEA PASTA ROLLS

KHANDVI (PRON: KHAANDVEE)

Khandvi was once described by a friend as the 'Gujarati pasta'. I suppose it is! Made from chickpea flour and yoghurt with a light spice tempering, I would go to the extent of saying that when made well they are much better than pasta! Silky-smooth, melt-in-the-mouth rolls – I find a plateful of them irresistible. The Gujarati cook or *Maharaj* seems to have the knack of blending, cooking, spreading and rolling with great speed. If you've ever made gougères or choux pastry, the method is similar. It's all about timing. Khandvi is ideal for anyone who loves the texture of pasta but is intolerant to gluten.

Serves: 8 (or approx 70 pieces)

INGREDIENTS

For the batter

2 cups chickpea flour
4 cups yoghurt
2¼ cups water
2 tsp salt
1 tsp turmeric
2 green chillies and a small piece of ginger, made into a paste
5 tbsp oil

For the tempering

2 tbsp oil (traditionally sesame or peanut)
¼ tsp asafoetida
1 tsp mustard seeds
10 curry leaves
2 green chillies, slit vertically

For the garnish

2 tbsp coconut, grated
½ cup fresh coriander, chopped

METHOD

Pour all the ingredients for the batter into a saucepan and cook on a low heat. Stir with a wooden spoon till there are no lumps or whisk with a small steel whisk. When the mix reaches a soft dough consistency and starts coming off from the sides of the pan (this should take around 5 minutes), remove from the heat. If you are unsure, remove a small ball and see if you can roll it on your kitchen platform. If it sticks, then it needs to cook further. Brush some oil on the reverse side of a steel thali or a kitchen worktop and roll the dough as thinly as possible while it's still hot. Cut into 1½-inch wide strips and roll each strip like a Swiss roll. Place all the khandvi pieces on a plate.

Heat the oil for tempering and throw in the asafoetida, mustard seeds, curry leaves and green chillies. When the spices splutter, pour it on top of the khandvi rolls. Garnish with grated coconut and chopped coriander. Serve at room temperature.

CORN IN A CREAMY SAUCE

MAKAI NU SHAAK (PRON: MUCKAY NOO SHARK)

This is my version of the Gujarati favourite *makai nu shaak*. Although I live in India, where fresh coconut is nearly always accessible, I often find it painful to clean and grate. To concede to my sheer laziness, I tweaked the original recipe from grated coconut to coconut milk. I now actually prefer my new version with chunky cobs of corn swimming in a pool of silky-smooth coconut curry.

Serves: 6

INGREDIENTS

3 fresh sweet corn cobs, each broken into 3
1 tsp salt
⅛ tsp sugar
4 green chilies
4 tbsp fresh coriander leaves, chopped
1-inch piece of ginger
1 cup coconut milk
2 tbsp oil
2 tsp mustard seeds
8 curry leaves
½ cup yoghurt, whisked
½ cup coriander leaves, chopped (for garnish)

METHOD

Place the corn into a large saucepan or handi and add enough water to just cover. Add a teaspoon of salt and a pinch of sugar. Boil till the corn becomes soft – this should take about 5–7 minutes. Remove the boiled corn from the water but don't throw away the water in which they were boiled. Grind the green chillies, ginger and fresh coriander leaves together with a few spoons of the coconut milk to make a paste. Add this paste to 2 cups of water that we used to boil the corn and whisk till it reaches a liquid consistency. Throw the excess water away.

Heat the oil in a small pan and add the mustard seeds and curry leaves to it. Add the tempering to the liquid prepared above and simmer on a low heat. Add the remaining coconut milk and whisk in the yoghurt. Season to taste and add the corn cobs. Cover and continue to cook on a low heat for at least 5 minutes. Serve hot with plain boiled rice and garnish with some chopped coriander leaves.

SWEET AND SOUR MANGO CURRY

FAJETO (PRON: FUDGE-AYTOE)

I never knew my father-in-law but by all accounts he was a great guy and a visionary who died before his time. He was, I hear, a great gastronome who travelled widely in Europe and brought Scandinavian designers to work with him in his furniture business in Bombay. A Gujarati Vaishnav by birth, he had a steak named after him at the Bombay Gymkhana Club! He loved fajeto and felt that it should be served in fancy French restaurants as a cold soup. Consommé à la mangue? Well, we serve it at our fancy Indian restaurant in London, Colonel Saab, and it is one of the most popular dishes on the menu!

Serves: *3–4*

INGREDIENTS

For the fajeto

1¼ cups full cream yoghurt
1¼ tbsp chickpea flour
4 green chillies, each slit vertically
20 curry leaves
¼ tsp turmeric powder
1 tbsp jaggery, chopped
1 tsp salt
¾ cup mango puree
3 tbsp coriander leaves, chopped (for garnish)

For the tempering

1½ tbsp ghee
1½ tsp cumin seeds
1 whole dried red chilli, crushed

METHOD

Whisk the yoghurt and add approximately 1½ cups of water to make buttermilk. Whisk in the chickpea flour. Pour this mixture into a saucepan and cook it over a gentle heat for about 10 minutes, stirring constantly, until it turns slightly thick. Add the green chillies, curry leaves, turmeric, jaggery and salt and then simmer. Mix the mango puree into the curry and cook for a further 10 minutes. Heat the ghee in a small pan and throw in the cumin seeds and chillies. When they splutter, pour them into the *kadhi* or *fajeto*. Garnish with coriander leaves and serve hot with boiled rice or have it as a soup.

Note: *Do not compromise on the ghee. Not only does it taste wonderful and is much healthier than refined oil, it also gives the fajeto a smooth, velvety finish.*

LENTIL STEW WITH FLAT DUMPLINGS

DAL DHOKLI (PRON: DAAHL DHOKLEE)

This dish reminds me of the Italian *pasta e fagioli*, a thick bean and pasta soup. This is a much tastier version! Dal dhokli is a thickish sweet-and-sour spicy dal with flat dumplings (dhokli) made from whole wheat flour. The dumplings can be uneven, thick and handmade or rolled with a rolling pin to the thickness of a lasagna sheet. This is Heena Suraiya's recipe. It is light and the dumplings are thin and melt in the mouth.

Serves: 4–6

INGREDIENTS

For the dal

2 cups tuvar dal (yellow)
1 tsp salt
3–4 cloves
4–5 pieces of kokum
¼ tsp turmeric powder
½ tsp red chilli powder
10 curry leaves
1 tbsp jaggery
¼ cup coriander leaves and stalks

For the dhokli

2 cups whole wheat flour
1 tbsp oil
½ tsp red chilli powder
¼ tsp asafoetida
½ tsp salt
¼ tsp turmeric
¼ tsp carom seeds

For the tempering

1 tbsp ghee
1 tsp mustard seeds
2-3 dry round red chillies (*boriya mirch*)
¼ tsp asafoetida
¼ tsp fenugreek seeds

METHOD

Soak tuvar dal for about an hour and drain the water. Add ten cups of fresh water and some salt and pressure cook until the dal turns soft – this should take about 20 minutes. The dal should not be too thick; whisk until smooth. Keep on a low flame. If you slow cook the dal (not pressure cook it), it may take up to an hour to cook.

For the dhokli

Place the whole wheat flour on a large plate or *thali*. Make a well in the centre and add the oil. Add all the remaining ingredients for the dumplings and as much water as you need to make a firm dough. Knead well. Roll out into thick rotis. Cut into diamond shaped pieces and keep aside. In a small frying pan, heat ghee and add mustard seeds, chillies, asafoetida and fenugreek seeds. When the mustard starts spluttering, pour the tempering into the dal. Add the kokum, jaggery and curry leaves into the dal and stir. Gently slide the dumplings into the hot dal. They need no longer than 5 minutes to cook.

Lastly, throw in the coriander leaves and stalks and cloves. Eat as is with an onion and tomato salad (*kachumber*). You don't really need rice because of the dumplings.

FRIED CHILLI PEPPERS

MARCHU NU SHAAK (PRON: MURHCHOO-NOO SHARK)

This is one of those instant recipes made with big green *Bhavnagari* chillies which are not too spicy when cooked. If you live outside India, you can substitute with Italian pepperoni sweet peppers, cherry peppers or Iberian roasting pimentos. Falguni Gokhale makes this in the most unorthodox way and the result looks somewhat like a mess – but that's the idea! It should look like a rough scrambled egg with chilli.

Serves: 4

INGREDIENTS

10–12 big green chillies, about 6–7 inches long
2 tbsp oil
1½ tsp carom seeds
2 tbsp chickpea flour
½ cup water
1 tsp turmeric

METHOD

Cut the chillies into ½-inch rounds and deseed them. Heat the oil in a kadhai or pan. Add carom seeds and turmeric powder and roast the spices. Mix the chickpea flour with water to make a paste and toss the chillies to this batter. Add the chickpea-coated chillies to the pan, stir and cook on a low heat for 5 minutes till the chickpea paste dries up and clings to the chilli slices. Season with salt.

Note: *If you can't find these chillies, use green bell peppers (capsicum) and throw in a couple of long green chillies for the spice quotient.*

WINTER VEGETABLE STEW

UNDHIYO (PRON: OON-DHEE-OH)

Undhiyo is a celebration of winter and is a dish to be shared with many. It is made throughout Gujarat but this version is from Surat and the *Surtis* (people from Surat) are considered to have the most refined palate in the state. This recipe has been passed on through three generations of my husband's family, the Sankalias, and shared with me by his first cousin, Mala. It is no doubt a complicated recipe but if you are sitting in New Jersey and longing for undhiyo, this is a sure-shot winner, tried and tested over many years and generations. In Gujarat today, winter is celebrated with much excitement after a hot summer and, although this is a dry state (no alcohol is sold), I have never felt thirsty, if you get my drift. Personally, I am not a huge fan of this root vegetable stew but for many Gujaratis the world over the mere mention of the word 'undhiyo' can stir up huge excitement.

Serves: 8–10

INGREDIENTS

For the stew

1 kg *Surti papdi* (from the area of Katargam traditionally. A mix of 500 g tender and 500 g mature ones with beans inside. After discarding the tough pods of the mature ones, you will be left with approx 700 g tender pods and beans)
1 cup fresh tuvar beans
6–8 aubergines (small, stubby, dark purple ones)
300 g yam, peeled and cut into 1½-inch cubes
400 g purple yam, peeled and cut into 1½-inch on the diagonal
3 sweet potatoes, peeled and cut into thick rounds
10 small or medium-sized potatoes, peeled
3 *Rajali* banana or regular banana, ends discarded and cut into 3 pieces with skin

METHOD

To prepare your green masala, finely chop and mix the ingredients. Keep the masala aside. Do not grind this as we do not want a paste.

Next, for the green garlic chutney, combine all the ingredients with a little water and grind into a coarse-textured paste. Keep aside.

The preparation for this recipe is quite laborious, so ideally do it the day before you plan to eat the undhiyo. Firstly, each papdi is opened like a pea pod. The spine is discarded and only the tender pods and the beans are kept. If the beans are large, it usually means the pods are tough and need to be thrown away. So you should end up with approximately half the amount of full pods like mange tout or sugar snap peas and half beans like peas from a pea pod. Wash and drain these in a colander and allow to dry completely. Keep some beans aside for use later.

Make a slit along the length of each piece of banana and stuff some green masala into each slit. For the aubergines, cut off the stem, make a slit and stuff with green masala. Make a cross slit on each potato and repeat the masala stuffing process. Mix the yam, sweet potato and purple yam with the green masala in a bowl. You should still have a little green masala left.

Take a very large heavy-bottomed pot (preferably brass) and heat the oil in it. Add carom seeds and, when they splutter, add the asafoetida and soda. Add the tender papdi and most of the beans. Season with salt and cover the pan. Cook for approximately 5–10 minutes. Do not add any water. When the papdi is half cooked, remove from the heat, add any leftover

For the tempering

1½ cups peanut oil
2 tsp carom seeds
A pinch of asafoetida
A pinch of soda bicarbonate

For the green masala

1 big bunch of coriander leaves
1 tsp carom seeds
1 coconut, freshly grated (white part only)
2 tbsp green chilli-ginger paste (2:1)
3 tsp salt
1 tbsp cumin-coriander powder (or ½ tbsp each)
½ tsp turmeric powder
1 tsp garam masala
1 tbsp sesame seeds
1 tbsp sugar
1 cup roasted peanuts, crushed
A pinch of soda bicarbonate

For the green garlic chutney

1 large bunch of green garlic, chopped (green and white part)
½ cup fresh coriander leaves and stalk, finely chopped
½ cup coconut, grated
3–4 green chillies, stems removed
2-inch piece ginger, peeled and chopped
1½ tsp salt
Juice of 1 lime
1 tsp whole cumin, roasted and ground to a powder
A pinch of sugar

green masala and start layering the vegetables – the purple yam, then yam, potato, aubergine and sweet potato. Coarsely grind the remaining papdi beans and the fresh tuvar beans and throw them in between the layers. Cover with a lid and pour a little water on top, which when hot indicates that the steam is forming inside and your food is cooking.

Add the bananas at the end, when the root vegetables are almost cooked, since they would take the least amount of time to cook. Traditionally, this dish is slow cooked over a wood fire. You can shake the whole pot from time to time but do not stir. The whole dish takes between 45 and 60 minutes to cook.

To serve, you can either go in with a big spoon or the more elegant way is to take each vegetable out separately and let people help themselves to what they like.

My *Surti* cousins pour a little cold-pressed sesame oil on the undhiyo before serving. Fresh green garlic chutney and crispy *sev* are served on the side. The more rural style of serving (certainly not *Surti*) is to take a bowl of undhiyo, mash it and add the sesame oil, green garlic chutney and sev in your bowl. I can imagine that would be very soul-satisfying – sitting on a farm on a charpoy eating it hot off the fire.

Note: *The Gujaratis believe that the addition of soda bicarbonate in their vegetable dishes retains the green colour. In my opinion, if you overcook green vegetables, there is precious little you can do to retain the colour and nutrients anyway. Undhiyo is a case in point. The best way to retain the colour and nutrients of any vegetable is to cook them briefly by steaming or blanching and then arresting the cooking by immersing in cold water or ice.*

There seem to be two schools of thought on when to add the surti papdi to this dish. One suggests that they all go in right at the beginning so they form the bottom layer of the undhiyo. The other, that you layer after each root vegetable so you get some papdi (considered a great delicacy) in every bite.

Tip: *Fresh tuvar beans are not easy to find but edamame or fresh fava are good substitutes.*

MILLET PURIS

DHEBRA (PRON: DHAYBRA)

Sandwiched between Surat in the south of the state and Ahmedabad further north, is a rich farming community called the Patels. Most people internationally would have heard of them because they are all over the UK (after they were ousted by Idi Amin from Uganda in the early 1970s), the US and Canada and are known for their enterprising business acumen. The 'Motel Patel' in the US is not fiction. This affluent community owns more than a third of US motels and small hotels. Dhebra are traditional millet flatbreads made on farms in Gujarat and very much part of the Patel diet. I love them and my friend Falguni Gokhale takes great pride in making them since it reminds her of the childhood spent on her grandparents' farm at Karamsad near Anand.

***Serves:** 4 (or 12 puris)*

INGREDIENTS

1½ cups millet flour (*bajra*)
1 tbsp chickpea flour
½ cup buttermilk (or ¼ cup water mixed with ¼ cup natural yoghurt)
1 cup spinach leaves, finely chopped
2–3 green chillies, finely chopped
1 tsp coriander powder
½ tsp cumin powder
1 tsp chilli powder
½ tsp turmeric
2 tbsp sesame seeds
1 tsp ginger paste
Salt to taste
Oil for deep frying

METHOD

Mix all the ingredients together in a large bowl and work out a firm dough. Grease your palms with oil. Pluck out a small amount (the size of a ping pong ball) and roll into a round roti with a rolling pin – about 5 inches in diameter and about ⅛-inch thick. Sprinkle sesame seeds on each one and slightly flatten them into the dough with the palm of your hand. Place them on a sheet of greaseproof paper. This makes it easy to remove them later. Do this with all the dough. Heat enough oil to deep fry in a wok or kadhai. Keep the heat on medium and slide two rolled rotis at a time into the wok and fry until they turn light golden brown on both sides. They should puff up while cooking, leaving a pocket of air in the centre. If they become very brown quickly, just lower the heat. Transfer them to a plate lined with kitchen paper to soak the excess oil. Deep-fry the remaining dhebra. Eat piping hot as is or with green chutney or plain yoghurt. Dhebra are really the tastiest breads ever.

Note: *Traditionally, fenugreek (methi) is used to make dhebra but Falguni prefers using spinach which is milder in flavour and differentiates the roti from the thepla.*

STEAMED RICE PANCAKES IN BANANA LEAVES

PAANKI (PRON: PAAN-KEY)

I first had paanki at Swati Snacks in Bombay which is an institution and a 'must-try' for anyone interested in authentic Gujarati cuisine. It is a modest eatery started by Minakshi Jhaveri in the 1960s, then run by her daughter Asha in the late 1970s and now by her brother and their children. It serves street-style and homecooked Gujarati snacks at very affordable prices and initially catered to the many Gujaratis who flocked to the city for work. This recipe was shared by Heena Suraiya who made it look very simple. Like everything, practice makes perfect.

Serves: 4

INGREDIENTS

1 tbsp ghee
6 banana leaves, cut into 7 x 7 inch pieces
2½ cups rice flour
5 cups yoghurt
¼ tsp turmeric powder
1 tsp salt
1 tbsp ginger-green chilli paste (1:1)
¼ cup chopped coriander leaves
1 tbsp oil

METHOD

In a bowl, mix rice flour, yoghurt and turmeric. Cover with a lid and leave overnight to ferment. The next morning, remove the lid. The batter should have thickened to just pouring consistency. Stir in the salt, ginger-chilli paste, coriander and oil.

Brush a little ghee onto each banana leaf to prevent the batter from sticking. Pour the batter with a ladle onto the banana leaves. Lightly cover with another banana leaf, but do not press down. Heat a non-stick tawa or frying pan. Place the banana leaf parcel onto it. When hot, turn once and cook on the other side. Repeat with the remaining batter. Frying this way instead of steaming imparts a lovely smoky flavour to the paanki. To eat the paanki, simply peel off the top banana leaf, then remove the paanki from the bottom leaf. Serve warm with green coconut chutney.

SAVOURY LENTIL CAKE

HANDVO (PRON: HAAHND-VOH)

A great eat-anywhere-anytime kind of savoury snack that is as satisfying as it is travel worthy. Every community in Gujarat has their own version and each one says theirs is the best! This one comes from Falguni Gokhale née Patel and is a typical recipe from the Patel community.

Serves: 4

INGREDIENTS

For the *handvo*

½ cup rice
¼ cup tuvar dal
1 tbsp urad dal
1 tbsp whole moong dal
1 tbsp chana dal
¼ cup yoghurt (few days old)
1 cup bottle gourd, peeled and grated
½ cup carrots, grated
1 tsp oil
1½ tsp sugar
½ tsp red chilli powder
¼ tsp turmeric powder
2 tsp ginger-green chilli paste (1:1)
Salt to taste

For the tempering

2 tsp oil
½ tsp mustard seeds
1 tbsp sesame seeds
¼ tsp asafoetida
1 dried red chilli
A pinch of Eno fruit salt or soda bicarbonate

METHOD

Clean, wash and soak the rice and dals together in enough water and cover for at least 4–5 hours. Drain and keep aside. Grind this mixture to a coarse texture and stir in the yoghurt. Cover and keep aside this batter to ferment overnight. The next morning, add the bottle gourd, carrot, oil, sugar, chilli powder, turmeric powder, ginger green chilli paste and salt and mix well. Keep aside.

Heat the oil in a kadhai or small pan and add the mustard seeds. When the seeds crackle, add half the sesame seeds and asafoetida and the whole dry chilli. Pour this crackling mix over the batter. Add Eno fruit salt to fluff up the batter – this will happen almost immediately. Quickly pour the batter into 2 greased baking trays approx 8 x 6 inches and about 3 inches high. Sprinkle the remaining sesame seeds on the batter and bake in a preheated oven at 200°C for 30–35 minutes till the crust turns golden brown. Cool the *handvo* slightly and cut into square pieces.

Note: *Gujaratis love to put soda bicarbonate or baking soda in everything. Granted it does make grains and lentils cook quickly and the end result is lighter as it is in a cake. However, used in many dishes on a Gujju table, this can have an adverse affect and cause bloating and discomfort or as we Indians say openly 'gas'. Eno, though called a fruit salt, is made up of baking soda, citric acid and salt. There's no fruit in it. Use with caution!*

HOMESTYLE KHICHIDI

KANKI BHAAT (PRON: KANKEE BHAATH)

Khichidi, like kedgeree or risotto, is a dish of slow-cooked, soft rice – perfect comfort food. *Kanki* is a Gujarati version and a great favourite in the Sankalia household, my husband's family who now live in Baroda. Although it looks a bit sloppy, it is quick comfort food for many Gujaratis away from home. This is Mala Sankalia's recipe, passed down to her from her grandmother and mother.

Serves: 4

INGREDIENTS

For the *kanki bhaat*

2 cups broken rice (*kanki*), washed a couple of times
2 cups yoghurt. 2 cups water
Salt to taste
½ tsp turmeric powder
1 tsp red chilli powder
¼ cup fresh coriander, chopped
1 tsp *sambhariyu* masala (also called *methiyu* or pickle spice)

For the tempering

2 tbsp ghee. 1 tsp cumin seeds
A large pinch of asafoetida
8–10 curry leaves
3 green chillies, slit vertically

METHOD

Combine the yoghurt and water in a bowl and whisk to get buttermilk. Cook the broken rice, just covered with water, in a heavy-bottomed brass vessel or in a pressure cooker for 5 minutes with the water to rice ratio as 3:1. Remove from heat and mash gently with half the buttermilk to prepare the *kanki*.

For the tempering, heat the ghee and add in the cumin seeds. Once it splutters, add asafoetida, curry leaves and green chillies. Pour onto the cooked *kanki* and stir it for a minute or two on a low heat. Add salt, turmeric powder and red chilli powder. Continue to mix well. Add in the remaining buttermilk and keep stirring continuously to avoid lumps. The mix should have the consistency of a thick porridge or *khichidi*. Remove from the heat. Sprinkle with chopped coriander and *sambhariyu* masala and serve with a simple dal, *kachumbar* (a salad of finely chopped tomatoes, onions and cucumber salted and with a squeeze of lime) and a dry vegetable (*sabzi*) like potato or okra with potato or *tendli*.

SIMPLE DAL OR VARAN TO GO WITH THE KANKI BHAAT

INGREDIENTS

1½ cups tuvar dal
1 tsp salt
4 cups water
1 tsp turmeric
1 tbsp jaggery powder

For the tempering

1 tbsp ghee
A pinch of asafoetida

METHOD

Soak the dal for an hour. Drain and wash. Boil the dal in a pressure cooker for 5–7 minutes with 3 cups water or in a pot with 4 cups water until the lentils are really soft. This dal should be quite thin and runny so you may need to add a little water. Add the turmeric, jaggery and the tempering. Cook on a medium heat for another 5–7 minutes till the dal is completely smooth and the spices cooked.

TWO VERSIONS OF FENUGREEK ROTIS

METHI THEPLA (PRON: MAYTHI THAPE-LAA)

Methi thepla must be the quintessential Gujju roti or flatbread. Thepla is a soft-dough roti or chapati with the addition of fresh fenugreek, that are especially good in winter when the leaves are at their most tender. It is made on a griddle or tawa with a little oil. Fresh fenugreek is also very healthy, rich in anti-oxidants vitamin C and vitamin A. This method of kneading the fenugreek into the dough and the quick cooking preserves all the essential nutrients. *Methi* is also an excellent immunity booster.

This is Mala Sankalia Sinha's recipe. She adds more *methi* than the standard 1:1 ratio of flour to *methi* so the dough is even softer.

MALA'S THEPLA

Serves: 4

INGREDIENTS

2¼ cups of whole wheat flour (*atta*)
¾ cup oil
1 tsp red chilli powder
½ tsp turmeric powder
1 tsp carom seeds, crushed slightly
2 tsp ginger-garlic paste
1 tsp sesame seeds
3 cups fenugreek leaves, washed and roughly chopped
1½ tsp salt
½ cup rice flour

METHOD

Put the flour onto a *thali* or work top. Make a well in the centre and pour in ½ cup oil. Add all the ingredients and then the fenugreek and salt. Mix well and knead into a soft dough with a little water. Add a little oil to your hands to remove any excess dough. Set the ball of dough aside, covered with a damp cloth, for at least 1 hour. Divide into equal portions – each portion the size of a large ping-pong ball – and roll out each ball into a thin *chapati*. Dust each thepla with rice flour. Heat a tablespoon of oil from the remaining oil on a tawa or frying pan and fry the theplas one at a time on a medium heat. Turn once. When the thepla is golden brown, remove at once and serve hot with a sweet mango pickle like *chhundo*.

HEENA SURAIYA'S THEPLA

Serves: 4

INGREDIENTS

¼ cup chickpea flour
1½ cups whole wheat flour
½ tsp turmeric powder
1 tsp ginger-garlic paste
1 cup fenugreek leaves, roughly chopped
1 tsp salt
2½ tbsp oil

METHOD

Mix the wheat and chickpea flours. Form a dough by making a well in the centre of the flour and add all the ingredients and 1½ tbsp of oil. Mix well and add enough water to make into a pliable dough. Knead into a smooth ball and set aside for at least 20 minutes, covered. Again, knead the dough well and divide into equal portions, the size of ping-pong balls. Roll out each ball into a thin chapati.

Heat the remaining oil on a tawa and shallow fry the theplas. Once the thepla puffs with small air bubbles, turn it over to the other side. Turn the thepla over once again. When the thepla has golden brown spots on it, remove at once and serve hot with green chutney and plain yoghurt or a sweet mango pickle like *chhundo* (recipe follows).

MANGO CHUTNEY

CHHUNDO (PRON: CHHOONDOH)

Gujaratis love their sweet, sour, salty and spicy flavours – what we like to call '*chatpata*'. Nothing exemplifies that more than a chutney. This is really a bit of tradition that I love and can manage simply because I live in India where we have a scorching summer and I have a garden where the jars of chutney can cook under the hot summer sun. The only thing to remember is to take the jars in every evening. I've never quite figured out why. It may be in case it rains (the mouth of the jar is covered with a piece of muslin only) or it may have something to do with the change of temperature at night. One day a scientist will explain it to me!

INGREDIENTS

2½ kg raw mango, peeled and grated (net weight)
2 kg sugar
10 g turmeric powder
25 g cumin, roasted and powdered coarsely
25 g red chilli powder
50 g salt

METHOD

Traditionally, this is prepared right at the very beginning of the mango season with inexpensive mangoes like *totapuri* or *rajapuri* or any local variety. The mangoes must be absolutely raw with green skins. Now that julienne cutters are available, I peel and then cut my raw mangoes using one, which gives me nice, even strips or juliennes instead of a messy pile of grated mango. You could also use a microplaner with large holes.

Place the grated mango, salt, turmeric and sugar in a large bowl and toss (this is usually done with your hands, but you can use a big spoon if that's more comfortable). Leave the mixture to rest for upto 2 hours. The traditional recipe says to squeeze any excess water from the mango, but I don't. I'll tell you why – if you do squeeze out the water, your chutney will probably last much longer but it will get thick and gloppy. You will have to add at least 30 per cent more sugar to ease the texture out which is what tradition demands. I like my chutney a bit watery and less sweet, so I keep the liquid in there. Consequently, I also have to refrigerate my jars.

Place the mango mixture into one large glass jar or divide between 2 or 3 glass jars. Cover the neck of the jar with a muslin cloth and secure it with string or a rubber band. Do not be tempted to screw on a lid. This will cause condensation and ruin your chutney. Place the jars in the sun between 9 a.m. and 4 p.m. for 8 days. You have to take the jars indoor every evening and take the muslin cloth off every morning and stir the mixture. I just shake it well and do the removal of muslin routine every 2 days. On the 9th day, mix in the chilli powder and cumin and continue the routine for 3 more days.

After 12 days, you should have the most delicious mango chutney or *chhundo* you have ever tasted. You can carry on this routine for 3 days more if you really want to be sure that your chutney won't spoil. Purists often do this because the chutney is made once a year only to last until the next year. If you are not sure of having two weeks of continuous sunshine and hot weather, you can still make *chhundo* by slow cooking the ingredients together on the stove (uncovered) on a very very low heat till the mango feels soft and cooked but not mushy.

SWEET YOGHURT

SHRIKHAND (PRON: SHREE-KHUND)

This is my version of the relatively healthier sweet (compared to the myriad of ghee, reduced milk and sugar laden sweetmeats available in India) made in Gujarat and Maharashtra. I used to make it to accompany an Indian meal when I lived in Paris. There would be an exclamation of delight when at the end of the meal somebody would invariably shout '*La mayonnaise Indienne est arrivée!*' (Karen's Indian mayonnaise has arrived!). The consistency of shrikhand does, I have to admit, resemble mayonnaise.

Serves: *4*

INGREDIENTS

1 kg yoghurt made from full cream milk
200 g castor or powdered sugar
2 tbsp almonds, slivered
2 tbsp unsalted pistachios, slivered
¼ tsp ground nutmeg
½ tsp ground cardamom
½ tsp saffron, dissolved in a little warm milk
2 tbsp rosewater or a few drops of rose extract

METHOD

Pour yoghurt into the middle of a large piece of muslin cloth, gather the corners together and tie them with a string or a rubber band. Hang the muslin over a bowl overnight to drain off the excess water. You should be left with around 400 g thick yoghurt. Turn yoghurt into a bowl, add the sugar and whisk energetically until the texture is completely smooth. Stir in half the cardamom, saffron and rosewater. Turn into a large bowl or individual small bowls and sprinkle the nuts and the remaining cardamom and nutmeg on top. Serve chilled.

Fresh fruit also tastes wonderful in this dish. Add 1 cup of mango pulp to the mixture for *amarkhand*. Don't mix it too well as it looks and tastes very attractive if it is marbled.

Tip: *Greek yoghurt is a good substitute and you may only have to hang it for an hour or so because it is already quite thick.*

CHICKPEA FLOUR SWEET TREAT

BESAN KA LADDOO (PRON: BASIN KA LUDDOO)

This is a very easy *mithai* or sweetmeat made all over India but those made in Gujarat and Maharashtra with pure ghee and roasted chickpea flour are by far the best I've had. My husband always says his grandmother's were the best because they had so much homemade ghee in them that each *laddoo* would plop down on itself bottom heavy, which gives rise to the term 'sitting like a laddoo' (couch potato). They should just melt in the mouth. You can eat laddoos anytime of the day or, in my husband's case, at night too. They don't necessarily have to accompany or follow a meal.

Serves: 40 laddoos

INGREDIENTS

250 g ghee
450 g chickpea flour
350 g fine powdered sugar or castor sugar
2 tsp cardamom powder
A handful of yellow raisins (*kismis*)

METHOD

Heat the ghee in a heavy-bottomed saucepan (I use a steel lined copper pan) and add the flour. Roast the flour in ghee on a low heat till the flour turns a light golden colour. This should take 15–20 minutes. Be careful, it can turn brown very quickly. The result is a granular texture and slightly bitter aftertaste. Take off the heat and continue stirring for a couple of minutes. While still warm, transfer to a bowl and stir in the powdered sugar and mix well till the sugar dissolves. Add the powdered cardamom and cool. Roll portions of the mix between your palms into balls the size of small limes. Put a raisin or two on top of each laddoo and press down slightly. Lay on a plate. Serve at room temperature. No need to refrigerate. The laddoos can last for a few months, if you can resist gulping them down!

Tip: *For the powdered sugar, just take normal granulated sugar and run it through a dry grinder so that it looks like icing sugar or use castor sugar. Traditionally, mithai wallas would make what is known as an inverted sugar syrup, i.e., melt granulated sugar with a little water and then dry it out and crumble it to a very fine texture. It then melts easily and lends a finer texture to sweets.*

KERALA

My first visit to Kerala – which translates to 'the land of coconuts' in the local language of Malayalam – was in 1985, soon after I had returned to India. It was my first real adventure within India, with neither my husband nor an entourage to greet me at the other end. My impressions were innocent, naive and full of a freshness that only comes with the passion and energy of youth. It was a wonderful interlude and proved that you could have marvellous experiences on a shoestring budget. One of my most memorable experiences with food was when Sethu, my majestic mundu-clad friend who was the production head behind the films of the avant-garde filmmaker Aravindan, took me on a boat ride through the backwaters. Somewhere along the way, someone mentioned food. Sethu asked the boatman to stop at a spot where all we could see were a little hut and plenty of coconut palms. We leapt out. The boat continued down the backwaters. We sat in the shade of a coconut palm and were brought fantastic little fried fish called *podimeen* or *kozhuva* (similar to whitebait or anchovy) and a flat fish called *karimeen* – both specialties of the backwaters, we were told. We had, in fact, just seen the fish being caught a few minutes ago. They were tossed into the sand and cleaned while live, rubbed with red chilli, turmeric, salt and fried. Nothing can erase the memory of that taste, nor of that peaceful afternoon, sipping toddy, followed by a nap on the banks of the backwaters.

When I revisited, more than a decade later, friends and spouses in tow and budgets considerably more solid, Kerala hadn't really changed, but we had. Our old friend and guide, Sethu, was older and wiser and not as agile to jump on and off boats. We felt the sun was hotter. We judged. We compared. We rediscovered the little, now more formal, *toddy* shop (as they are known in Kerala), where we had experienced the amazing fish and *toddy* on that distant afternoon. Nothing much had changed except that other people had discovered our little haunt too. The *karimeen* was good but was now served on steel plates and the *toddy* was stored in plastic containers instead of the older terracotta pots. Two decades later, we took a proper houseboat down the backwaters – a luxury *kettuvalem* with air-conditioned bedrooms, spotless bathrooms and a dreamy deck with planter chairs. The boat also came along with a boatman. I was determined to find that little hut and relive the memory of the old *toddy* shop and I drove the boatman batty, plying up and down the backwaters till I finally found the place, known today as 'R' block. It was the same *toddy* shop of many moons ago but in its new avatar and infused, no doubt, with some Vitamin M from the Gulf; it had morphed into an ugly cement structure. The place was serving all the backwater staples and continued catering to the *toddy* needs of the locals. The food thankfully hadn't changed much but what was most memorable was the magical ride down the backwaters to get there.

Today, you can hire a houseboat like this, a *shikhara* (a covered moto-boat with cane seats) or an old-fashioned country boat which is manually pushed (a bit like a gondola), perfect for meandering down the tiniest of canals past fields of fuchsia-coloured lotus so thick and profuse that you can't see the water underneath. Time slows down in one of these. My Kerala escapades have come full circle and today I choose the old, inexpensive gondola over the air-conditioned houseboat as a means to discover the backwaters or rather to enjoy the journey.

The cuisine of Kerala is inseparable from its climate. The warm, green Malabar coast has for centuries been the focal point of the world's spice trade, first with the Arab spice traders and then the Portuguese, Dutch, French and British colonists. This state is the home of the much-prized black pepper, cardamom and a variety of fragrant spices. Malabar pepper has been one of the most sought-after commodities and was paid for by the Romans with gold in the olden days! The coastal area of Kerala is a strong fish- and meat-eating region. It is reported that the first Jewish settlers came to Kerala along with King Soloman's merchants, bringing with them the notion of slaughtering livestock as humanely as possible so that the meat was acceptable or kosher. There were other waves of Jewish settlers after the destruction of the Second Temple and a last migration from Spain and Portugal in the sixteenth century to escape persecution. Hindus, Jains and Buddhists were the predominant religious groups in the state until the Syrian Christians settled in Kerala.

There is some doubt about whether they came to be called Syrian Christians because their liturgy of worship was Aramaic (Syriac language) or whether they were in fact from Syria. One of the twelve disciples of Jesus, St Thomas, the apostle, is said to have landed here in CE 52 which prompted their arrival. Kerala became home to all these communities.

Not influenced by traditional Hindu prohibitions on beef, Kerala's Christians have developed a variety of beef dishes where the meat is tenderized (usually by boiling before transforming it into a rich coconut-milk curry, a dry roast or fry). They are also renowned for their wild duck dishes.

Around CE 550–800, the Arabs had a virtual monopoly on trade with Kerala, resulting in the spread of Islam in the region. With the arrival of the British in the eighteenth century, many Syrian Christians became rubber and tea plantation owners which made them a wealthy community. They were also a powerful trading community with an almost aristocratic and elegant lifestyle, which reflected in their homes, and their great love of food. Many of the dishes that are associated with 'Kerala cuisine' – fish *polichattu*, *meen moilee*, *appam* and mutton stew, duck roast and the famous beef *ularthiyathu*,

are all Syrian Christian dishes. The community doesn't observe any food restrictions and enjoys all manner of meats, poultry, seafood and vegetables. Pre-independence Kerala was basically split into the princely states of Travancore and Kochi in the south, and Malabar district in the north. The influence of this geographical divide is evident in the food even today. Along with the influence of its trade links with the Arab world, some 'Moplah' or Muslim dishes were also developed, like the wonderfully aromatic *Thalassery* biryani made with lamb (not goat). This is cooked, as tradition demands, in a large degchi on a wood fire. What is distinctive about this biryani is the aroma and taste of the pungent black pepper from Thalassery and the inclusion of dry fruits. Links with the Middle East have been retained till now. A large number of *Malayalis* work in the Gulf regions, making Kerala the biggest remittance economy in India with an estimated ₹3000 crore (over $400 million) coming in every year.

After several journeys to 'God's own country', I feel I can now taste the clear distinctions between the bland austerity of the vegetarian *sadya* or a simple banana leaf vegetarian meal, seafood dishes from the backwaters, the spicy offerings from Travancore in the south, to the meaty richness of the Malabar coast in the north of the state. This is the land of fish. They fry little ones whole, make a variety of coconut curries and shallow fry the rest – snapper, kingfish, prawns of all sizes, mussels (the meat is a great delicacy here and often more expensive than fish), squid and the pearl spot or *karimeen*. When in Kerala, you must try *karimeen*. It is the tastiest fish with succulent white flesh but a few bones to deal with. It comes from the backwaters so it's neither salty nor sweet. They dust it with salt, chilli powder and rice flour and deep or shallow fry it. Alternatively, a more glamorous recipe is *pollichattu* where the fish is cooked whole, bathed in a thick red masala, wrapped in a banana leaf which is then cooked in an open terracotta dish.

Over the years, I have fortunately come across places and people who have added to my knowledge and experience of Kerala's rich cuisine. I always christen my Kerala visits with an Ayurvedic massage for which Kerala has become world renowned. Don't expect relaxing massages. These are essentially medical treatments where there is much pummeling, pushing, shoving and oil application involved. Most of the local Ayurvedic massage places are hardcore and the oil application is done on hard wooden slabs. Something I suppose you have to get used to. I have found the perfect balance between the rigours of tradition and relaxation at **KUMARAKOM LAKE RESORT** where their girls do a synchronized oil application, gently pounding away with hot medicated poultices (*patrapodala*) which completely takes away any trace of flight fatigue. I have had a variety of treatments here over the years – all have left me in a state of calm euphoria and cured whatever ache and pain I had.

After my massages here, I generally sashay down to the Vembanad lake for a lunch of crispy *podimeen* and a glass of chilled rosé – a winning combination – and my staple lunch at the resort, which lulls me into that afternoon nap I rightfully deserve. The resort also serves excellent local food and their chefs have, over the years, been gracious enough to teach me a thing or two.

A visit to a local home for Sunday lunch is the pinnacle of pleasure, and I have been fortunate enough to know **JOSE DOMINIC**, founder of CGH Earth hotels. The lunch is a typical Syrian Christian banana leaf extravaganza at his ancestral home and farm. He is probably the first hotelier in India to talk about sustainable tourism and responsible luxury in the world of hospitality. With several gorgeous properties all over South India, his passion has now turned to farming – medicinal white turmeric, rubber trees and miniature cows! I must mention that all his stunning heritage hotels take pride in serving excellent local food.

Kochi is a 'must visit' for anyone going to Kerala for the first time and a good place to begin your South Indian odyssey. Fort Kochi has transformed from a tree lined, touristy enclave with Chinese fishing nets and Dutch colonial bungalows to an artsy, edgy neighbourhood with good restaurants and boutique hotels, galleries and cafes. It is also home to the Art Biennale which attracts hundreds and thousands of visitors from all over India over a period of three months every two years. A stroll through the sunlit, leafy lanes of Fort Kochi reminds me that this was a land of many cultures. It still remains an area full of relaxed charm with a great deal to see. Have tea at the utterly gorgeous Brunton Boatyard hotel overlooking the Arabian Sea or a coffee at David Hall, a space built by the Dutch India Company in the seventeenth century which is now an art gallery and cultural space with a beautiful garden and cafe – very bohemian chic.

A visit to Jew town with its old lace shops may seem a touristy thing to do but the lace is exquisite and a dying craft brought to the state by the Portuguese. Thomas at the Little Queen Embroidery Store is a gem. I buy something

every time I'm there. He will show you photos of himself and Prince Charles but what he doesn't brag about is that Camilla, the Duchess of Cornwall, regularly orders embroidered linen from him for her homes in the UK; delicate pinpoint, cross-stitch and lace which would compete with Bruges any day.

On my first trip to Kerala in the 1980s, we stayed at Bolgatty island in a hotel called Bolgatty Palace Hotel run then by Kerala Tourism Development Corporation (KTDC). It had modest rooms on stilts with a mesmerizing view over the Arabian Sea. The hotel is still there but there's also an impressive Grand Hyatt right next door with equally stunning views. The original palace built in the eighteenth century is one of the oldest Dutch palaces outside Holland.

SAJI THOMAS, a hotelier by profession and a cook by passion, took me to a local Kochi institution called Vella Kanthari (White Chilli) on the Kochi backwaters near the beautiful Bolgatty island for a local seafood lunch. Local ladies cook and bring you as many as twelve local specialities on a tray from which you choose. Quite a vernacular experience! In his spare time, Saji scours the city and countryside in search of culinary nuggets, ferreting out family tables laden with robust traditional dishes, eateries that serve up authentic local fare, however humble, and farms, backyards and backwaters that harvest the freshest fish, coconuts, home grown spices and other regional bounty of the land. In this chapter, I include his recipes for Malabar biryani, mutton pepper fry and Kerala fried chicken.

Breakfast offerings are aplenty in Kerala and you should try something new every morning, like *puttu* – grated coconut and rice powder layered in a cylinder and steamed served with a dish of black *channa* or with smashed baby bananas and milk. I devour the *kozhukotta* – a sort of *modak* or balls of rice stuffed with jaggery and coconut and steamed. There are also crisp Udupi style *dosas*, chutneys, simple *sambhars* and *idlis*, but why try those when you can have the rice spaghetti like *iddiappam* with a mouthwatering egg roast?

Kerala has a mystical magic that stands still in time, maintaining a sense of purity and sincerity. Even in resorts, everything moves as it should, slowly, with great respect for local traditions and local recipes. The prices are reasonable and locals fall over themselves to help you. Kerala is a revival tonic and the monsoon, I feel, is the best time to be there; light rain, cool breeze, warm, sultry days and, most of all, few tourists.

I love this state – it's a real celebration of the unity as well as the diversity of people and their cuisines, of different communities with myriad influences of centuries wafting out of their kitchens.

1 Stir-fried Pappadum – Pappadum Thoran

2 Shallot Curry – Ulli Theeyal

3 Kerala Vegetable Stew and Appam

4 Egg Roast – Mutta Roast

5 Fish in a Light Coconut Sauce – Meen Moilee

6 Boatman Fish Curry

7 Masala Fish in Banana Leaf – Karimeen Pollichathu

8 Alleppey Yellow Prawn Curry

9 Claypot Crab

10 Kerala Fried Chicken – Kozhy Varutha

11 Duck Roast – Varutha Tharavu

12 Slow-roasted Coconut Beef – Beef Ularthiyathu

13 Mutton Pepper Fry

14 Malabar Mutton Biryani

15 Coconut Milk Pudding – Payaru Payasam

STIR-FRIED PAPPADUM

PAPPADUM THORAN (PRON: PAPPADUM THORUN)

Thorans are quick stir-fried vegetable dishes made in homes all over Kerala. It is always part of the traditional *sadya* or wedding feast meal served on a banana leaf. The most common thorans are made with cabbage, long beans and okra. The two components of a classic *thoran* are the spice and coconut mixture – garlic, green chilli and grated coconut and a tempering of spices – usually mustard, red chilli and curry leaves. A quick fix for *thoran* is to add all the ingredients, splash a bit of water, stick a tight-fitting lid on and steam cook. Surprisingly easy! I love this one from the Kumarakom Lake Resort, where, instead of green vegetables, they use crushed pappadum (papad). It gives a fantastic texture, taste and twist to predictability and tastes spectacular with a glass of wine or beer as you sit sipping and eating at sunset, overlooking lake Vembanad.

Serves: 4

INGREDIENTS

10 big or 15 small pappadum (papad)
½ cup fresh coconut, grated
A pinch of turmeric powder
6 small onions or shallots, finely chopped
¼ tsp cumin seeds
2 green chillies, finely chopped
2 cloves of garlic, crushed
2 tbsp + ¼ cup coconut oil
½ tsp mustard seeds
3-4 dried whole red chillies, torn
A few curry leaves
Salt to taste

METHOD

Fry the pappadums in ¼ cup coconut oil till they turn crisp, drain on a paper towel and then crush them roughly with your hands. In another bowl, mix the grated coconut with turmeric powder, shallots and cumin seeds, green chillies and garlic.

Heat 2 tbsp oil in a pan and throw in mustard seeds and, when they start to splutter, add dried red chillies, curry leaves and sauté for a minute. Add the coconut mixture and a pinch of salt to the tempering in the pan. Stir and remove. Mix in the crushed pappadum. Serve at once.

SHALLOT CURRY

ULLI THEEYAL (PRON: OOLLEE THEEYEL)

A traditional dish with sweet and sour notes which packs a lot of flavour. *Ulli* are small shallot-like onions which add a sharp onion flavour to any dish. *Theeyal* means 'burnt', probably because of the dark brown colour from the roasted coconut and tamarind. I first had this dish years ago at the gorgeous Kumarakom Lake Resort on Lake Vembanad. They have a little restaurant overlooking the lake, and my lunch used to be crispy *podimeen*, ullitheeyal, an appam and a glass of chilled rosé.

Serves: 4

INGREDIENTS

100 ml coconut oil
1 coconut, grated
5 tbsp ginger-garlic paste
2 tbsp fennel seeds
3 tbsp red chilli powder
4 tbsp coriander powder
A few curry leaves
2 cups small onion (shallots), peeled and each cut into two
2 green chillies, each cut on the slant into 3 pieces
¼ cup tamarind pulp
⅓ cup jaggery, crumbled
A pinch of asafoetida
2 dried red chillies
1 tsp mustard seeds
1 tbsp turmeric powder
Salt to taste

METHOD

Heat a large frying pan and add 1 tbsp oil. Roast the grated coconut with fennel seeds, ginger and garlic till golden brown. Add chilli powder, coriander powder and salt, and continue to roast on a low heat for a few minutes. Make sure that the mixture doesn't burn as the coconut releases its own oil. Cool and grind this mixture to a thick paste without water.

In another pan, heat the remaining coconut oil (leave 1 tbsp for the tempering) and fry the onions for a minute. Add the green chillies and 2 cups water, jaggery, tamarind pulp and asafoetida. Stir and add the coconut paste. Bring to the boil and simmer. Meanwhile, in another pan, heat the remaining 1 tbsp of oil and throw in the mustard seeds, red chillies and curry leaves. When they sizzle, pour this into the onion mixture. Serve fresh with rice.

KERALA VEGETABLE STEW AND APPAM

Pronounced *shtew* locally, this Kerala stew is made with coconut milk and whole spices. The meat version used to be served with soft rice bread called *appams* as a starter at Syrian Christian weddings, but today the vegetarian version is served up at breakfast throughout the state and is part of the traditional banana leaf meal called *sadya*.

Serves: 4–6

INGREDIENTS

For the stew

4 tbsp vegetable or coconut oil
6 pods of green cardamom, whole
6 cloves, whole
1 inch cinnamon stick
1 green chilli, slit vertically
2 tsp ginger, cut into julienne strips
½ cup onion, sliced
¾ cup carrots, peeled and sliced
1 cup potato, peeled and sliced
1½ tsp salt
1½ cups water
½ cup French beans, cut into fine slices
1 cup cauliflower, cut into small florets
10–15 curry leaves
1 tsp black peppercorns, coarsely crushed
2 cups coconut milk

For the *appam*

500 g rice flour or raw rice
25 g semolina (*rawa*)
Salt to taste
5 g yeast
1 tsp sugar
Coconut milk from half a coconut
Water to mix

METHOD

For the stew

In a medium-sized pan, heat oil and sauté the cardamom, cloves and cinnamon sticks for half a minute on medium heat. Add green chillies, ginger, onion and sauté for 2 minutes. Add carrots, potatoes, salt and water. Cover the pan with a lid and cook for 5 minutes. Stir in the French beans, cauliflower and the curry leaves and continue cooking for another 8 minutes or until tender. Add the crushed peppercorns and coconut milk and simmer for a minute at very low heat so that the coconut milk does not curdle. Adjust salt if needed and serve hot with appam or rice.

For the *appam*

If using raw rice, soak the rice for 2 hours and make a fine paste of it without adding too much water. If using the rice flour, mix with water (make sure that you don't make a very thin batter).

Heat a little water and cook the semolina, keep stirring to avoid forming lumps. Allow to cool a little and mix with the rice flour batter. Add salt, sugar and yeast. Keep the batter aside for a minimum of 6–8 hours and let it ferment. Once fermented, add coconut milk and keep aside for another half an hour. Start making appam in a nonstick or cast-iron traditional *appam* kadhai by swirling the batter around. A little batter will sink to the bottom, giving you thin crisp edges and a soft belly at the bottom.

EGG ROAST

MUTTA ROAST (PRON: MOTTAA)

This is a popular breakfast dish in Kerala. *Mutta* is egg all over South India. This version is a bit like an egg curry but the masala is onion-based and sticks to the eggs rather than the eggs floating in a pool of sauce. It tastes fabulous with hot *appams* and is a great spicy start to the day. The word 'roast' is very deceptive in Kerala and has nothing to do with any oven-roasting at all. It has a great deal to do with frying, mainly onions in oil or ghee and browned masala into which your boiled eggs, duck or chicken are tossed.

***Serves:* 2**

INGREDIENTS

100 ml coconut oil
¼ tsp mustard seeds
6–8 curry leaves
4 large onions, sliced
2 tbsp ginger, chopped
1 tbsp garlic, chopped
3 tbsp coriander powder
2 tbsp red chilli powder
1 tbsp turmeric powder
1 tsp green chillies, chopped
2 cups tomato, chopped
¼ cup coconut milk
2 boiled eggs, halved
1 tbsp garam masala powder
Salt to taste

METHOD

Heat a pan and add 2 tbsp of the coconut oil. Add in the mustard seeds. When the mustard seeds start to pop, add curry leaves and sliced onions. Fry on low heat until the onions are very lightly browned and soft. Add ginger and garlic and sauté for a minute. Now add all the dry spice powders – chilli powder, coriander powder and turmeric powder. Fry for a minute on low heat. Then add the tomatoes and green chillies along with 1 cup of water. Cook on a medium heat until the tomatoes turn soft. Add salt to taste. You should have a thick masala like gravy. Add in some coconut milk and stir through. Lastly, add the boiled eggs and allow to cook for 2 minutes. Do not stir as the point is to keep the egg halves and yolk intact. Sprinkle with garam masala. Serve hot with steamed rice or *appam*.

FISH IN A LIGHT COCONUT SAUCE

MEEN MOILEE (PRON: MEAN MOYLEE)

Nobody is quite certain where this dish originated. It is likely of Portuguese origin or the word 'moilee' may have come from 'Malay' but is associated with both the Syrian Christian community and Kerala. It is a delicious light yellow fish curry, creamy with coconut milk and very gentle spices. In West Bengal, the prawn dish *chingri malai* is said to have similar origins because of trading with Asia.

***Serves:* 4**

INGREDIENTS

¼ cup coconut oil
10–12 curry leaves
½ tsp mustard seeds
½ tsp fenugreek seeds
1 onion, sliced
3–4 cloves of garlic, chopped
2-inch piece of ginger, cut into juliennes
2–3 green chillies, slit vertically
1 tsp turmeric powder
1 cup thin coconut milk
1 tsp vinegar, preferably coconut vinegar or any light-coloured natural vinegar
2 cups thick coconut milk
½ kg kingfish or any white fleshy fish, cut into 2-inch pieces
1 tomato, sliced lengthwise into 6 pieces
½ tsp salt to taste

METHOD

Rub around a teaspoon of salt into the fish and keep aside. Heat oil in a pan and fry the curry leaves, mustard seeds and fenugreek seeds for a few seconds. Add the onions and sauté for 2–3 minutes until cooked but still white. Add garlic and ginger, then turmeric powder and the green chillies and stir for a few minutes. Wipe the fish pieces dry and slide them into the pan. After a minute, add the thin coconut milk and vinegar. Bring the mix to just under a boil till the fish is cooked. Now add the thick coconut milk and reduce to a simmer. Stir and take the *moilee* off the heat immediately. Serve hot with rice, *appam* or bread.

This is quite a thick velvety curry.

Tip 1: *You can add a few peppercorns, cloves and cardamom to the oil when frying the curry leaves but remember to remove them before serving. It brings a gentle spice flavouring to the dish.*

Tip 2: *Instead of the thin coconut milk, you can add ½ cup fish or chicken stock.*

COLONEL
SAAB
COLONEL
SAAB

BOATMAN FISH CURRY

The *karimeen*, or pearl spot fish, is particularly popular in this region. The perfect place to savour the *karimeen* is on a houseboat, floating along Kerala's tranquil estuaries or in a 'toddy shop' somewhere along the way. The boatmen often double up as cooks on these boats and they all seem to produce local fish, tossed in spices and fried in coconut oil and a fish curry, at the drop of a hat. Fish curry is traditionally served with tapioca or *kappa* in the backwaters. Thick tapioca roots are either steamed, boiled or mashed and garnished with coconut, but rice is more popular as an accompaniment today.

Here's the one we had on one of our trips; it was made by our boatman.

Serves: 4

INGREDIENTS

For the curry

3 tbsp coconut oil
12–15 curry leaves
½ tsp mustard seeds
¼ tsp fenugreek seeds
4–5 sambhar onions, peeled and lightly crushed
3–4 hot green chillies, slit vertically
1-inch piece of ginger, peeled and crushed
5 cloves of garlic, crushed
2–3 pieces of kodampuli or
2 tbsp tamarind paste
1½ tsp salt
750 g karimeen, fish steaks or slices, about ½-inch thick
3 hot dried red chillies, broken

For the coconut paste

1 tsp red chilli powder
3 tbsp coriander powder
1 tsp turmeric powder
1 cup coconut, freshly grated

METHOD

In a mixer/grinder/blender, combine the ingredients for the coconut paste with a little water and grind to a paste. Heat the oil in a kadhai and throw in the curry leaves, mustard seeds and fenugreek seeds. As the seeds start to crackle, add the onions, green chilli, ginger and garlic. Stir and cook on medium heat until the onions become lightly golden – this won't take long. Add the paste to the pan with 1½ cups water and bring to the boil. Lower the heat and cook for 5–7 minutes to cook the spices. Add the *kodampuli* or tamarind and the broken dry chillies. Season with salt and slip in the fish. Cover and simmer gently for 10 minutes, or until the fish is just cooked.

MASALA FISH IN BANANA LEAF

KARIMEEN POLLICHATHU (PRON: CURRYMEEN POLEECHAADH)

It is almost worth going to the backwaters of Kerala for this fish alone. Known as pearl spot in English, *karimeen* is a plumpish flat fish which resembles a pomfret in size and shape but has a thicker black/grey skin. The flavour is neither salty nor sweet since it is caught in the backwaters of Kerala. It is coated with a little salt, turmeric and chilli powder and crisp-fried or smothered in a spice paste, wrapped in a banana leaf and cooked traditionally in an *urli*. Both versions taste divine. This version of *pollichathu* which is not wrapped entirely in banana leaf is the creation of Chef Deepak from the gorgeous Kumarakom Lake Resort where we often go for a bit of R&R.

Serves: 1

INGREDIENTS

1 *karimeen* (pearl spot), approx 300 g

For the marinade

1 tbsp ginger-garlic paste
2 tbsp mild red chili powder
Juice of 1 lime
Salt to taste

For the paste

1 tsp ginger, chopped
1 tsp garlic, chopped
2 tsp Kashmiri chilli powder
1 tsp hot red chili powder
½ tsp turmeric powder
1 tsp coriander powder
¼ tsp cumin seeds
15 small shallots, fried 1 *kodampuli* bulb, soaked for an hour in warm water and strained. Use ¼ cup of the juice

A few curry leaves
4 tbsp coconut oil (to fry the shallots and for the fish)
Coarse ground pepper to taste
1 banana leaf
⅓ cup coconut cream or thick coconut milk

METHOD

Clean the fish and make gashes on both sides. Marinate in the spice mixture and keep aside for 10 minutes.

Combine all ingredients for the paste and grind using a little water. Heat some coconut oil and cook the ground spice paste for 5–10 minutes. Add the *kodampuli* juice and salt to taste. Once this masala paste cools, coat the fish with it and keep aside for another 15 minutes.

Heat a heavy cast-iron pan and sprinkle a few drops of coconut oil in it. Place the banana leaf on it. Put the marinated fish on top of the banana leaf with a few curry leaves. Smother the fish with the remaining masala paste. Add coconut milk and crushed pepper. Allow the fish to cook for about 5 minutes. Then cover the pan with a lid and allow the fish to steam cook through for a further 7–8 minutes or until just done. The coconut milk and masala paste should be reduced to a thick paste. To serve, remove the fish with the banana leaf and place on a plate.

Note: *A good substitute for karimeen in India would be pomfret or, if you would prefer a fish steak without bones, any white fleshy fish like rawas or bhetki in India or snapper or sea bass abroad.*

Tip: *Use coconut or any natural vinegar as a substitute for kodampuli.*

ALLEPPEY YELLOW PRAWN CURRY

This is the delicious, velvety smooth, yellow prawn curry that is referred to in restaurants as 'Alleppey' prawn curry. It comes from the middle of the state and most people know the area because this is where the backwater houseboats or *kettuvalams* start from. Locally it is known simply as 'yellow curry'. I had this curry at my old friend Bindu Panicker's home and she convinced her mother to part with the recipe. I think Mother Panicker was reluctant at first because 'It is really so easy', she said! There's no complicated grinding of a masala paste; it's just made with a few spices and powders and is a specialty of Hindu non-vegetarian homes in Kerala.

Serves: 4

INGREDIENTS

For the curry

¼ cup coconut oil
½ tsp black mustard seeds
10–12 curry leaves
3 tsp ginger, chopped
4 tsp garlic, chopped
¾ cup *sambhar* onions, peeled but left whole (shallots)
3–4 green chillies, slit vertically
1 medium-sized raw mango, peeled and cut into 2-inch pieces without skin
2½ cups thick coconut milk
500 g medium-sized prawns, peeled, cleaned and deveined
1½ tsp salt

For the spice paste

1 tsp turmeric powder
½ tsp coriander powder
1 tsp red chilli powder

METHOD

Mix the spice powders with ¼ cup of water to prepare the spice paste. Heat oil in a stone pot or pan on medium heat and toss in the mustard seeds and curry leaves. When the mustard seeds start to splutter, add ginger, garlic, whole onions, green chillies and lastly the spice paste and cook on a low heat for a few minutes till the spices are cooked. The mixture should not turn brown. Add 1 cup water and raw mango. Bring to the boil, then lower the heat to simmer and pour in the coconut milk. Stir continuously and add prawns. Continue to cook on a very low heat till the prawns are cooked – for around 6 minutes. Taste and season with salt. Serve with hot steamed rice.

Tip: *If raw mango is unavailable, substitute with 2 tbsp light tamarind pulp (not the dark block).*

CLAYPOT CRAB

I have always wondered how human beings decided to eat crab. Delicious creature though it is, for me it falls in the same category as a custard apple or an oyster, those 'difficult to eat or open, but addictive once you get hooked' foods. Along the west coast of India, small sea crabs are relatively common, but nobody really thought much about the big mud crabs in the great culinary circles of this country until a little restaurant in south Bombay, called Trishna, started serving something called 'Salt, Butter, Pepper, Garlic Jumbo Crab'. It was as much of a mouthful as the description on the menu; succulent, sweet flesh surrounded by devilishly sinful melted butter spiked with oodles of garlic. Somehow it was this combination of the melted garlic butter, the whopping size of those claws (which also makes it easier to get to the flesh) and the 'bohemianness' of being in a then-unfashionable back alley, that somehow hooked us all.

Going into a fish market in India can be a frightening ordeal if you are not used to it. Large fisherwomen beckoning, shouting different prices and different species like madams of their domain. If you don't already know, please buy crab live, not dead. This is because crab flesh goes off very fast after it has been killed.

In India, our jumbo crabs are sweet, moist and tasty and I hear that many of them, especially from Kerala, now go straight for export, mainly to Singapore where they command a hefty price. In Asia, they are referred to as mud or, mangrove crabs since they are usually found in mangroves, rivers or estuaries. This is a traditional clay pot recipe using small mud crabs found near Kerala's shores. It would have been cooked in a stone or clay pot, but any large utensil will work. I often do it in a wok.

Serves: 4

INGREDIENTS

5 crabs (appox 200 g each)
½ tsp turmeric powder
5 tbsp coconut oil
4 onions (medium-sized), sliced
4 tbsp ginger-garlic paste (1:1)
2 tbsp Kashmiri chilli powder
1 tsp coriander powder
½ tsp fennel powder
2 medium-sized tomatoes, chopped
4 green chillies, chopped
A few curry leaves
2 pieces *kodampuli* (soaked in water to soften)
Salt to taste
½ cup thick coconut milk

METHOD

Clean and cut the crabs into pieces. Put the crab pieces in a big pot with some salt, turmeric powder and ¼ cup water. Cover and cook on high heat for 10 minutes. Keep the pot aside. In a pan, heat some coconut oil, add onion and fry on a high heat for a couple of minutes. Add the ginger-garlic paste and fry well until the mix becomes aromatic. Lower the heat and add all powders – chilli, coriander and fennel – and mix well. Once the raw smell of the spices has gone, add curry leaves, chillies and chopped tomatoes to it and continue to cook on a low heat until you have a paste-like consistency. Now add the *kodampuli*, the cooked crab and any of its water to the masala. Cook it for 10 minutes on low flame. Finish with thick coconut milk.

KERALA FRIED CHICKEN

KOZHY VARUTHA (PRON: KOREE VAHRTHA)

Let's face it, there is nothing quite as scrumptious as a piece of deep-fried, crispy chicken. There's a reason why KFC is a global brand. Chicken was only 'local' or free range when this recipe originated. They were sold in markets live or reared by someone you knew. Today of course you can do it with a commercial broiler but it won't taste the same, so please try and source a good, organic or farm bird. Deep-frying chicken is popular all over the south, including Kerala. I guarantee, you'll never eat Kentucky fried chicken again after tasting this one! This recipe comes from Saji Thomas's kitchen. It is his go-to Sunday special. Malayalis clearly knew that brining a chicken or cooking it with salt and spices first was the key to a flavourful bird long before Colonel Sanders 'invented' it!

Serves: 4

INGREDIENTS

1 free range chicken – approx 1 kg, cut into 8 pieces
1½ tsp salt
3 tsp chilli powder
1 tsp turmeric powder
3 tsp ginger-garlic paste
1 tsp garam masala

1 cup rice powder or rice flour
2 tsp cornflour

Oil to deep fry
1 cup curry leaves

METHOD

Cook the chicken till soft in a pot with a tight lid with half the chilli powder, turmeric, salt and ½ cup water. Remove the boiled chicken and marinate with the remaining chilli powder, ginger-garlic and garam masala for an hour. Mix the rice flour with the cornflour in a bowl and dip each piece of the chicken in this to coat it thoroughly. Heat the oil in a kadhai or wok and slip in a few pieces of chicken at a time till each piece turns golden. It is better to do this in batches. Throw in the curry leaves and fry till crisp. To serve, sprinkle with the crispy curry leaves and any crispy bits from the kadhai. The more rustic this looks, the better.

DUCK ROAST

VARUTHA THARAVU (PRON: VAHRTHA THAARAAVE)

Duck is my favourite protein, even more than seafood which I adore. Whenever I've cooked or eaten duck in Europe, it is usually the plump breast, *magret*, or the full leg *confit*, slow cooked in its own fat. So I was quite excited to discover that Kerala has duck and that duck roast is a traditional dish amongst the Syrian Christian community. A note on the word 'roast' – you'll find 'ghee roast' and 'beef roast' on India's southwest coast from Goa down to Kerala. This has nothing to do with an oven, so don't expect perfectly crispy skin or a juicy joint of meat cooked lightly and left pink in the middle. 'Roast' in this part of the world means to fry something, often in ghee, till brown. The roasting refers to roasting spices in oil or ghee in a heavy skillet or kadhai. In Kerala, the duck is wild, so it is a tough, skinny bird but full of flavour. The duck pieces are first boiled to soften the meat and then *fried* in a pan with spices till dry. The two common recipes with duck are a curry with coconut milk and a roast duck, which I prefer. Even though everything is cooked to smithereens, the flavour is still intact. This recipe was shared by a young cook at Kumarakom Lake Resort. I was so excited about the prospect that he actually arranged a little cooking class to show me what roasting actually meant.

Serves: 3–4

INGREDIENTS

1 duck, cut into 10 pieces (around 1 kg)
4–5 curry leaves
1 tbsp coriander powder
1 tbsp pepper, coarsely crushed
1 tsp salt
¼ tsp turmeric powder
2 tbsp ginger, chopped
3 tbsp garlic, chopped

1 cup coconut oil
10 small onions (shallots), sliced
2 green chillies
½ tsp garam masala powder
¼ cup coconut milk

METHOD

Boil the duck with the curry leaves, coriander, pepper, salt, turmeric powder, ginger, garlic and enough water to cover. Cook till tender – 1½ cups of water should be enough if you are using a pressure cooker. You will need 3 cups of water at least if you're cooking in a pot or pan.

Heat 3 tbsp of oil and fry the onions till they turn almost crisp. Remove from the heat and keep aside. To this pan, add the stock of the boiled duck and cook and reduce it to half a cup. Then add the duck and green chillies and cook on a slow fire till dry. Add garam masala powder and check the seasoning. Heat the remaining oil in another kadhai. If you're wondering what happened to the 'roasting', here it is – now fry the duck pieces till they turn brown on all sides. Add the coconut milk and cook on a low heat till the sauce clings to the duck pieces. Serve with the fried onions on top and fried potatoes on the side.

SLOW-ROASTED COCONUT BEEF

BEEF ULARTHIYATHU (PRON: OOLYERTHIYADH)

I had the most tasty, succulent Beef *Ularthiyathu* made by Chef Gejo Joseph at the Fort Kochi boutique hotel. Situated right at the heart of Fort Kochi, a couple of minutes' walk from the waters' edge in a house which belonged to a well-to-do Jewish merchant in the nineteenth century. The menu at Fort Kochi is extensive and caters to the international traveller, but their traditional Syrian Christian dishes are the stars here. This is one of our most popular dishes at Colonel Saab in London.

***Serves:** 3–4*

INGREDIENTS

300 g boneless beef (tenderloin or rump)
½ tsp red chilli powder
1 tsp coriander powder
¼ cup coconut bits
30 ml coconut oil
½ tsp mustard seeds
1 tsp fennel seeds
1 green chilli
1 tsp ginger, sliced
1 tsp garlic, chopped
2 dried red chillies, chopped
10 curry leaves
2 onions, sliced
2 tbsp coconut slivers
1 tbsp coriander powder
¼ tsp turmeric powder
2 tsp chilli powder
½ cup tomato, sliced
Salt to taste
½ tsp garam masala powder
2 tsp fennel seed powder
½ tsp crushed black pepper

METHOD

Cook the beef in a pressure cooker or pot until tender, with the coconut bits, red chilli powder, coriander powder and 1 cup of water. If cooking in an ordinary pot, you'll need more water.

Heat the coconut oil in a thick-bottomed pan. Add the mustard seeds and fennel and let them crackle. Add in ginger, garlic, green chilli, curry leaves, red chilli, coconut slivers and onion. Sauté on a medium heat till the onions are golden, then add turmeric powder, chilli powder, coriander powder and the sliced tomato. Add the cooked beef and coconut bits along with the cooking liquid to the pan, stirring continuously. When almost all the gravy has reduced and the masala starts sticking to the beef, add garam masala, fennel seed powder, pepper and salt.

Serve hot with Kerala paratha or *appam*.

MUTTON PEPPER FRY

Mutton and beef pepper fry are common in small, unassuming roadside eateries in Kerala. The meat is often not of great quality, but you sit and chew away because the spices are so lip smacking. This recipe allows you to replicate the dish at home, ensuring melt-in-the-mouth meat and the same spice quotient. You can also make it with beef. For beef fry, the pieces are cut much smaller and cooked first with cloves, cinnamon, star anise, ginger, garlic, spice powders, coconut and water till the beef is tender. The onions are then fried separately in coconut oil till brown, and then the meat pieces with their spices and curry leaves are added and cooked till the masala turns dry. Thank you for the recipe, Saji Joseph!

***Serves:* 4**

INGREDIENTS

For the mutton fry

1 full leg of mutton/lamb (approx. 750 g, after removing the bone, you should be left with around 500 g boneless mutton, cut into 1½-inch chunks)
3 tbsp coconut oil (2 tbsp to fry, 1 tbsp for just before serving)
5 cloves of garlic, finely chopped
1 inch piece of ginger, thinly sliced
1 large onion, finely chopped
10 curry leaves
¾ tsp salt
4 tbsp black pepper, freshly crushed
2 tsp fresh coconut, cut into ½-inch bits and fried till golden
½ cup fried onions

For the marinade

1 tsp cumin powder
1 tsp red chilli powder
1 tsp coriander powder
½ tsp turmeric powder
1 tsp salt
2 tsp lemon juice

METHOD

Mix all the marinade ingredients and marinate the mutton for 2–3 hours or overnight in the fridge. Heat 2 tbsp of coconut oil in a pan (though traditionally this is cooked in an *urli*) and fry the garlic and ginger for a minute. Add onions and curry leaves. Cook on a medium heat till the onions turn soft. Add marinated mutton, salt, pepper and coconut pieces, and mix well. Continue to cook on medium heat for 4 minutes. Now add 2 cups of water and mix well. Cover and cook on a low heat until the mutton is tender and the water has dried up. Garnish the mutton pepper fry with fried onion slices and fried coconut chips. Pour a tablespoon of coconut oil on top before serving.

MALABAR MUTTON BIRYANI

Saji and Pinky Thomas are great foodies. This is their easy-to-do version of the Moplah or Malabar biryani. Saji's family, although Syrian Christian, live in Calicut in north Kerala where this biryani comes from, so they have grown up eating it. The origin of biryani can be traced back to Persia where they had a fried rice dish known as *birinj*. A version called *plov* is eaten all over Central Asia and was brought to India by the Mughals. Malabar biryani is miles away from what developped in Lucknow and Hyderabad, although it can be considered a local version. It is made with local kaima rice and, besides the spices which are common in all biryanis, it also contains cashews and raisins.

Serves: 8

INGREDIENTS

1½ kg mutton with bone, cut into 1½-inch pieces
6 large onions, thinly sliced
6 whole shallots
100 g garlic
50 g ginger
2 sprigs of curry leaves
15 green chillies
1 bunch or 4 cups coriander leaves, chopped
½ bunch or 2 cups mint leaves, chopped
½ cup yoghurt, whisked till smooth
2 tbsp garam masala
1 tbsp fennel powder
1 tsp turmeric powder
4 tomatoes, roughly chopped
¾ cup coconut oil
Salt to taste
1 kg *Kaima* rice
4 pods of cardamom
1-inch stick of cinnamon
4 cloves
1 star anise
Rose water

To serve

½ cup fried cashews
¼ cup raisins
½ cup sliced onions, fried till crisp

METHOD

Clean and coarsely crush the shallots, 6 cloves of garlic, quarter of the ginger and 3 chillies. Heat 2 tbsp oil in a large pan and add the curry leaves followed by the crushed shallot mixture. Fry on medium heat till golden. Add mutton, salt and enough water to cover the mutton. You could either use a pressure cooker or cook mutton the traditional way till it turns soft. Remove the mutton pieces with a slotted spoon and keep the liquid aside to use as stock later – you should have about 2 cups or more of it. Soak the rice for 20 minutes and drain off the water. Heat 2 tbsp of oil and fry the cardamom, cloves, star anise and cinnamon on low heat. Add the rice and mutton stock in 1:2 ratio; so for 1 kg rice you need 2 litres of stock or stock + water. Add in some salt and cook till almost done.

Make a paste of the remaining ginger, garlic and chillies by grinding them. In a large, thick-bottomed pot, heat the remaining oil and fry the onions till golden. Add the ginger-garlic-chilli paste and fry for a few minutes on a medium heat. Add in the tomatoes, garam masala and fennel powder, followed by the cooked mutton, fresh coriander, mint and yoghurt. Cover and cook for 5 minutes. Lower the heat and spoon all the rice over the meat mixture. Sprinkle some rose water and cover and cook on low heat for 15 minutes. Garnish and serve with cashews, raisins and fried onions.

Note: *Jeerakasala or Wayanadan Kaima rice is a short grained aromatic variety of rice used especially for Calicut biryani.*

COCONUT MILK PUDDING

PAYARU PAYASAM (PRON: PAYAR PAYAASUM)

This is one of the two most common *payasams* or milk puddings in the state. One is made with rice and milk, rather like a rice pudding. The other one is made with whole green moong and coconut milk and is, to my mind, much more delicious. It's also good for those who are lactose intolerant. It is served at all traditional dinners along with a milk-based *payasam*. I have also seen big vats of it made for a temple feast, stirred like a witches' cauldron, but in Kerala it will be a shallow bell metal *urli*.

Serves: 2

INGREDIENTS

250 g jaggery powder
1 cup whole green moong (green gram or *cherupayaar*)
2 tbsp rice powder
1 cup thin coconut milk
½ tsp cardamom powder
1 cup thick coconut milk
A pinch of salt
3 tbsp ghee
¼ cup whole cashews, fried
¼ cup raisins (soaked in a little water to soften)
¼ cup fresh coconut chips (cut into ½-inch pieces from the white flesh of the coconut)

METHOD

In a saucepan, mix the jaggery with 1 cup of water and cook on a low heat till dissolved. Cool and strain. Cook the moong in plenty of water (to which you add a pinch of salt) till it turns extremely soft. There should be some water left. It's best to soak the moong overnight or cook in a pressure cooker. Add the rice powder to the thin coconut milk and mix thoroughly. Add the jaggery syrup and the thin coconut milk mixture to the moong and bring to the boil. Lower the heat and add the thick coconut milk along with the cardamom powder and allow it to come to just under a boil. Remove from heat. Stir in the ghee to finish and top with fried cashew nuts, raisins and fresh coconut chips. Serve warm.

यशवंत गुलाबराव नाईक
ढोल-ताशे व्यापारी
मो. : 9371015532

MAHARASHTRA

I live in Pune, a city of just over 3 million. It's around 200 km from Mumbai, on the Deccan plateau, with a reputation as the centre of higher education – an Oxford of the East so to speak because of its many colleges and a significant university. Although the city has a cosmopolitan culture and attracts people from all over the country, it has managed to retain its Maharashtrian soul. I feel I am in a pole position – living within but not belonging to the city – to have some fun in the pursuit of a few home truths.

Maharashtrian cuisine is one of the lesser-known Indian cuisines and suffers because there is very little written down about it. It has not been actively promoted, perhaps because it lacks the glamour and sophistication of some other Indian cuisines. Generally speaking, Maharashtrians are regarded as quietly understated and not prone to fuss, pampering or excess; their food follows similar patterns. When you are invited over for a meal in Pune, you will get home-cooked food, nothing store bought, and it will most likely be a very traditional meal not borrowing from any foreign or even other Indian cuisines. There may be a sweet dish if there is a special occasion, rotis stuffed with a mixture of jaggery and chickpea flour known as *puran poli* or a simple yoghurt-based *shrikand*. In between meals, if you have a sweet tooth, you can snack on flaky pastries dusted with icing sugar known as *chirothas* and, during the festival of Ganpati, you are likely to find sweet, steamed dumplings called *modaks*.

The *Puneri Brahmin* (Brahmin belonging to Pune) is a strange creature. I can say so because I'm married to one (well he's half a Puneri Brahmin and I constantly hope that he takes after the other half). The Puneri Brahmin speaks plainly and is fiercely proud, sometimes to the point of rudeness. He will not bend backwards to help and is often outspoken. He likes a well-ordered, disciplined life and his expectations aren't high. In Pune, the Brahmin community is generally vegetarian and their daily diet is frugal; almost spiritual in its simplicity. You'll have a green vegetable made with dill, spinach or a baby brinjal rich with a peanut masala, an *amti* or dal, a couple of chutneys, a *koshimbir* or chopped salad, millet roti or *bhaakri* and local *ambemohr* or mango blossom rice with a dollop of ghee. This does not however mean that the dishes are either easy to prepare nor have they been thrown together in an ad hoc fashion. Many of them require a deft hand, are time-consuming and take years of experience to get just right. Each meal is prepared to an almost mathematical precision for the number of people at the table. I am a big salad person and, when I first sat down to lunch at my mother-in-law's home many years ago, I noticed a *vati* or small bowl of chopped salad right next to my thali. I took it, presuming it was for me since I am such a big salad eater; there was pin-drop silence. The *koshimbir* or chopped salad was for everyone to share! After that, the cook, Sarubai, was kind enough to make a larger helping every time I went over. On a Maharashtrian thali, you have the principle of *ujwa-dava-sagla-hava* which means that the placement of the items both raw and cooked on the left and the right of the thali must be balanced. There is a place for the lemon and raw chilli just as there is a place for the salad. I clearly screwed that up.

Every evening in Pune you see fresh leafy vegetables from nearby farms piled high on carts – bundles of red and green amaranth, fresh fenugreek, spring onions, spinach and kohlrabi and beetroot with their greens. People buy a bunch or two for their evening meal and stick them into little cloth bags. They buy exactly what they need for one meal. There are no leftovers because it's all available fresh on the corner the next evening.

Of the other three cuisines within this state, the communities from the Konkan coast are the most complicated: you have the Konkanastha Brahmin who is vegetarian, a community called CKP who eat everything, another one called Pathare Prabhu who were amongst the early settlers in Bombay and eat fowl, fish and meat, and the Saraswat Brahmins who are vegetarian with the exception of seafood. Most of this coastal region is known for its delicious spicy seafood, chicken and mutton dishes from the region of Malvan – baby shark fry, prawn masala with kokum, Bombay duck and Malvani chicken made with a dry spice blend of sixteen ingredients. The chicken is always hacked into around twelve pieces through the bone with no care to joint it. Many small eateries in

Mumbai still serve authentic Malvani food. They set up their eateries at the turn of the century to cater to migrant workers from the region who flocked to Bombay to work in the city's textile mills, factories and docks. The blue and white collared workers, who were mainly men, lived in tenement housing known as *chawls* with single rooms and no kitchen. The Irani cafes in the city owned and run by Zoroastrians, who fled Persia because of persecution, also started catering to the various communities in Bombay around the same time. They didn't serve Maharashtrian food though, they were famous for their chai and snacks – samosas and puffs, *kheema pau*, homemade biscuits, cakes and colourful soft drinks.

The Portuguese impact was not just limited to Goa but extended its wing to Bombay as well, as their policy was also the 'evangelization' of the 'Province of the North' (Província do Norte), i.e., Bombay. There were already Christians in Bombay whom the Portuguese succeeded in converting to Catholicism along with several Hindus. The Christians (Marathi-speaking unlike the Goans who spoke Konkani) were sometimes referred to as 'Portuguese Christians'. After Portugal handed over Bombay in 1661 to the British East India Company, the latter began recruiting Christians from other parts of the Konkan – Mangalore and Goa. In order to differentiate the ethnic community of Bombay from the migrants, they began to call themselves the 'Original East Indians'.

East Indian food is a mix of Goan Christian with British influences and Indian spices. Like Goans, they have Portuguese-inspired dishes like *vindalho*, *balchao* and *guisado*. Like other Christian communities from Kerala, Madras, Mangalore and Goa, they also have tongue roast, pan rolls and potato chops stuffed with mince, in common. But their little bread rolls or *fugias*, *frithad*, ball curry and their famous dry spice mix commonly referred to as 'bottle masala', are totally their own.

I remember my father always asking my mother to make ball curry in the UK. My sister and I giggled like it was our private little joke. There was much cross pollination between Goans, East Indians and the Anglo Indians living in Mumbai in those days and when they immigrated to far off shores, so did the potato chops, *bafat* and ball curry.

This was further aided by a lovely old lady who did her own range of dry ground spices called Kenny's from a tiny store in Byculla. I can still remember the aroma of spices roasting in a kadhai in the back of the shop while I waited for her to pack the spices. My mother bought insane quantities every time she would visit Bombay and many of the Indian dishes that she churned out in London were permutations and combinations of Mrs Kenny's pepper masala, *bafat* masala and *frithad* masala.

Kolhapur in central Maharashtra is where you'll find the heavier and spicier dishes from the state. The city was home to the Marathas who ruled from the mid-seventeenth century for around 150 years. Marathas love their mutton. Angre, Mohite, More, Bhonsle, Pawar are all Maratha surnames, so if you're invited to dinner by one of them, you can maybe expect Kolhapuri mutton – rich in spices, *pandhra rassa* – a dish of soft mutton in a gentle thin white coconut soupy curry, *tamda rassa* – a red coloured gravy or *kaala* (black) mutton from the north of the state but made by famous families in Baramati.

This is also the sugarcane belt, so jaggery is a predominant ingredient in cooking. *Bhaakri*, flatbreads made with millets, replaces rice. Lastly, *Vidarbha* (Varadhi) food, from the north of the state around Nagpur and Jalgaon, concentrates on fiery hot, oily tempering of chilli and garlic, and mouthwatering hand-pounded rough chutneys of chilli and garlic known as *thecha*. *Khadaknath* black chicken, an old variety of poultry said to have healing properties, is making a revival in local restaurants as have local farm eggs.

The other thing worth mentioning here is street food. India is famous for its street foods. They are simple, tasty and affordable. The origin of this type of food can be traced to food stalls in the fairs and weekly markets held in small towns and villages of India. Slowly, these dishes found their way to the larger towns and cities and were modified to suit urban palates. The appeal of street food is pan-India – it is a great leveler. The sounds and smells of *pakodas*, *bhajiyas* and *samosas*, as you walk by, is irresistible. The ingredients used are affordable and easily available. If you have grown up on the sweet, sour, tangy and spicy flavours of Indian street food, at least one

of these snack foods will find a part in your childhood memories. While the whole of India has amazing street food, Maharashtra's (and Uttar Pradesh's, I have heard, although I must confess to knowing very little about the food there) is pretty spectacular. Both Mumbai and Pune have a wealth of street food that is almost more famous than home cooking. In Pune, it's the *vada pau* – a sort of vegetarian hamburger made with deep fried potato stuffed inside a soft bread roll and eaten along with fried green chillies and a dry chutney made with peanuts, chilli and garlic; *misal pau*, a thin red gravy called 'sample' to which are added *usal* or sprouts, crispy sev and *chevda*, raw onion, tomato and a wedge of lime on the side; and the onion *bhajiya*, which are deep fried crispy onions. In Mumbai, it's the Bombay sandwich – soft white bread stuffed with slices of cooked potato, cucumber, tomato, raw beetroot and onion and slathered with green coriander chutney. And Mumbai is also where *pau bhaji* was created. Although chaat – the tangy, sweet sour spicy roadside snacks – are found all over India, Mumbai's *bhel puri* and *pani puri* are considered the best in the country.

And now to the mystery of the name Bombay duck or *bombil* as it is known locally. It is unlike any other fish and to my knowledge is not as popular anywhere else in India except in the waters around Mumbai. It has a strangely soft white almost gelatinous flesh which falls apart easily and an even stranger pinkish head – pretty ugly all around. They are eaten fresh at the end of summer when the fishing season reopens or dried for use throughout the year. It has a high almost fermented fishy smell but the communities in Mumbai – the Maharastrians, Christians and Parsis – love it. There are a few claims to the origin, but the one I like is from Farrukh Dhondy's book *Bombay Duck*, 'In fact, it should be spelt as Bombay Dak ... when the British introduced the railway system to western India under their Raj, it (bombil) started going in wagon loads to the interior from Bombay. The crates stank of dried fish ... They were marked "Bombay Dak", literally "Bombay Mail". At the time, the railway was run by the British. They referred to the fish euphemistically as "Bombay Dak", the Bombay Mail.'

Here are some of my friends and family who made this collection of recipes possible.

RAMABAI BAKHLE

Ramabai Bakhle was my husband's grandmother known fondly to everyone as '*jijee*' (granny). Her home in one of Pune's old bylanes stood resplendent under a large old laburnum tree which burst with a plethora of bright yellow flowers all summer. The whole family, including all the grand- and eventually great-grand children, would meet there on every holiday and be fed with *jijee's* amazing food. She started Pune's first finishing school for Maharashtrian girls in the 1930s. Part of the training included the art of cooking and serving traditional Maharashtrian food, including helpful hints and shopping tips which was revolutionary for the time. In the 1970s, she compiled her recipes into a book in Marathi called *Shakhambari*. I'm thankful to her granddaughter Nandita for translating some of the recipes for me and keeping those delicious food memories alive. Her recipes are simple, easy to follow and always work.

SUMITRA NAREN

When I first came to Pune in the late 1980s, I had little knowledge about the city, the culture, the communities, or the nuances of the cuisines. Sumitra Naren did a great deal of handholding and introduced me to many things about the old city in particular that many locals wouldn't know. Her table is a mix of traditional Maharashtrian, Konkan and Mangalorean food. She now lives in Holland, but fed up with the Dutch staple – the stodgy *stamppot* – she has returned to her vast repertoire of Maharashtrian home cooking to create some memorable dishes as part of something called the 'Indian Supper Club'.

RAM HUDLIKAR

The Hudlikar family are in some way related (I still haven't found out how) to my husband. Ram Hudlikar is an outstanding cook, meticulous to the last detail in all matters of Maharashtrian Brahmin home cooking with an insightful, deep knowledge and a wicked sense of humour. His mother Alka, a speech therapist for children with special needs, was the same. She reminds me of Gayatri Devi, the Princess of Jaipur. She wears a simple sari with the elegance of a queen, and has an accent as British as women on a postwar BBC Radio show.

SAGAR DESHMUKH

I discovered a little restaurant in Pune called Maratha Samrat, serving Maharashtrian food from all over the state, when I was doing the restaurant reviews for *Pune Times* a few years ago. I was astounded by the quality and authenticity of the dishes from Kolhapur, Vidarbha and the coastal area of Malvan. It is a task serving local food to locals in this state with the constant issue over pricing and authenticity. Pune is a very price-sensitive market. I'm happy to say that the handsome young owner Sagar Deshmukh went out on a limb, and it has paid off. He now has multiple branches of his restaurant in the city with long queues outside. The *thecha* prawns – his creation using the spicy green chutney from Nagpur, the plump, pan-fried prawns – the mutton fry, the almost soupy mutton *tambda* and *pandhra rassa* from Kolhapur and *kaala* mutton – a spicy dish of mutton with individually roasted spices – is difficult to find in homes, let alone in a restaurant. Maratha Samrat is one address outside a home where you can get a whiff of authentic Maharashtra in all its glory.

1 Tomato and Coconut Curry – Tomato Saar

2 Crushed Lentil and Yoghurt Salad – Chana Dalachi Chatni

3 Crispy Coriander and Lentil Toasts – Kothimbir Chi Vadi

4 Fresh Dill with Moong – Shepu Chi Bhaji

5 Everyday Sprouts – Matki

6 Baby Aubergines with Sesame and Peanut – Bharleli Vangi

7 Peanut Curry – Shengdaanyachi Aamti

8 Sweet and Sour Masoor Dal – Masoor Chi Amti

9 Prawns with Green Chilli – Prawns Thecha Fry

10 Prawns in a Coconut Chutney – Kolambi Che Vatnache Kalvan

11 Malvan Prawn Curry – Kolambi Che Kalvan

12 Spring Onions and Dry Prawns – Paaticha Kanda Ani Sukki Kolambi

13 Malvani Chicken – Malvani Kombdi

14 Blackened Mutton – Kaala Mutton

15 Kolhapuri Mutton

16 Spiced Rice Pullao – Masala Bhaat

17 Semolina Halva – Sheera Naivedya

TOMATO AND COCONUT CURRY

TOMATO SAAR

This is one of Jijee's (Ramabai Bakhle's) comfort dishes which Madhur Jaffrey loved and included in her book, *A Taste of India*. I have upped the decadence by adding thick coconut milk and ghee for the tempering which makes the texture all the more velvety. *Saar*, *kadhi*, *amti* and *moilee* are all from the same family of thin *curries* with a coconut milk base. You can drink them as a soup or serve them with rice.

Serves: 4

INGREDIENTS

700 g tomatoes
1 cup coconut milk
1 tbsp ghee
8–10 curry leaves
1 fresh hot green chilli, finely chopped
½ tsp salt
1 tsp sugar or jaggery
¼ tsp black pepper, freshly ground
1 tbsp green coriander, finely chopped

METHOD

Drop the tomatoes into boiling water and cover with a lid. After a couple of minutes, remove the tomatoes from the water and peel. Chop up the tomatoes and put them into a small pan. Cover and simmer for about 15 minutes until the tomatoes are soft and pulpy. Put the tomatoes into a blender and blend until smooth. Strain and place the tomatoes back onto the stove on a low heat and stir in the coconut milk. Simmer for 5 minutes till the saar turns thick. Heat ghee in a small pan and throw in the curry leaves and green chilli. Let it cook for 30 seconds. Pour this tempering on the saar. Stir once. Add salt, sugar or jaggery (only if the tomatoes are sour) and ground black pepper. Cook uncovered on a low heat for about 5 minutes, stirring every now and then. Garnish with fresh coriander.

Note: *If the mixture looks more like a sauce than a soup, which could happen if the tomatoes are very fleshy, add half cup of water.*

CRUSHED LENTIL AND YOGHURT SALAD

CHANA DALACHI CHATNI (PRON: CHANYA DAHLACHEE CHUTNEY)

Chutneys and pickles are hugely important in this state because they are used to perk up the sometimes-bland fare of everyday home cooking. For rural workers, who can only afford bread or *bhaakri* (millet roti), chutneys are an important source of vitamins, minerals and proteins. For many, '*chutney bhakar*' is a meal. In Maharashtra, chutneys are not wet; they can be made of powdered or smashed ingredients to be eaten fresh. Popular amongst these are peanut chutney made with ground peanuts, chilli, salt and sugar or *thecha* made with green chilli, garlic and salt, curry leaf mixed with dry lentils and tamarind, and many more made with left-over bitter gourd or pumpkin rind and hot *khardas* from Kolhapur. This is another one of Jijee's recipes translated and shared by Nandita Khaire. It was a family favourite and a cross between a raita and a chutney.

***Serves:** 3–4*

INGREDIENTS

1 cup chana dal, soaked overnight in plenty of water
1 cup fresh natural yoghurt
1 tsp salt
1 tsp chilli powder
1 tsp jaggery powder
1 tbsp oil
½ tsp mustard seeds
A pinch of asafoetida
3 dried red chillies, torn
10 curry leaves

METHOD

Drain the chana dal and throw out the water. Grind/blend in a mixer to a coarse texture.

In a bowl, whisk together the yoghurt, chilli powder, salt and jaggery. I find a small balloon whisk most efficient. Add the chana dal to the yoghurt mixture and mix well. Heat the oil in a small pan and add the mustard seeds, asafoetida, chillies and curry leaves. When the mustard splutters pour this on top of the yoghurt mixture. Chill and serve this raita/chutney as part of lunch or dinner or serve as a dip with any salty biscuits.

CRISPY CORIANDER AND LENTIL TOASTS

KOTHIMBIR CHI VADI (PRON: KOHTHIMBEEREE CHEE VUHDEE)

Vadis or savoury cakes made with lentils are eaten all over the country but I love the Maharashtrian ones, eaten most often as a snack. These are mixed with fresh coriander and traditionally deep-fried. I often find them over-fried and unnecessarily brown, destroying the steamed texture and fragrance of the fresh coriander. So I lightly sear mine in a frying pan in some olive oil.

***Serves:* 4**

INGREDIENTS

1 cup chana dal, soaked for 4–6 hours and drained
1 tsp cumin powder
4–5 cloves of garlic
3 green chillies
1 tsp salt
½ cup chopped coriander
3 tbsp oil

METHOD

Coarsely grind the soaked lentils (chana dal), cumin, garlic, salt and chilli with no added water. Remove the ground mixture from the mixer and throw in the chopped coriander by hand.

Take a large handful of the mixture and make into an oval cutlet. You should get 5 cutlets from this quantity. Steam the cutlets in a steamer or in a sieve over a pan of boiling water with a tight-fitting lid for 10 minutes. Cool and cut into ½-inch slices. Toast them on a frying pan or griddle over medium heat with a couple of spoons or so of oil until crisp. Unorthodox, but I like to use olive oil. Deep frying obviously achieves the best crispy texture but for this recipe you will have to be vigilant all the time. I feel the griddle method works well if you're doing more than one thing at a time!

Tip: *You should not need a binding agent. If, however, you live out of India and are forced to use some kind of other lentil, you may need to use a bit of egg white to bind.*

FRESH DILL WITH MOONG

SHEPU CHI BHAJI (PRON: SHAYPOO CHEE BHAAJEE)

In the evenings in Pune, and in many towns and villages all over Maharashtra, you'll find carts stacked high with leafy greens. It's tradition that you buy your fresh leafy veggies for the evening meal and maybe for lunch the next day. Indian shepu or dill is wonderfully aromatic, but I have to say – you either love it or hate it. Here's a family story. It is oral history so I'm sure it has been exaggerated and tweaked along the way. It would be really funny if it was completely true! My husband's great-grandmother was an overbearing, domineering sort of woman. She had three sons who turned out to be very successful young men – all exemplary students educated in England and two returned to take up senior positions as civil servants in independent India. They were all united in their dislike of *shepu chi bhaji*. As young boys, the more they made their feelings known, the more it would appear on the dining table. Shepu is a vegetable known to induce gas if you eat too much. One day, out of total rebellion which was very uncharacteristic of these fine young men, they decided to fart 'God save the King' in front of their mother, after eating bowls of the stuff, to make her stop serving it once and for all. At this point in the retelling of the story everyone is doubling over with laughter, so nobody remembers the ending – did they succeed or not? The mystery continues …

Serves: 4

INGREDIENTS

¼ cup moong dal
2 tbsp oil
1 medium onion, chopped
1 tsp garlic, finely chopped
3 green chillies, finely chopped
1 big bunch dill, chopped

METHOD

Soak the moong in a cup of water for 1 hour and drain. Heat the oil and fry the onion on a medium heat till translucent. Add the garlic and chilli and continue frying for a minute. Add in the chopped dill and the soaked moong. Toss, cover and cook on a low flame for 5–7 minutes. Add ¼ cup of water if you feel the vegetable is drying out but if the dill is fresh, you don't normally need to add water. Eat as is or with chapati.

This recipe can be made with spinach, spring onions (in which case you don't add onion) or any green leafy vegetable.

EVERYDAY SPROUTS

MATKI (PRON: MUTTKEE)

We all know sprouts are healthy and the Chinese eat them a lot but so do Maharashtrians, especially for breakfast. It's a healthy way to start the day and a good addition to the rice dishes and salads. Markets and roadside stalls sell a variety of sprouted beans and whole lentils but you can quite easily sprout the beans yourself in a dark, warm place. It takes 2 days and they do not need to be more than a centimetre long.

***Serves:** 4*

INGREDIENTS

1 cup *matki* (moth), soaked overnight and sprouted for 2 days in a muslin cloth
1 tbsp oil
A large pinch of asafoetida
1 tsp turmeric powder
½ tsp chilli powder (mild or hot according to preference)
1½ cups water
1 tsp salt
1 tbsp tamarind pulp
½ tbsp jaggery

For the garnish
2 tbsp coriander, chopped

METHOD

In a kadhai or wok, heat the oil and throw in the asafoetida, turmeric and chilli powder, in that order. Cook for 30 seconds and add the sprouts along with the water and salt. Cover and cook on a medium heat for about 7 minutes till they become soft but still have a bite. Remove the lid, lower the heat and cook till most of the water has evaporated. Add the tamarind and jaggery or a couple of teaspoons of date and tamarind chutney. Stir through. Garnish with freshly chopped coriander.

Tip: *To sprout matki or any whole bean or lentil, first soak overnight (8 hours) in plenty of water. Wash, rinse and tie in a muslin cloth or large handkerchief. You can put a plate or light weight on top (this usually speeds up the sprouting). I sit this potli or pouch of wet beans over a colander which sits on a bowl so that the water drips into the bowl, somewhere near the window sill where it is constantly warm. Sprinkle water on the cloth twice a day. It shouldn't get dry. In the intense Indian summer heat, it takes two days to sprout the beans. In the UK, a friend keeps the beans in a warm cupboard under the stairs. In this case, it may take three days. You'll see the tiny white sprouts appear out of the cloth. Sprouts for this dish need to be no longer than half an inch. They do not resemble Chinese beansprouts in any way.*

BABY AUBERGINES WITH SESAME AND PEANUT

BHARLELI VANGI (PRON: BHARLEHLEE VAANGHEE)

This is a typical Maharashtrian recipe given to me by my dear friend Sumitra Naren. For me, this is the quintessential Maharashtrian '*sabzi*' which unites an unusual vegetable with sweet, sour and spicy notes. The spice is called *goda masala*, a roasted spice blend which goes into dals, rice and vegetables.

Serves: 3–4

INGREDIENTS

For the sabzi

12 small aubergines
2 tsp *goda* masala

For the stuffing

1 tbsp peanuts, finely ground
1 tbsp sesame seeds, finely ground
2 tbsp coconut, freshly grated
2 tbsp fresh coriander, chopped
2 tbsp jaggery

For the tempering

3 tbsp oil (preferably peanut or any vegetable oil)
½ tsp mustard seeds
10 curry leaves
½ tsp turmeric powder

1 tsp salt
1 cup water

METHOD

Cut the stalks off the aubergines, leaving a little of the green on. Make a cross slit on the other side. Mix all the stuffing ingredients together in a bowl. Add the *goda* masala into this spice mix. Stuff the masala into each aubergine piece.

Heat the oil in a kadhai or big frying pan and add the mustard seeds, curry leaves and turmeric. Stir-fry on a low flame. Ease in the stuffed aubergines, sprinkle with 1 tsp salt and add 1 cup of water. Cover and cook till the aubergines are soft. Season to taste and serve with rice, chapati or millet roti (*bhaakri*).

Note: *A particular variety of aubergine is used for this recipe. They are about three inches long, purple and white striped with a few prickly thorns near the stem. If you can't find them, then use the big aubergine which you don't need to stuff. Just stir together with the spice paste. Take care not to overcook.*

If I'm not in the mood to do the peanut/sesame/coconut grinding, I take a jar of my satay sauce (K's Kitchen in India), mix in the goda masala and add 3 tbsp of that instead of the stuffing ingredients. Works like magic!

PEANUT CURRY

SHENGDAANYACHI AAMTI (PRON: SHAYNG-DAANYA-CHEE AAMTEE)

This is another one of Jijee's staples. Her faithful maid Kusum would rustle it up at a moment's notice if anyone popped by unexpectedly for lunch and serve it with piping hot *ambemohr* or mango blossom rice or millet rotis (*bhaakris*). The rice is called 'mango blossom' because in the old days it actually had the fragrance of mango blossom as it cooked. The rice would always be served with a dollop of ghee. This is the basic version of peanut kadhi. You could add a tempering of dried red chilli and some ground spices like cinnamon and cloves for added flavour, but this is the recipe I know and love in all its simplicity.

Serves: 2–4

INGREDIENTS

For the peanut curry

1 cup roasted peanuts, without skin
5 green chillies, chopped
2 pieces of kokum
2 tbsp jaggery
Salt to taste
2 or more cups of water

For the seasoning

1½ tbsp ghee
1 tsp whole cumin
A pinch of asafoetida

For the garnish

Chopped coriander leaves

METHOD

Grind the peanuts and chopped green chillies to a fine paste with a little water. If preparing in winters, use lukewarm water to grind the peanuts and chillies. Keep this paste aside. In a kadhai or handi, add the ghee. Once hot, add in the cumin and asafoetida. Now add the peanut chilli paste, kokum, jaggery, salt and about 2 cups water and stir. Bring to the boil and then simmer for 3–5 minutes until you have the consistency of a thin sauce or runny custard. Take the kadhai off the heat. Sprinkle some coriander to garnish.

SWEET AND SOUR MASOOR DAL

MASOOR CHI AAMTI (PRON: MUSSOOR CHEE AAMTEE)

Aamti is a dal from Maharashtra that is called so because of the 'ambat' or sour note. It almost always has a tinge of sweetness in it too. Aamti from the Konkan coast tends to be made with *goda* masala and is soured with kokum. This is a Khandeshi recipe from north Maharashtra, given to me by my dear friend Sumitra Naren and is a scaled-down version of her mother's original recipe which had 22 spices in it!

Serves: 4–6

INGREDIENTS

1 cup whole masoor dal, soaked for 2–3 hours in plenty of water
3 tbsp sunflower oil
½ tsp mustard seeds
2 red chillies, broken
5 cloves of garlic, crushed
10–12 curry leaves
A large pinch of asafoetida
1 large onion, roughly chopped
4 tbsp light brown tamarind pulp (if using the dark brown, almost black, tamarind, add half the amount since it is concentrated)
2 tbsp jaggery
1 tsp coriander powder
1 tsp cumin powder
1 tsp hot chili powder
½ tsp garam masala
½ tsp curry powder
½ tsp turmeric powder
Salt to taste
½ cup coriander, stalks and leaves chopped

METHOD

Wash the soaked lentils in several changes of water until the water is completely clear. Cook with 6 cups water in a casserole till the lentils turn soft. Alternatively, cook the lentils in a pressure cooker using 4 cups of water. Keep the cooked lentils aside.

Heat the oil in a large saucepan or kadhai and toss in the mustard seeds. As soon as they pop, add the red chillies and garlic. Swirl them around till the garlic is just golden, then add the curry leaves and asafoetida. Cook for a minute and then add the onion. Lower the heat and cook till the onion turns translucent and soft. Pour in the cooked lentils and water and add all other ingredients, except the fresh coriander. Bring to the boil, lower the heat and simmer semi-covered for 7–10 minutes till the spices are cooked. Garnish with the chopped coriander and serve it with rice, wheat or millet rotis (*bhaakri*).

Note: *Always remember that whole pulses thicken while cooking and if you make it in advance you may need to add as much as a cup of water more when you reheat it.*

Tip: *You should use whole masoor lentils which are similar to puy lentils in Europe. If you can't find this, then the orange polished masoor is also fine.*

PRAWNS WITH GREEN CHILLI

PRAWNS THECHA FRY (PRON: THAY-CHA)

When Sagar Deshmukh started his second restaurant Maratha Samrat in the more cosmopolitan part of Pune, he recognized the need for more vegetarian and seafood options on his menu which otherwise leaned more towards the chicken and mutton dishes of Maharashtra. He explored recipes from Malvan for his fish *thali* but needed something a bit special and different for regulars. So he came up with prawn *thecha*, a marriage between a traditional chutney (eaten by farmers with millet flatbread) and super fresh prawns. It is my favourite dish on his menu and oh so easy! If you are chilli-hesitant, please reduce the number of chillies by half.

Serves: 4

INGREDIENTS

3 tbsp peanut oil
1 tbsp cumin seeds
12 green chillies
12 cloves of garlic

1 small onion, finely chopped
20 medium-sized prawns, peeled and deveined
1 tbsp lime juice
Salt to taste

Coriander leaves for garnish

METHOD

Heat 2 tbsp oil in a wok or kadhai. Add cumin seeds, chillies and garlic and fry for just a minute on medium heat. Put this mixture into a mixer/grinder/blender and grind it into a coarse paste. This is *thecha*.

Heat the remaining 1 tbsp oil in the same kadhai. Add finely chopped onion and the *thecha*. Sauté on medium heat for a minute till onions are translucent. Then add the prawns, lime juice and salt to taste. The prawns should be cooked in 5–7 minutes. Sprinkle with fresh coriander leaves and stir through.

PRAWNS IN COCONUT CHUTNEY

KOLAMBI CHE VATNACHE KALVAN (PRON: KOLUMBEE CHAY VAATNACHAY KAALVUN)

This is a delightfully different prawn recipe from my friend Prasanna Gokhale née Dhurandhar. A passionate cook who decided to reinvent herself with a recent pop-up of food from the Pathare Prabhu community of Mumbai, to which she belongs. Pathare Prabhus were one of the earliest communities in Mumbai who came from Gujarat in the thirteenth century. They became wealthy and progressive landowners and merchants and so their cuisine was known to be quite rich (and somewhat oily – a sign of wealth) with a variety of seafood and mutton dishes. They have some unique stone-ground masalas essential to their dishes like *bhuzna* and *baffat*. The kalvan is coriander coconut chutney with prawns, one of their lighter offerings.

Serves: 4

INGREDIENTS

For the curry

500 g prawns, shelled and deveined
½ tsp turmeric powder
2 tbsp oil
3–4 garlic cloves, finely sliced
8–10 curry leaves
Juice of 1 lime
¼ tsp asafoetida
Salt to taste

For the paste

¾ cup coconut, grated
4–5 green chillies, roughly chopped
1 heaped cup of coriander leaves, washed well
2 tsp rice powder or flour
6–8 peppercorns
8–9 garlic cloves, peeled

METHOD

Wash the prawns well and marinate with the turmeric powder and a little salt. Combine the ingredients for the paste in a mixer and grind to a fine chutney.

Heat the oil in a heavy-bottomed pan and add the finely sliced garlic. Sauté for a few minutes until it turns golden brown. Add the asafoetida and curry leaves. As soon as they crackle, add the ground chutney and sauté for a couple of minutes on a low heat. Splash some water if you find the masala sticking to the pan. Add upto ¾ cup water to make the consistency of the chutney like that of a sauce. Allow it to come to just under a boil and then simmer for a few minutes. Add prawns and lime juice and cook until the prawns turn pink (around 7–9 minutes). Add salt to taste and serve hot with rice.

Tip: *For a richer sauce, add ¼ cup thick coconut milk to the curry towards the end of cooking.*

MALVAN PRAWN CURRY

KOLAMBI CHE KALVAN (PRON: KOLUMBEE CHAY KAALVUN)

Malvani fish curries can be distinguished from Goan ones further down the coast by their use of fiery chillies in the spice paste and a slightly different spice blend. The Hudlikars had an old cook called Kamalbai, who came from the Malvan region of the Konkan coast in Maharashtra. Their puritanical Brahmin taste buds were jolted by her heavy hand and her fiery curries (which they secretly adored). Here's their favourite one.

***Serves:* 4**

INGREDIENTS

For the spice paste

3 tsp coriander seeds
3 bay leaves
25 dried red chillies (from *Sankeshwar*)
15 cloves of garlic
Half a coconut, grated

For the curry

500 g small-sized prawns, peeled and deveined
1 tsp turmeric powder
½ tsp red chilli powder
4 tbsp oil
½ cup curry leaves
4 green chillies, slit vertically
6 pieces of kokum soaked in ½ cup water
½ cup cashews, fried
1 cup coconut water
1½ cup coconut milk
Salt to taste

METHOD

Marinate the prawns with the turmeric and chilli powder and set aside for 10 minutes.

Roast the chillies, coriander and bay leaves in a frying pan and grind to a smooth paste along with the grated coconut and garlic.

Heat oil on a high heat in a heavy-bottomed vessel and add the curry leaves. Stand far away because they will spit and splutter vigorously. Add the green chillies and then the coconut paste. Fry this well till the aroma of spices fills the air and the oil starts to separate from the mixture. Add the marinated prawns and the kokum along with water in which the kokum has been soaking. Stir gently on a low heat. Add the coconut water and the coconut milk followed by the cashew nuts. Add salt to taste. The prawns should be cooked in about 5–7 minutes. Do not allow the curry to boil; always keep it on a gentle simmer.

***Note:** Sankeshwar chillies are traditionally used for this recipe simply because they are grown near Malvan. Beware, they are treacherously hot. I'm not that brave and I use a mix of local 'gavthi' for heat and Kashmiri or Bydagi chillies for flavour and colour.*

SPRING ONION AND DRY PRAWNS

PAATICHA KANDA ANI SUKKI KOLAMBI (PRON: PAATEECHA KAANDA AANEE SOOKKEY KOLUMBEE)

Edwin Andrews (no relation to Julie Andrews) has been working with us for many years. He is one of those fiercely loyal, dependable employees who is often the nut and bolt in many work situations. We would like to think he'll be with us forever. Every day, his mum (by all accounts a competent cook) packs him a lunch tiffin. Everyone in the office sits around a common lunch table and shares. Edwin is the first to generously offer his, probably because he wants to try everyone else's too! There is one dish that crops up frequently on his tiffin menu which I adore, so I asked Mrs Andrews for the recipe. It's absurdly simple. I can't bring myself to use the amount of oil she does so here's my slightly refined version.

***Serves:** 4*

INGREDIENTS

1 cup dry prawns with shell (or ½ cup without the shell)
1 big bunch of spring onions (around 15), cleaned, washed, wiped dried and chopped
1½ tsp garlic, crushed
4 green chillies, finely chopped
4 tbsp oil
Salt to taste

METHOD

If the prawns have shells, toast them in a frying pan till golden and crispy. If without, reconstitute in a little warm water for 10 minutes. Drain but keep the water. Toss the prawns in a hot frying pan with a teaspoon of the oil and fry for 2 minutes. Keep the prawns aside. Heat the remaining oil in the same frying pan or wok, ideally a kadhai. Throw in the garlic and green chillies. Cook till golden and add the spring onions. Mix well till the greens just wilt and do not add any water. Now add in the prawns. If the greens stick to the bottom, add a tablespoon or two of the water in which you soaked the prawns. Cover and cook for 2 minutes. The entire cooking should take no more than 5–7 minutes. Eat this warm with a roti or serve as an accompaniment to rice and a yellow dal.

Note: *Dried prawns are available in fish markets and stores along India's coasts and online. They are also readily available in many markets and local stores all over Southeast Asia and China. In the West, you will probably find them in an Asian or Chinese supermarket.*

MALVANI CHICKEN

MALVANI KOMBDI (PRON: MAALVANEE COMBDEE)

Sumitra Naren shared this recipe with me for my first Indian cookery book, *Lean Cuisine Curries*, and I've been making it ever since. Again, the spice blend is very particular – I call it Malabar, but technically it isn't from that part of the coastline at all. It has a nice ring to it though! All you need is a teaspoon or so of it, a little lemon juice and salt to liven up any seafood. The main ingredients are dried red chillies, coriander seeds, black pepper, black mustard seeds, nutmeg, cloves, cinnamon and asafoetida. Very different from anything else on the coast!

***Serves:* 4**

INGREDIENTS

For the chicken curry

1 kg chicken, cut into 8–10 pieces
2 large onions, roughly sliced
3 tsp *Malabar* masala
1 cup coconut, grated and roasted on a griddle until golden
2 cups chicken stock
2 tbsp peanut oil

For the paste

3 green chillies
2-inch piece of ginger
½ cup fresh coriander
½ tsp turmeric powder
6 cloves of garlic
Juice of 1 lime
1 tbsp oil
Salt to taste

METHOD

Combine and grind all ingredients for the paste till it reaches a fine consistency. Coat the chicken with the paste and marinate for at least one hour. Heat the oil and fry the onions for a few minutes on a high heat in a wok. Add the chicken pieces, Malabar masala, coconut and 2 cups of stock. Stir well, bring to a boil and then simmer uncovered until the chicken is cooked – which will take approximately 40 minutes on low heat. You should get the consistency of a thick gravy. Serve hot with rice, *bhaakri* (flat rotis made of ground rice) or crusty bread.

***Note:** In the old days, this recipe would have been made with free range chicken or fowl. Today, with broiler chickens, you simply don't get that full chicken flavour which is why I add chicken stock, not water, to cook the chicken.*

BLACKENED MUTTON

KAALA MUTTON

This is the devilishly complex black or *kaala* mutton from Khandesh in north Maharashtra. The masala is distinctive because each spice used, the onions and the coconut are roasted till they turn dark brown, almost black. Originally this would have been done over a coal fire (*sigdi*) and then ground to make a really dark brown masala paste. Families are hesitant about giving away the recipe, but Sagar Deshmukh gave me his willingly.

Serves: 4

INGREDIENTS

For the garam masala

3 bay leaves
3-inch stick of cinnamon
3 green cardamoms
1 black cardamom
4 cloves
2 tbsp coriander seeds
2 cups grated coconut

For the mutton curry

6 tbsp oil, preferably peanut
4 medium-sized onions, sliced
1 tbsp cumin seeds
1 kg mutton
½ tbsp turmeric powder
4 cloves of garlic
1 tbsp ginger paste
2 tbsp garlic paste
1 tbsp hot red chilli powder
1 tbsp *kanda lasun* masala
1 tbsp *goda* masala
1 tbsp garam masala, ground
Salt to taste
½ cup coriander leaves

METHOD

Heat a kadhai or large frying pan and dry roast all the garam masala ingredients along with coriander seeds on a medium heat. When brown, add grated coconut and roast it till it turns dark brown and keep aside. Heat half the oil in a kadhai or large frying pan and add cumin seeds and 3 of the sliced onions. Fry till really dark brown. Take care that they don't burn. Grind the roasted spices and coconut to a fine powder and the onions to a paste separately.

Cook the mutton along with the garlic, one sliced onion, turmeric powder and about a teaspoon of salt. You can slow-cook the mutton in a handi or casserole with enough water to just cover it, or pressure cook the mutton with 1 cup of water for 10 minutes till the meat turns soft.

In another kadhai, heat the remaining oil and add the onion paste followed by the ginger and garlic pastes. Once golden brown, add the coconut paste. Cook till the mixture turns brown and add red chilli powder, turmeric powder, *kanda lasun* masala, *goda* masala, garam masala and salt. Cook on medium heat. Once the oil starts to ooze out from the masala, add the boiled mutton and stir. Add the stock from the mutton and give it a good stir till you get a thick gravy. Garnish it with fresh coriander leaves and serve with bhaakri.

KOLHAPURI MUTTON

Kolhapuri is often a synonym for spicy or chilli hot in traditional Maharastrian cuisine. While it is true that they enjoy their chilli in Kolhapur, not all dishes are fiery. This one, however, usually is. I asked Hemlata Angre for her recipe because I simply couldn't get enough of her version of this dish. She has slightly tweaked the recipe after leaving her hometown, near Kolhapur, for the fields of Ujjain near Indore in Madhya Pradesh. I have played around with it further, lessening the fire and brimstone, simplifying the cooking process and going easy on the amount of oil used. It is still a delicious but complex dish, heavy with masala.

***Serves:* 4–6**

INGREDIENTS

1¼ cups cooking oil
½ tsp asafoetida powder
6 medium-sized onions, sliced
3 tomatoes, chopped
1 tsp turmeric powder
1 kg mutton, cut into 2-inch pieces with bone
3 tsp salt
2 whole pods of garlic, peeled and made into a paste
3 tbsp ginger paste
1 cup coconut, grated and roasted (or ½ cup desiccated coconut, roasted)
2 bay leaves
4 tbsp Kolhapuri masala

METHOD

Stage 1

Heat ¼ cup oil in a large casserole or pressure cooker. Add asafoetida and one sliced onion. Fry for a minute till it turns golden and then add 1 chopped tomato, 1 tsp turmeric powder, the mutton, 1 tsp salt and 3 cups of water. Pressure cook for 10–15 minutes. Traditionally, this would have been slow cooked in a heavy-bottomed degchi for at least an hour.

Stage 2

Heat ¾ cup of oil in a large frying pan or kadhai and add the remaining onions, ginger and garlic pastes. Sauté on a medium heat till golden. Add the leftover tomatoes and roasted coconut. Cook on a low heat till it all turns brown. This may take about 15 minutes. Grind this into a paste and keep aside.

Stage 3

In a large casserole or handi, heat the remaining ¼ cup oil. Add bay leaves, onion-coconut paste (that you prepared in stage 2), 4 tbsp Kolhapuri masala and sauté for 4–6 minutes until the oil leaves the mixture. Add the mutton and stock. Cover and cook on low heat till the gravy becomes quite dry. Enjoy hot with millet roti (*bhaakri*).

Note: *The original recipe for Kolhapuri masala has around six more ingredients which can only be found in Maharashtra and South India. This is my abridged version. The masala can be quite spicy especially if you use hot red chillies in the spice mix. My recommendation is 4 tbsp for this recipe. You can add or subtract, depending on your spice tolerance.*

SPICED RICE PULLAO

MASALA BHAAT (PRON:BHAATH)

Bhaat in Marathi means rice. This is a basic rice preparation in Maharashtrian homes and comes closest to a biryani or pullao in this state. It was shared with me by Sumitra Naren many years ago and, although it really doesn't compare to a biryani in terms of depth of flavour, it is a lovely fragrant pullao which goes well with most of the vegetarian dishes in this chapter.

***Serves:** 4*

INGREDIENTS

For the pullao

1 cup *ambemohr* or any short grain rice
2 or more cups of hot water, depending on your rice
¼ cup Indian gherkin (*tendli*), peas and sliced cashews
2 tsp *goda* masala
Salt to taste
A squeeze of lemon juice
1 tsp jaggery

For the masala paste

2 tbsp grated coconut (roasted golden)
¼ tsp cumin seeds
1 green chilli

For the tempering

1 tbsp oil
A few curry leaves
½ tsp black mustard seeds
A pinch of asafoetida
¼ tsp turmeric

For the garnish

1 tsp chopped green coriander

METHOD

Put the rice with hot water and salt to taste into a large pan. Add the vegetable and cashews, the ground masala paste and *goda* masala and stir on a low flame. Add a squeeze of lemon juice and the jaggery. Cover and cook until the rice is soft. Heat the oil in a pan. Throw in the curry leaves, mustard, asafoetida and turmeric in that order. When the mustard begins to pop, pour the tempering on the rice. Garnish with coriander and serve hot with a raita.

SEMOLINA HALVA

SHEERA NAIVEDYA (PRON: SHEERAA NAIVAIDYUH)

The basic recipe for the Sheera 'naivedya' comes from the Revakhand segment of the eighth-century religious Hindu texts of the Skanda Purān, which contains the legend of the Satyanarayan prayer ritual. In Hindu mythology, Skanda is the son of Lord Shiva and Parvati. The Revakhand was added sometime in the twelfth century, making this recipe pretty old! It makes you wonder how, amongst 81,000 verses containing legends, parables, hymns and stories, which cover topics such as temples, discussion about good and evil, of theology and of the nature and qualities of Shiva as the Absolute and the source of true knowledge, they thought about food! As part of tradition, Ram Hudlikar makes this very special dessert on certain days only and his recipe is much sought after.

Serves: 4

INGREDIENTS

2 cups full cream milk
1 cup ghee
1 cup coarse semolina (*rava*)
1 cup sugar
2 very ripe bananas
1 tsp cardamom powder
A generous pinch of saffron, lightly heated to crisp up the strands and coarsely powdered
¼ cup almonds, slivered and lightly roasted
2 sheets of silver leaf (optional)

METHOD

Heat the milk and keep it aside. Heat the ghee on a low flame in a heavy bottomed casserole or handi. When hot, pour in the semolina. Roast in ghee while stirring continuously till the mixture changes colour slightly, but does not turn golden. Once roasted, add in the hot milk. Be careful as the mixture splutters viciously. Keep stirring on a low heat. It will look glutinous and gloppy initially. Cover for a minute. Then stir in the sugar. Cover again for 2–3 minutes. Slice the bananas quickly and stir in. Cover and turn off the heat after about a minute. Add the cardamom powder and the saffron and stir well. Serve warm, garnished with silver leaf (*varq*) and lightly roasted almonds.

WEST BENGAL

I was first introduced to Bengali culture when I was at university in England. We had a cinema club and Satyajit Ray's award-winning *Pather Panchali* was the first film to be screened there, followed by an onscreen interview. I was mesmerized; he was elegant and erudite and politically aware, with that mane of thick white hair (just what a 19-year-old girl is impressed by!). I remember wanting to leave for India right away . . . and, as fate would have it, I did.

On returning to India in 1984, I met the Director of the National Film Development Corporation at a dinner, where we discussed the state of my Hindi (pretty bad!) and my love of cinema. 'Why don't you help us subtitle Indian films?' he had suggested. 'Someone will do the basic work. You need to spruce up the English, you'll see all your favourite new wave movies, and hopefully learn some Hindi as well.'

In my excitement, I said yes. The first film I worked on was by Mrinal Sen. I didn't know who he was or that he made films in Bengali. My Hindi was shockingly bad but surely not so much that I couldn't understand a word of the film. My colleague, who was actually doing all the hard work with the translation, laughed and said, 'Look at the credits . . . if you see Chatterjee, Banerjee or Sen more than three times in a row, it's a Bengali film!' And of course he was right – no wonder I was having such a hard time with this one!

I met Mrinal Sen a few years later in Kolkata, as he waxed lyrical about his films and everything else under the sun. I was captivated by how much time he spent talking to an absolute stranger for hours. 'Do you know how to recognize a Bengali?' he said. 'Look around you. We men love to sit in cafes and procrastinate all day long . . . chatting about any subject. Others will come and go but the Bengali will only leave when it's time for dinner. The other thing the Bengali man will willingly do is go to the fish market; such is his obsession with good food.'

I remember a scene from one of the Bengali films on which I worked, where two zamindars were sitting on the floor, wearing their crinkly dhotis and having a meaningful discussion about their lands, devouring what looked like the most divine crayfish, probably *golda chingri* in a *chingri malai kari* – freshwater giant shrimp bathed in a rich coconut sauce – a dish which they say comes from Malaysia (hence Malai or Malay). I had never seen food depicted so brutally well, and it spoke reams about how serious Bengalis are about eating.

Food in Kolkata has been influenced by many cultures – British, Portuguese, Baghdadi Jewish, Armenian, the Mughals, royal kitchens, neighbours in Tibet and Burma and the newer Marwari business community from Rajasthan. In this chapter, I am simply going to focus on the Bengali food I know and love. Kolkata is a city of fantastic people, whether they are Bengali or not, and gracious hospitality that is a result of leisure time and a past steeped in culture, literature and art. Bengali food is a big part of that, executed with much care to detail, served course wise and is often compared to French sophistication.

The chronology of dishes served is based on ancient beliefs relating to the digestive process. Since lunch is the main meal, they start with a bitter vegetable, then comes a saag or green leafy vegetable, dal and a *chhenchki* (stir fried vegetable) and *bhaja* (fritters), a vegetable like a *chorchori* followed by the fish, first the small ones then the large, and lastly the crab or prawn. Then comes the poultry or game birds, mutton, chutney and, finally, dessert. Leafy and bitter vegetables are never served in the evening. *Lucchi* (Bengal's answer to the *poori*), *pullao* or white rice is served to accompany the meal.

There are also ingredients particular to this region, which are very special, like the fish *ilish* or hilsa, a member of the herring family which has numerous small bones. Deboned and smoked, it is superior to even the best smoked salmon. When smothered in a paste of mustard and green chilli and steamed in a banana leaf (*paturi*), it is indescribably delicious. *Kolkata bhetki* is a soft-fleshed white fish which can be compared to European sea bass or Australian barramundi. Bhetki is to Kolkata what the pomfret is to Mumbai. *Nolen gud*, palm jaggery, which is used in *sondesh* and *rosogullas* in winter and stored in hard, semi-circle cakes or in syrup form for the rest of the year, is so much better than any average maple syrup. Mustard, pungent black and mild yellow, ground into a paste has long been added to give a significant punch to dishes, before the chilli came to India. I discovered the *gondhoraj lebu*, the most fragrant lemon India has to offer, which adds a new dimension to any dish. This fantastic green lemon (as opposed to lime or *nimboo*) fills the air with a heady lemony fragrance and can be compared to the Thai *magrut* from which we also get the aromatic kaffir lime leaf. Unlike kaffir, which is used mainly for its heavily scented leaves, *gondhoraj* has precious little juice and bitter leaves but a wonderfully scented rind which adds magic to a gin and tonic! Traditionally, it would only have been used, and that too sparingly, to add a sour note to dal before serving or placed on the table as a gesture rather than an ingredient.

I used to believe that the most flavourful fish in India came from the west coast – from Mumbai down to Kerala. That was until I discovered fish from West Bengal. Bengalis prefer what we call sweetwater fish, from their many lakes, ponds and rivers rather than fish from the sea which tends

NIKE
WB 04
E6108
CHANK
LUNGIES
HAJRA STORES
HAJRA STORES

to be salty in comparison. And it's for that reason that I feel we who live on the west coast always traditionally add a sour note of either kokum, tamarind or lime to our fish dishes. Bengalis never add any sourness. Their seafood is either smothered in a strong mustard paste (*paturi*), cooked in a light coconut curry with onions and fragrant Bengali garam masala (*chingri malai*) or in milk (*doodh maachh*). *Maachher Jhol* is probably the only exception, a home-style fish cooked in a light broth of whole spices and tomato. After many visits to Kolkata over several years, I have grown to love the sweet soft flesh of a lake and river fish like *chitol*, *katla* (carp), *rui*, *hilsa* (*ilish*) and *bhetki* (barramundi), although the latter two are also caught in estuaries, but that's more a technicality.

During my early visits, apart from eating fish, I was keen to see fish in the flesh, so to speak, and so I asked the people at *Calcutta Walks* to take me on a tour of North Kolkata food spots. My day started with the freshness of the day's catch – *ruimaachh*, shiny silvery *hilsa*, live crab, soft shell crab and mounds of other smaller fishes, in an environment that smells of ponds and not stale fish. This was Manicktala market. Placed on mounds of crushed ice, like bejeweled deities or laid out neatly on bright green banana leaves, fish is worshipped in this city.

Small, ugly bottles of *kasundi*, a tart delicious mustard paste once available only in reused rum bottles and traditionally made by married women of certain families only, were sold in markets. Today, they are commercially produced and found in supermarkets and even online – not in reused rum bottles though! Bags of the famous Bengali five spice, *panch phoran*, which adds life to many vegetarian dishes is another familiar market sight. Bengalis love their veggies almost as much as their fish and mounds of maroon-coloured banana flowers, baby aubergines, bitter gourd, wax gourd, baby cauliflower and various green leafy vegetables are particular to a Bengali market scene. Bengalis also use green chillies as opposed to dried red ones. Before the Portuguese introduced the chilli to India in the early sixteenth century, Indians used black pepper and long pepper to perk up their dishes. These were incidentally also used in Ayurvedic medicine.

In Bengal and in much of Northeast India, Burma,

Malaysia and Thailand – I am reliably informed – another condiment called *choijhal* (hot horseradish) preceded the chilli. It is still found in some remote areas of the northeast and used with fish.

> *A bit of trivia: Christopher Columbus actually brought the chilli to Europe from South America when he went looking for India. He named it chilli pepper after Chile. The chilli went all over southern Europe, including Portugal from where the seeds were brought to India.*

Bengalis love their sweetmeats. Some 'must visit' stops in North Kolkata are the Girish Chandra Dey and Nakur Chandra Dey mithai shops near Beadon Street. Some Marwari families that I know send their drivers all the way to these rather shabby shops, from their fashionable addresses in the south of the city, just for a box or two of fresh *sondesh*, a melt in the mouth sweetmeat, which is considered healthier than others since it is made with *chhena*, a soft, curd-like cottage cheese as opposed to *mewa*, *khoya* or *ghee* (*thick cream and butter*).

Our next 'must visit' stop is Nobin Chandra Das for the *rosogulla*. I never liked the dense spongy texture and sweet syrup in which this spongy ball is immersed. Not until, that is, I tasted them in Kolkata. Here, the rosogulla is light and airy and the syrup is watered down to a bearable sweetness. Venturing into North Kolkata can frankly be a bit of a trek. A very convenient address for all traditional Bengali sweets is Mithai near Park Circus and their sister concern Vien right off Park Street. They also happily pack everything for you to take on a flight, including a very authentic *mishti doi* (yoghurt made in a terracotta pot and sweetened with palm syrup or palm jaggery).

The drive through 'colonial Kolkata' is an experience and a whole stratosphere away from the bylanes and cycle rickshaw pullers of the north. The city was the capital of the British Indian Empire until 1911. The regal Governor's mansion (Raj Bhavan), Victoria Memorial, St Paul's, Dalhousie Square, the vast expanse of gardens and parks to Chowringee, are all testament to that. The first food stop down the magnificent Chowringee is New Market which was originally called Hogg's Market after Sir Stuart Hogg. Today, like many buildings in the city, it is a shadow of its past glory. I always visit J. Johnson's, an otherwise non-descript store, for a small, smoky, crumbly local cheese called *Bandel*. It is named after a town on the banks of the river Hooghly where cheese-making began with the Portuguese. An old friend, Chef **SHAUN KENWORTHY**, who has lived and worked in Kolkata for many years, introduced me to this cheese some years back.

I always pay a visit to Nahoum, the old cake shop in the centre of the market established in 1902 by a Baghdadi Jew called Nahoum Israel Mordecai. They started with selling fish *pantaras* (fish-stuffed pancakes), cheese samosas and walnut brownies. Today, Nahoum does a brisk business in coconut macaroons and fruit cake.

My favourite place to stay in the city is The Oberoi Grand which is over 100 years old and was also the residence of a Colonel Grand in the early nineteenth century. It passed through the hands of an Armenian businessman from Isfahan and was finally bought by Mr M.S. Oberoi in 1943, who refurbished the heritage property but changed very little in terms of the structure and design.

Around the corner, tea is a must at the iconic pink and brown Flurys tearoom on Park Street. The Viennese coffee and collection of teas are excellent and the rum ball and asparagus sandwiches, memorable.

Let's talk about undivided Bengal or *Bangaal* as it is called. 'There doesn't seem to be such a distinctive divide anymore between West and East Bengal (now Bangladesh) dishes,' says food historian **PRITHA SEN**. Pritha has an encyclopedic knowledge of Bengali food and presides over the much talked about Bengali menu at the award-winning Mustard in Mumbai – a restaurant that celebrates the ingredient mustard through both Bengali and French cuisines. Pritha's interest in *Goalondo Fowl Curry* grew after reading about it in Sayyed Mujtaba Ali's writings. She wanted to enlighten people about the huge repertoire of East Bengal cuisine which was somehow buried during Partition. Pritha is my 'go-to' girl, on the other end of the phone, for anything to do with Bengali cuisine. I have learnt much from her about the use of green chillies (as opposed to dried red which is a modern-day phenomenon in Bengal) and the enormous variety of vegetarian dishes in a cuisine we often think of as fish-centric. She tells me, 'for example, traditional Bengali fish curries have no onion or garlic. This is because the *Vaishnavs* of West Bengal, like the Vaishnavs everywhere in India, were forbidden onion and garlic in their diet. However, the Bengali Vaishnavs did eat fish (fruits of the sea!) and cooked these without onion and garlic out of habit.'

Bengali food is one of the few Indian cuisines I can eat in restaurants. This simply isn't so of other Indian cuisines, where the restaurant versions are in no way representative of the real deal. Restaurants in Kolkata, like the modest Suruchi (run by women), Kewpie's, Aheli, Oh! Calcutta, Sonar Tori, Bhojohori Manna (which has several branches) and 6 Ballygunj Place, do Bengal proud as do the plethora of Bengali chefs in our hotel industry. Below are some great chefs and friends who made the collection of recipes in this section possible.

Chef **SAURAV BANERJEE** is a seasoned and senior executive chef who balances the demands of a luxury hotel (The Oberoi) with an uncompromising attitude towards traditional Bengali food, both in terms of ingredients and preparation. If the *Kosha Mangsho* says slow cooked, then he assures me that it must be slow cooked and not pressure cooked. When the recipe calls for ghee, he'll even specify the brand. I have discovered much about real Kolkata, and by extension Bengali, food through his eyes.

The bloggers of Kolkata are another breed apart – passionate, often with hundreds of thousands of followers. I met **MADHUSHREE AND ANINDYA BASU** when we were doing our market events in the city. They blog about Bengali food, cook and now are proficient professional food photographers (Pikturenama Studios). They have shot the recipe images in this book.

ITI MISRA is almost eighty. I have to tell you this because she doesn't look a day over fifty. They say it's the fish oil that keeps the hair strong in Bengal. I wonder if it works for wrinkles too because she doesn't have those either! In her seventies and encouraged by her daughter, PR Queen Radhika Misra, Iti decided to embark on a life of pop-ups serving classic Bengali dishes, some of which she shared with me. She loves what she does and it shows through her food and her elegant table.

LUX cozi
KMC

1 Mulligatawny

2 Breakfast Dal – Ghugni

3 Stir-fried Pumpkin and Potatoes – Kumro Chhenchki

4 Fried Aubergines – Beguni

5 Mixed Vegetables with Mustard – Chorchori

6 Chana Dal – Chholar Dal

7 Prawns in Creamy Coconut Milk – Chingri Malai Kari

8 Prawn and Potato Rissoles – Chingri Alur Chop

9 Homestyle Fish Stew – Maachhher Jhol

10 Fish in a Milk Sauce – Doodh Maachh

11 Mustard Fish in Banana Leaf – Fish Paturi

12 A Fish Callled Bhetki – Bhetki Gondhoraj

13 Pritha Sen's Steamer Fowl Curry

14 Mutton Curry – Kosha Mangsho

15 Tomato and Date Chutney – Tomato-Khejur Chutney

MULLIGATAWNY

(PRON: MULLAGATORNY)

This for me is the quintessential Anglo-Indian soup/dish served all over the country and in Indian restaurants abroad, each region in India claiming it as its own. When underdone and watery, it resembles dirty dish water. At its best, it is velvety deliciousness and was, in fact, served at one of the banquets of Queen Elizabeth II's coronation. The soup is said to have been invented in the Madras Club and the name derives from two Tamil words – *milagu*, meaning pepper, and *thanni*, meaning water. In the south, it is served with a spoonful of rice, a slice of lemon and sweet mango chutney to balance out the spice in the soup. Curry powder is the main ingredient that gives this soup such a distinctive flavour. The recipe involves curry powder, red lentils, carrots, apples and coconut milk to which you add white rice, chopped boiled eggs and shredded cooked chicken.

By the time the British Raj had been firmly established, the English women had accepted living in the East and had set a standard of living that not only became the accepted way of life during the Raj but lingered long after. Once the Suez Canal was opened and getting to India by sea within a month became possible, not only the wives of men employed in India, but also bevies of young girls who were sisters, cousins, nieces, friends or daughters of friends came pouring into India, sometimes only for the winter, often in search of husbands and easy living. They brought along an air of excitement and had ready reasons for elaborate entertainment, made easy by the abundance of servants here.

The Englishwoman fought against eating Indian food for more than one reason. Highly spiced food often upset her poor digestion and through ignorance she regarded Indian food as hot and unpalatable. It also gave her a sense of superiority to despise the food of the natives. French cuisine was considered fashionable and food cooked in wine was the last word in good taste. But the Englishman who had come alone long before the woman had acquired a taste for Indian food and was no longer content to eat his roast beef, potatoes and boiled vegetables. So, gradually, very subtly, Indian spices were introduced into English dishes and Mulligatawny being the first course of a meal, which lead the repertoire of Anglo-Indian dishes to follow. This recipe is from Chef Bikram Das while he was at the East India Room at Raajkutir in Kolkata.

Serves: 2–3

INGREDIENTS

For the soup

¼ cup butter
1 red onion, chopped
1 carrot, peeled and diced
1 fresh red chilli, seeded and diced
3 garlic cloves, minced
2 tsps ginger, peeled and minced
2 small firm apples, peeled, cored and diced
1 cup tomatoes, diced
1 tbsp curry powder
1 tsp cumin, ground
½ tsp paprika
½ tsp cinnamon powder
½ tsp turmeric powder
¼ tsp cardamom powder
¼ tsp black pepper, freshly ground
½ tsp thyme, dried
½ cup orange lentils (masoor dal), washed and soaked in water
3 cups chicken or vegetable stock
2 or 3 cups coconut milk
Salt and black pepper to taste

For the garnish

½ cup coriander, freshly chopped
½ cup chicken, shredded and cooked
1 egg, boiled and chopped
2 tbsp cooked rice

METHOD

Melt butter in a large pot over medium-high heat. Add the onion, carrot and chilli, then sauté for 4–5 minutes or until the onions have softened. Add the garlic, ginger, apples and diced tomatoes to the pot. Sauté for another 3 minutes, then add all the spices and toss to coat. Add the lentils and stock and bring to a boil. Turn the heat down to medium-low and simmer uncovered for 30 minutes.

Puree about 75 per cent of the soup. Leave some of the chunks whole, as it adds a nice texture and consistency to the soup. Return the soup to the pot and stir in the coconut milk. Simmer until heated through. Taste, and adjust salt and black pepper as needed.

Serve topped with shredded chicken, boiled egg, 1 tablespoon or two of cooked rice and fresh coriander.

BREAKFAST DAL

GHUGNI (PRON:GHOOG-NEE)

Anirban Dasgupta is a terrific chef and was the executive chef of the Hyatt Regency in Pune. Although he was proficient in many cuisines, as they say, you can take the boy out of Kolkata but you can't take Kolkata out of the boy (I think they say this about London and the girl but the same applies). He has done an inordinate amount of research around the cuisine of East Bengal (now Bangladesh) where his family originally came from but at heart he is a Calcutta boy who loves his breakfast of ghugni with *radhaballavi* (stuffed *luchi*). Ghugni is also eaten as a savoury snack at teatime and, with the addition of boneless mutton pieces, transforms into a centrepiece for dinner or Sunday lunch.

Serves: 2

INGREDIENTS

For the dal

200 g whole dried white peas, *matar* dal. 2 tsp salt
1 cup onions, thinly sliced
3 tbsp ghee
2 tbsp coconut, thinly sliced
4-inch stick of cinnamon
2 pods of green cardamom
2 bay leaves. 1 dried red chilli
¼ tsp cumin seeds
¼ tsp cloves
¼ cup potatoes, cut into 1.5 cm cubes
¼ cup tomatoes, diced
2 tbsp ginger paste
2 green chillies, ground to a paste
¾ tsp turmeric powder
½ tsp Kashmiri red chilli powder
½ tsp cumin powder
½ tsp coriander powder
3 tsp sugar. Salt to taste

For the garnish

2 tbsp date and tamarind chutney
½ tsp *bhaja* masala
1 tsp green chilli, chopped
1 tbsp onions, chopped
1 tsp fresh coriander, chopped
¼ cup potato *salli*

METHOD

Rinse and soak the dal in water overnight (at least 12 hours). Drain and transfer to a saucepan. Add 800 g of water, some salt and the half a cup of onions to the saucepan. Cover and boil the dal on low heat. The dal should be soft but remain unbroken. Once cooked, strain the dal and reserve the water for later.

Set a large pan on medium heat and add ghee. Once hot, add the coconut slices and fry them until they are golden-brown. Remove and set aside. Add the dried red chillies, bay leaves, cardamom, cinnamon, cloves and cumin seeds. Once the whole spices begin to crackle, add the remaining onions and fry them until brown. Next, add the potatoes and fry for 3 minutes before adding the tomatoes. Cook until the tomato is soft (about 2 minutes). Add the green chilli and ginger paste to the pan. Fry for about 3 minutes. During this time, make a paste of turmeric powder, coriander powder, cumin powder and Kashmiri red chilli powder in 100 ml water. Add it to the pan. Fry until the smell of raw spices is gone. This should take about 8–10 minutes. If the spices dry out, add a splash of the dal water that we reserved earlier and continue frying. Once the spices have started releasing their oils, add the boiled *matar* dal to the pan. Fold it with the spices and cook for 2 minutes before adding the reserved water. Season with salt and sugar and turn up the heat. Bubble on high heat for about 6 minutes until the curry loses its watery consistency and the dal is thick. Stir in two slit green chillies and the fried coconut. Cover and rest for 2 minutes.

Garnish with *bhaja* masala, chopped onions, chopped green chillies and top with date and tamarind chutney (shared later in the book) and *salli* (crisp fried potato cut into matchsticks).

STIR-FRIED PUMPKIN AND POTATOES

KUMRO CHHENCHKI (PRON: KUMRO CHECHKEE)

A simple Bengali vegetarian dish – all the flavours of Bengal with minimum effort, shared with me by Iti Misra. The kind of recipe I love and use very often! You can make it with any vegetables lying around your house, but these are a traditional combination. It's the Bengali five-spice which gives it that extra dimension.

***Serves:** 4*

INGREDIENTS

2 medium sized potatoes
250 g red pumpkin (butternut squash)
500 g ridge gourd
2 tsp *panch phoran* (five spice)
2 green chillies
2 tbsp vegetable oil
Salt to taste

METHOD

This dish requires the vegetables to be cut in a certain way so that they don't become mushy. Peel and chop the potatoes into ½-inch cubes. Peel and cut the pumpkin into 1-inch cubes. Peel the ridge gourd and cut into circles about 1-inch thick. If the ridge gourd is fat, cut each circle into half. Slit the green chillies lengthwise.

Heat a kadhai or wok and then add the oil. Once the oil is hot, remove the kadhai from the heat and add the green chillies and *panch phoran*. Put the pan back on the heat and add the potatoes and gourd. Stir, reduce the heat and cover and cook for about 4–5 minutes. The potatoes will cook in the water released by the gourd. Add the pumpkin and cook for another 3 minutes or till the vegetables are cooked but not mushy. Add salt according to taste and increase the heat to high, without covering the wok, till all the water is absorbed.

Serve with *puris*, parathas or chapatis or rice as a side dish.

FRIED AUBERGINES

BEGUNI (PRON: BAYGOONEE)

Bhaja or (deep-fried fritters) is always served at the beginning of a quintessential Bengali meal. It is also a popular snack. Made with *padwal* (pointed gourd), pumpkin, potatoes or aubergine. The aubergine ones are my favourite, either cut into rounds or long wedges. The plain ones just have salt and turmeric on them. This recipe has a bit of spice and the crunch of poppy seeds. The plain fried ones can also be added to yoghurt (*doi begun*) with a tempering of mustard seeds, cumin, a hint of green chilli and served as a substantial raita.

Serves: 2

INGREDIENTS

1 large aubergine
1 cup chickpea flour
½ tsp ginger paste
2 green chillies, deseeded and finely chopped
2 tsp poppy seeds
Salt to taste
Mustard oil for frying

METHOD

Slice the aubergines lengthwise into 6 pieces or in thick rounds and keep aside. The Bengalis do not salt the aubergines to remove the bitterness. Make a thick batter with chickpea flour, salt and a little water. Beat the batter well. Mix the ginger paste and green chillies into the batter. Keep aside for half an hour. Add the poppy seeds.

Dip the aubergines in the batter one slice at a time and deep fry in mustard oil till golden brown. Drain on paper and serve piping hot.

MIXED VEGETABLES WITH MUSTARD

CHORCHORI (PRON: CHOCHOREE)

This is one of my favourite Bengali vegetarian recipes. I first had it at Taj Bengal at the suggestion of their then PR manager Modhurima Sinha. Modhurima is an institution in Kolkata, and it was she who introduced me to many Bengali vegetarian dishes when I had a column in *BBC Good Food*. I arrived in Kolkata to do a piece on Kolkata and Bengali food only to hear from the editor, as I landed, that their policy had been changed and that the whole magazine in India had to feature only vegetarian food! All my plans for the fish market and seafood recipes went out of the window. 'That's no problem,' said Modhurima. 'There are so many homestyle vegetarian recipes I can introduce you to.' The first dish I had was *chorchori* and I simply loved it. It's a mix of seasonal vegetables tempered with *panch phoran*, flavoured with mustard paste and bathed in mustard oil. Chef Sujan Mukherjee who headed the Taj Bengal kitchens in those days explained that to elevate a *chorchori* from a simple homestyle dish, you should roast the *panch phoran* and then sprinkle it on top of the dish along with crisp roasted *bodi* (little crispy fritters made with masoor dal and then fried). This is tradition at its best and the use of all that oil was probably to preserve it in the days before refrigeration. If you want a lean version, you can avoid the first-stage frying of vegetables individually, but I warn you – it won't taste the same! You can use any combination of vegetables, but leafy greens, aubergine and red pumpkin (butternut squash) are a must. This recipe has no onion or garlic.

Serves: 4

INGREDIENTS

My preference of vegetables

400 g *tender poi* or spinach, leaves and stalks chopped roughly
1 medium-sized ridge gourd, scraped and cut roughly in triangles or 2 *padval* (pointed gourd), peeled and sliced into rounds
100 g red pumpkin, cubed with skin
200 g aubergines, cut in large cubes
1 medium-sized potato or sweet potato, cut into wedges

You can also add

100 g cauliflower, broken into large florets
100 g white radish or carrots, cut into chip-sized pieces
100 g French beans, cut in 2-inch pieces
1 tsp *panch phoran*
2 whole dried chillies
2 tbsp mustard paste (made with black mustard seeds, water and a pinch of salt)
½ cup mustard oil (to fry the veggies, for the tempering and to drizzle at the end)
2 green chillies, broken into two

METHOD

Fry each vegetable individually in a little mustard oil, except for the French beans (if using) and the spinach. The aubergines should be fried a bit more than the others.

Heat a tablespoon of mustard oil in a large kadhai and throw in the *panch phoran* and whole dry chillies. Add all the vegetables, except the aubergines and spinach and stir fry on high heat for about 5 minutes. Next, add the greens, cover and cook on medium heat, stirring from time to time. Season with some salt. When the vegetables are cooked and all water has evaporated, add the aubergines, the spinach and the mustard paste. Increase the heat and fry for 3–4 minutes. Add a drizzle of mustard oil and green chillies and take off the heat. Serve hot with rice.

CHANA DAL

CHHOLAR DAL (PRON: CHHOLAAR DAAHL)

Dal in every part of the country is so different. *Chholar* dal is a speciality not made every day in Kolkata but usually as part of an elaborate dinner and wedding banquet. It is thick and slightly sweet, easy to make and this recipe, given to me by Pritha Sen, features no onion, garlic or ginger.

Serves: 4

INGREDIENTS

200 g chana dal
2 bay leaves
2–3 pods of green cardamoms
2–3 cloves
2-inch stick of cinnamon
3 tbsp ghee
2 tbsp coconut, grated
1 tbsp coconut, slivered
2 tsp turmeric powder
2 tsp red chilli powder
½ tsp cumin seeds
2 whole dry chillies
1 tbsp small sultanas (*kishmish*), soaked in water for 10 minutes
1½ tsp salt
2 tsp sugar
2–3 green chillies

METHOD

Wash and soak the dal for an hour in plenty of warm water. Drain the water out and boil or pressure cook with 3 cups of water and green cardamom, cloves, cinnamon and 1 bay leaf. The dal is ready when each grain is separate yet cooked through (around 10 minutes in a pressure cooker). It should not be mushy. Add turmeric powder, chilli powder, salt and sugar and keep on a slow simmer. Meanwhile, heat half the ghee in a big pan and fry the coconut slivers to a golden colour and keep aside. In the same ghee, fry the grated coconut to a light brown and remove. Heat the rest of the ghee in a small pan and temper with a bay leaf, cumin and whole dry chilli. Pour this into the dal along with the coconut slivers and sultanas. Mix well. This dal thickens very quickly so you may need to add a little water, but the end result is still fairly thick. Adjust salt and sugar as per taste. Add in the green chillies and the fried grated coconut. Cover for a while and continue to simmer on a low heat for a few minutes. Traditionally, this dal is eaten with *luchi*.

PRAWNS IN CREAMY COCONUT MILK

CHINGRI MALAI KARI (PRON: CHINGREE MULLEYE CURRY)

Anjan Chatterjee started a hugely successful chain of Chinese restaurants in India in the 1990s. His dream though was to start a chain of Bengali restaurants in the country – which he did. He called them 'Oh! Calcutta' (unfortunate that the highly successful, raucous Broadway and West End play of the 1970s was called by the same name and I never had the gumption to mention it). Anyway, they had absolutely nothing to do with one another. Anjan was so full of passion and excitement about his ode to the food of his home that he offered to drive the 200 km from Mumbai to my home in Pune to show me a thing or two – all in the interest of journalism since I was doing a column for *Bombay Times* at the time. This is his recipe for this iconic Bengali dish of creamy prawn curry. I always thought that the word *malai* (cream in Hindi) referred to the texture of the curry which is very creamy. It seems although there are few references to substantiate it, the word '*malai*' here refers to Malay (Malaysia) from where this recipe drew its inspiration. By the way, Chatterjee has now realized his dream of taking Bengali food international and has opened 'Chourangi', along with Aditya Ghosh, in central London.

Serves: 4

INGREDIENTS

- 3 tbsp ghee
- 2 bay leaves
- 1-inch stick of cinnamon
- 2 pods of cardamom (skin removed)
- 3 cloves
- 2 onions, ground to a paste
- 1½ tbsp ginger paste
- 1 tsp turmeric powder
- 2 tbsp green chilli paste
- 500 g or 12 large prawns, peeled and deveined
- 1 cup coconut milk, thin
- 1 tsp salt
- 1 tsp sugar
- 1 cup thick coconut milk
- ½ tsp Bengali garam masala

METHOD

Heat 2 tbsp of ghee in a pan on medium heat. Add the prawns and stir for 2 minutes. Keep the tossed prawns aside. Add the remaining tbsp of ghee to the same pan and, when very hot, add bay leaves and whole garam masala. Then add the onion and ginger pastes, turmeric powder and green chilli paste and continue frying on medium heat until the spices are well fried. If the pastes start sticking to the pan, sprinkle a little water and continue stirring. Add the thin coconut milk, sugar and salt to taste. If you are using readymade coconut milk, dilute 200 ml of the coconut milk with 100 ml water. Simmer over a low flame until the gravy is reduced by half. Return the prawns to the pan. Add 1 cup of thick coconut milk and cook on a low heat for another 5–7 minutes. Add the Bengali garam masala just before serving.

Note: *In West Bengal, this curry is often made with large freshwater shrimp called golda chingri which have a sweet lobster-like flesh and an enormous head. You have to estimate the cooking time according to the size of your prawns.*

Tip: *If you are using red onions for the onion paste (which are quite sweet already), then omit the sugar from the recipe.*

PRAWN AND POTATO RISSOLES

CHINGRI ALUR CHOP (PRON: CHINGREE ALOOR CHOP)

Teatime snacks in India tend to be savoury, and often spicy and fried. The word 'chop' in India could mean a piece of meat with a bone. It could also mean a ball of mashed potato which has been filled with lamb or beef mince or chopped prawns. The latter is associated with the Christian communities of India and is a snack or first course in Goan and Mangalorean homes. Chops are round or flattened slightly, dipped in egg, coated with fine breadcrumbs, and fried. In Kolkata, they take on a fishy twist and are dipped in a chickpea flour batter before being deep-fried. People either make them at home or pay a visit to their neighbourhood *telebhaja* shop which sells all manner of fried snacks for teatime. This recipe was shared by Madhushree Basu Roy.

Serves: 4

INGREDIENTS

150 g small prawns cut into small pieces
½ tsp turmeric powder
1 tsp salt
2 tbsp oil
400 g potatoes, peeled and boiled whole
1 large onion, finely chopped
1½ tsp *Bhaja* masala (or *Bhajamoshla*)
3 dried red chillies
1 tsp freshly grated ginger
¼ cup chickpea flour
1 tsp garlic paste
¼ tsp baking soda
¼ cup water
Oil for deep frying

METHOD

Mix prawns, turmeric powder and a pinch of salt in a bowl and marinate for 10 minutes. Grate the potatoes (or use a ricer which has revolutionized mashing potatoes and which I now use for all my mashed potato needs) and keep aside. In a frying pan, take 2 tbsp of oil and lightly fry the marinated prawns on a low heat and remove when cooked. In the same frying pan, lightly fry the chopped onions and add the grated boiled potatoes. Mix them well and cook for 2–3 minutes on a high heat.

In a large bowl, mix the potato-onion mix, bhajamoshla, prawns and salt. In the frying pan, once again, take 1 tsp of oil and, when it becomes hot, add the dried red chillies. Fry them till they turn crispy and then remove from the heat. Crush the roasted red chillies in a mortar and pestle or with your fingers (it is advisable to wear gloves if you try the latter) and then sprinkle onto the potato mix along with some grated ginger. Mix everything well and make small balls – the size of a lime.

Make a batter with the chickpea flour, garlic paste, baking soda, salt and water. Whisk well so that the batter becomes smooth and thick. Heat enough oil in a kadhai or deep-frying pan to deep fry the balls. When the oil is hot, dip the potato balls into the chickpea flour batter and deep fry immediately in the hot oil till they turn golden brown. Control the temperature so as to not burn the outer shell. Drain excess oil on some kitchen paper. These chops are traditionally served with green chillies but I love them with the tomato and date chutney later in this chapter.

HOMESTYLE FISH STEW

MAACHHHER JHOL (PRON: MAACHHAYER JHOL)

In the not-so-distant past, when there were no direct flights from Pune to Kolkata, the journey, with a stopover in Mumbai, would take upwards of four hours. With the drive to and from airports, occasional delays and the airport check-in time, I would be travelling the better part of the day just to get to Kolkata! On one such occasion, I staggered into the Oberoi Grand after a day-long travel ordeal, to be greeted by the very charming Chef Saurav Banerjee in the lobby. 'Dinner?,' he quizzed. 'Straight to my room and a nice long soak in the tub,' I replied. 'Room service? Thai? Salad?' Room service had a nice ring to it. I insisted on something Bengali with fresh fish. 'Maachhher jhol will do the trick,' he said. 'This is my comfort food and usually we make this with bony river fish like *katla* or *rohu*. Being a hotel, we only have bhetki which is boneless but it has just come in and is super fresh.' After my hour-long soak, the fish curry arrived along with piping hot local *Gobindobhog* rice. I thought I would eat a small bowl but ended up devouring the whole serving. It was so good … perfectly fresh white fish in a thin broth-like curry with vegetables. When I asked Saurav for this recipe (which I have made several times since), he laughed, saying it is too simple to put in a book. I don't think so!

Serves: 3–4

INGREDIENTS

Traditionally made with river fish like *rohu* or *katla*
500 g *bhetki maachh*, large pieces
200 g potatoes, cut into wedges
200 g cauliflower, florets
1 tsp turmeric powder
150 ml mustard oil
2 bay leaves
2 dried red chillies
3–4 pods of green cardamoms
¼ cup raw onion paste
½ cup tomatoes, diced
1 tbsp ginger and cumin paste (both spices ground together in equal quantities)
A pinch of sugar
2 cups water
Salt to taste

2–3 green chillies, slit
2 tbsp coriander leaves, chopped

METHOD

Smear the fish, cauliflower and potato with turmeric and salt. Pan fry all of this lightly in half the mustard oil and keep aside. In another pan, heat the remaining mustard oil. Add bay leaves, dried red chillies and the cardamom pods. Add the onion paste and cook well on medium heat. Once the onion changes colour slightly, add the tomato and the ginger-cumin paste and cook well. Now add the cauliflower and the potatoes followed by a pinch of sugar, a cup of water, salt and green chillies and simmer till the vegetables are tender. Add the fried fish and cook till just done (should take a few minutes). Garnish with fresh chopped coriander. Serve with steaming hot rice and a slice of *gondhoraj* lemon.

FISH IN A MILK SAUCE

DOODH MAACHH

A stunningly simple homestyle recipe for river fish shared with me by Madhushree Basu Roy. I really thought it was too simple to be true so tried it with a few different fish, *katla* or lake perch, which is traditionally used, and then chunks of *rawas*. But the recipe turns out great every time. You must make sure that the fish pieces or fillets are thick, otherwise they tend to break. Bengalis have a similar recipe with yoghurt (*doi maachh*) instead of milk. This recipe is not suitable for frozen fish.

***Serves:* 2–3**

INGREDIENTS

400 g (4 large pieces) *katla maachh* or thick slices of any white fish
1½ tsp turmeric powder
4 tbsp mustard oil
1 tsp *paanch phoran*
½ tsp red chilli powder
Salt to taste
1 cup milk
3–4 green chillies, 2 torn, 2 slit vertically

METHOD

Wash the fish pieces and pat them dry. Rub half a tsp of turmeric powder and a little bit of salt to the fish. In a frying pan or kadhai, heat 2 tbsp of mustard oil till it almost reaches the smoking point and then gently slide the fish pieces into the pan to fry them. Fry the fish on each side for less than a minute, till lightly coloured. Take the fish out of the oil and keep aside. If the pan in which you have fried the fish is not full of bits of skin, etc., then use the same one. If the pan is messy, take a new one and add 1 tbsp of mustard oil, heat and add *panch phoran* and torn green chillies. Stir on medium heat for a minute till you get a whiff of the spice fragrance. Throw in the remaining turmeric and red chilli powder, fry for a few seconds and add the milk. Heat the milk mixture on a low flame and let it simmer for about 4–5 minutes. Then slide in the fish. Season to taste and let it come to a boil, uncovered. Once it thickens, lower the heat and cover and cook for 5 minutes. Uncover, drizzle the remaining tablespoon of mustard oil and add the slit green chillies. Turn off the heat and serve hot with steamed rice.

MUSTARD FISH IN BANANA LEAF

FISH PATURI (PRON: PAATOOREE)

This is one of my favourite ways to eat fish, smothered with mustard and chilli, wrapped in a banana leaf and steamed. Some people place the parcels on a griddle with a little oil, but this is the traditional way and, in fact, much easier. Iti Misra is the embodiment of Kolkata's good taste and fine manners. She is an accomplished Bengali cook and, at almost eighty years old, is now doing 'pop-ups' with well-known chefs throughout the country. This is her failsafe, foolproof recipe.

***Serves:* 4**

INGREDIENTS

For the paturi

4 large pieces of fish fillets (without skin and approx 4 x 3 x ¾-inch. Use firm white fish, preferably bhetki, mullet or sea bass.)
1 tsp turmeric powder

For the marinade

6 tbsp mustard paste
1 tbsp poppy seed paste (poppy seeds ground with water)
1 tsp ginger paste
2 tsp chopped green chillies
4 tsp chopped fresh coriander
4 tbsp mustard oil
Salt to taste

1 big banana leaf

METHOD

Smear the fish with ½ tsp of turmeric powder and around a tsp of salt. Set it aside for 5 minutes. Combine all the other ingredients in a bowl with the remaining turmeric. Mix well and spread all the marinade over both sides of the fish fillets and set aside for 15–20 minutes.

Remove the centre portion of the banana leaf and cut into 4 pieces (each 10 x 12-inches approximately). Soak the banana leaves in hot water to make them pliable and prevent splitting or soften over a gas flame. Drain and pat the leaves dry. Place one piece of fish on a piece of banana leaf with the marinade and wrap. Repeat with all other pieces of fish. Secure well with a string and ensure that there is no leakage. Place in a steamer and steam on high heat for 10 minutes.

Serve the fish paturi straight from the steamer, still wrapped in the banana leaf.

Tip: *If banana leaves are not available, use aluminium foil. Not as exotic but does the trick.*

Note: *Since chillies were not indigenous to India and black pepper grew on the Malabar coast – kitchens in Bengal used mustard paste to provide the hit of sharpness in food. Make the mustard paste ideally with a mixture of black and yellow mustard seeds, black being the sharpest. In restaurants, they tend to use the yellow only. Iti uses only black, for this recipe, ground with a little salt and water. In my 'go-to' version, I substitute fresh mustard paste with bottled wholegrain mustard. Not as authentic, but a real time saver.*

If you are hesitant about all this mustard, replace half the mustard paste with half a cup of fresh grated coconut made into a fine paste with a little water.

A FISH CALLED BHETKI

BHETKI GONDHORAJ (PRON: BHAYTKEE GONDHORAAJ)

I have been visiting Kolkata over the last thirty years. Each time I go, I discover something new about the cuisine. It's almost as if they are keeping well-guarded secrets to be shared a little at a time. One of the first things I came upon was the *gondhoraj* lemon. You will find this neither in a hotel nor a restaurant. The juice is negligible in quantity but the rind has a heady fragrance and a vanilla-sweet aroma, similar to the kaffir lime of Thailand. I love it! Mixed in with fresh lemonade, it becomes an exquisite and exotic summer drink; a sprinkling on fresh cream elevates a dessert. But it is this recipe by Chef Joy Bannerjee, given to me in 2003 when he was running the kitchens of the Oh! Calcutta chain of restaurants that is my favourite expression of its flavour. I would really like to give him due credit for bestowing on this lemon the cult status it truly deserves.

***Serves:** 4*

INGREDIENTS

500 g *bhetki* or any thick, firm, white flesh fish, cut into 2 x 2 x ¾-inch pieces or fillet
1 tsp salt
2 *gondhoraj* lemons, grated rind and juice
¾ cup thick fresh natural yoghurt or Greek yoghurt, whisked till smooth
1 tsp castor sugar
1½ tsp green chilli (ground to a paste with a little water)
1 banana leaf or foil
1 tsp oil

METHOD

Wash and pat dry the fish. Add salt and lime juice. Keep aside for 15 minutes. Drain any excess liquid. Mix the rind, yoghurt, chilli paste, salt and sugar together in a bowl and marinate the fish with this mixture for 20 minutes. Set up a steamer or large pot with a well-fitting sieve and lid. Place some pieces of the fish on a plate. Cover loosely with a banana leaf or foil (there is no need to wrap the fish) and place in the steamer. If you are using a banana leaf, brush it with some oil. Steam for 5–7 minutes. You will have to do this in batches for each piece or fillet. Serve hot with plain boiled rice.

***Tip:** If you cannot lay your hands on gondhoraj lemon, replace with Thai magrut or kaffir.*

PRITHA SEN'S STEAMER FOWL CURRY

This must be the easiest recipe for chicken curry I have ever come across but the most difficult to replicate in terms of flavour because the ingredients were particular to a place in time which doesn't exist today. You must try and find a free-range bird or '*gavthi*' chicken. It is just not the same with what we call a 'broiler' or commercial chicken.

Heady nostalgia – during the late 1800s, passengers took the East Bengal Express connecting urban Calcutta with Goalondo, from where people opted for the ferry service on the Padma River which took them to Narayanganj in Dhaka or to Barisal. They then took connecting country boats and steamers to Assam, Sylhet, Chittagong or Burma. The express train was discontinued in 1964 during the Bangladesh war but one particular thing was not forgotten – the famous Goalondo Fowl Curry. It was cooked by the boatmen who came from East Bengal and Chittagong Hill which is why it is also known as Boatmen's Chicken Curry. The steamers were slow. To cater to hungry passengers, a few enterprising boatmen, who were just villagers, rustled up a quick curry with a couple of country fowl they had just slaughtered and threw some readily available spices and oil into a pot and slow cooked it. There are several, almost poetic, accounts of the aroma and taste of this curry. Pritha Sen says that the umami flavour (could this originally have been cooked in salt water?) of the chicken is a mystery, so she recreates this in her recipe below with dry shrimps.

Meat from a large cock (a doodle do variety) is traditional. It should be a fiery thin red curry, with oil floating on top.

Serves: 4

INGREDIENTS

½ of a medium head of garlic
2 tsp dried shrimp, chopped
15 whole dried red chillies, soaked in warm water
1 kg chicken, cut into 12 pieces across the bones (not jointed), preferably with skin
2 medium-sized onions, roughly grated
1-inch piece of ginger, grated
1 tsp fresh turmeric (preferable) or 1 tsp turmeric powder, made into a paste with 3 tsp water
5 tbsp mustard oil
One whole head of garlic
2–3 boiled eggs, cut in halves
4 whole green chillies

METHOD

Make a paste of the ½ head of garlic, chillies and dried shrimps. Marinate the chicken pieces with the chilli-garlic-shrimp paste, grated onions, ginger, turmeric paste, salt and 2 tbsp mustard oil and set aside for about an hour.

Heat 3 tbsp mustard oil to smoking point in a kadhai or pan. Add the marinated chicken and fry well on high heat, stirring till dry and golden. Add water to cover the chicken, bring to the boil and cover the kadhai. Drop the whole head of garlic into the curry. Lower the heat to a simmer and let it slow cook. When oil floats on top and the chicken is tender, add the halved boiled eggs and green chillies.

Serve with a salad of raw onions and slices of lime.

MUTTON CURRY

KOSHA MANGSHO (PRON: KAWSHAA MAANGSHOW)

This is the Bengali version of an Indian pot roast or *bhuna* gosht. *Kosha* means to fry and in the original recipe, the meat was marinated and then fried with onions over a slow heat for a few hours. This also meant that you had to keep a watchful eye on it. Iti Misra shared her much easier version with me in which you add water to cook the meat and then continue cooking till the gravy thickens and becomes quite dry. *Kosha Mangsho* is always slow-cooked in a pot, never pressure-cooked.

Serves: 4–6

INGREDIENTS

For the tempering

150 ml mustard oil
A pinch of sugar
1 x 3-inch piece of cinnamon
6–8 pods of green cardamom
1 pod of black cardamom
4–5 cloves
3–4 dried red chillies, whole
2–3 bay leaves

500 g onions, sliced
⅓ cup ginger-garlic-green chilli paste (equal amounts)
2 tbsp coriander powder
Salt to taste
1 kg mutton, diced into 1½-inch cubes with bone
3 cups hot water
1 tbsp ghee
1 tbsp Bengali garam masala

METHOD

In a pot, heat the mustard oil upto smoking point and the lower the heat. Add a pinch of sugar and all the spices for the tempering together. After a minute, add the sliced onions and sauté till golden brown over medium-low heat. Add the ginger-garlic-chilli paste and cook for a few minutes. Add the coriander powder and mix well. Turn the heat up and add in the mutton pieces. Brown the meat pieces on all sides, then reduce the heat and continue cooking on a low flame. Add 3 cups of hot water and bring to a boil. Lower the heat and cover with a lid. Cook gently for about an hour so the meat turns soft. Remove the lid and stir until the gravy thickens and the masala just coats the meat. Check and adjust the seasoning. Finish by adding the Bengali garam masala and then a dollop of ghee. Serve with *luchis* or paratha.

TOMATO AND DATE CHUTNEY

TOMATO-KHEJUR CHUTNEY (PRON: KHEY-JOOR)

Chatni or chutney in India is a savoury relish usually made with freshly-grated coconut or peanuts, chilli, mint, coriander and a tempering. Colonial-style chutney was similar to making a jam with which the British were familiar. No one quite knows whether it was the Bengalis who took from the British or the other way around. Bengali aristocracy loved their lip-smacking sweet and sour accompaniments often with raisins and so did the British ... cross pollination perhaps?

Chutney is a Bengali homestyle staple which is eaten after the meal and before dessert. There are many sweet and sour chutneys in Bengali cuisine including one made with raw papaya, pineapple and, of course, mango. The idea of something sweet and sour and a bit spicy to perk up bland British food also encouraged British soldiers, like Colonel Skinner and Major Grey serving in India, to create their own chutney recipes based on what they tasted in Kolkata. Back in Britain, they used their own orchard fruit and vegetables like apples, plums and rhurbarb to substitute the exotic Indian ones. The base, however, was always the same – fruit or vegetable, sugar, vinegar, spices. Chutneys became so much a part of the British diet that Branston pickle and piccalilli eventually turned into household staples on the British table.

1 large jar

INGREDIENTS

4 tbsp mustard oil
2 whole, hot, dried red chillies, chopped
2 bay leaves
1½ tsp *panch phoran*
500 g tomatoes, chopped
1 tsp salt
150 g sugar or jaggery
4 dates, soaked, seeds removed and chopped
4 tbsp tamarind pulp (light brown not dark concentrated)
50 g raisins, soaked for 1 hour and then drained

METHOD

Heat the oil in a heavy-bottomed pan over a medium flame. When hot, put in the red chillies, bay leaves and *panch phoran*. Let the spices sizzle. Stir once and add the tomatoes and salt and simmer on low heat until the tomatoes become soft and mushy. This may take about 15–20 minutes. Add the jaggery, dates and tamarind and lastly the raisins. Continue cooking on a low heat until the dates are soft and the raisins plump.

The chutney goes really well with the Chingri Alur Chop shared earlier in this section.

MEMORABLE MEALS

In this section, I cover the many memorable meals I've had the good fortune to feast on from places as diverse and different as Ladakh in the far north to Assam in the east, and Coorg and Chettinad in the south. There are also recipes from Parsi and Sindhi communities known for some outstanding dishes that are very much part of Bombay food culture. I have known them at close quarters because of family ties. I have also chosen recipes from meals which have been taken out of their geographical context, like an Indian dinner I cooked in Hong Kong, a fantastic recipe from an Indian restaurant in London, a Mangalorean recipe cooked in Pune and a Tamilian one served in Coorg. Lastly, I have made a conscious effort to include some Indian family favourites, familiar recipes you look for on a Sunday when you have time to cook or when you want to entertain ... authentic Kashmiri rogan josh, Chettinad chicken and prawn *patia*. These are sure shot, straight from the source, with no fancy business or fusions. They work well every time and I urge you to try them once at least.

1 Okra and Beetroot Crisps – Kurkure Bhendi Aur Chukandar – Delhi
2 Green Chillies in Coconut – Safed Mirchi Ka Salan – Hyderabad
3 Bamboo Shoot Stir Fry – Baimbale Bharthad – Coorg, Karnataka
4 Pumpkin Curry – Kumbala Curry – Coorg, Karnataka
5 Sindhi Dal with Flaky Bread – Dal Pakwan – Sindhi
6 Fish Tikka with Dill – Delhi
7 Assamese Fish with Tomato – Masor Bilahi Tenga – Assam
8 Fish Steamed in Banana Leaves – Patra Ni Machchi – Parsi
9 Fish in Fresh Fenugreek Sauce – Methi Machchi – Sindhi
10 Prawn Ghee Roast – Mangalore, Karnataka
11 Hot, Sweet and Sour Prawns or Fish – Prawn or Fish Patia – Parsi
12 Chicken Fingers – Chicken Kainchi Kebabs – Lucknow, Uttar Pradesh
13 Chicken 65 – Chennai
14 Chicken Chettinad – Milagu Masala Kozhi – Tamil Nadu
15 Chicken with Dried Apricots – Jardaloo Ma Murghi – Parsi
16 Pork with Bamboo Shoot – Baanhgajor Lagot Gahori – Assam
17 Coorg Pork Curry – Pandi Curry – Coorg, Karnataka
18 Minced Mutton Kebabs – Shikampur Kebabs – Hyderabad
19 Mutton with Glass Noodles – Phing-Sha – Ladakh
20 Cardamom Mutton Stew – Foto Bhuno Gosht – Sindhi
21 Rajasthani Lamb – Laal Maans – Rajasthan
22 Kashmiri Lamb in a Rich Red Sauce – Rogan Josh – Kashmiri
23 Lucknowi Lamb Shanks – Nihari – Uttar Pradesh
24 Old Delhi-style Lamb and Lentils – Dal Gosht – Delhi
25 Date and Tamarind Chutney – Delhi
26 Lime and Chilli Chutney – Maharashtra
27 Raitas – Pan-India
28 Mishti Doi Cheesecake – Karen's Signature Recipe
29 Andraab's Kehwa – Kashmiri Tea – Kashmiri

OKRA AND BEETROOT CRISPS

KURKURE BHENDI AUR CHUKANDAR (PRON: KOORKOORAY BHAYNDEE OR CHOOKUNDAR)

I love *kurkure* or crispy okra which is a North Indian staple, but the addition of fried sweet beetroot crisps to the tangy hot spice blend adds a different dimension and an almost umami flavour. This is a great snack with drinks. It can be made well in advance as the crispy texture lasts long because of the mix of cornflour with the traditional chickpea flour. This recipe was shared by the chef and my partner-in-crime, Abhijit Berde, when we cooked a sit-down Indian dinner together for the India by the Bay Festival in Hong Kong. Even in the humidity of Hong Kong, everything stayed superbly crisp.

Serves: 6–8

INGREDIENTS

500 g okra
200 g beetroot
5 tbsp cornflour
½ cup chickpea flour
1 tsp carrom seeds
1 tsp turmeric powder
1 tsp red chilli powder
2–3 green chillies, chopped fine
1 tbsp cumin seeds, roasted and crushed
1 tbsp black pepper, crushed
1 tsp salt
1 tsp garam masala powder
2 tbsp chaat masala
½ tsp asafoetida
Oil for deep frying
Chopped coriander for garnishing

METHOD

Wash and slice each piece of okra into 6 thin, long strips. Combine the cornflour and chickpea flour with salt, carom seeds, turmeric powder, asafoetida and chopped green chilli in a bowl and toss the sliced okra in the mixture. Deep fry the okra in very hot oil till crisp, remove and drain in a bowl lined with kitchen paper. Wash, peel and slice the beetroot as thin as possible. Soak the sliced beets in cold water for an hour. Drain the beetroot and allow the excess water to dry off. Deep fry the beetroot in hot oil till crisp. Alternately, dry them at 60°C in the oven for 2 hours till crisp. Toss in with the okra. Combine the red chilli powder, roasted cumin, crushed pepper, garam masala powder and chaat masala. Sprinkle this spice mix over the fried okra and beetroot and toss to coat evenly. Garnish with chopped coriander.

GREEN CHILLIES IN COCONUT

SAFED MIRCHI KA SALAN (PRON: SUFAID MEERCHI KA SAALAN)

This is a slight variation of the normal *mirchi ka salan* shared with me by the soft-spoken, very genteel Mumtaz Khan, who was an extraordinary cook and ran a cookery school for predominantly Hyderabadi girls. Her daughter Parveen has brought out a book called *Hyderabad Khasa* in her mother's memory and it is choc-a-bloc with Mumtaz's recipes and tips for authentic Hyderabadi food. I find this 'white' version, made with fresh coconut, lighter. If you are using big, fat mild chillies, that's perfect. If you use smaller, thinner spicy ones, please remember to remove the seeds, otherwise the dish will become intolerably spicy. Like many Hyderabadi specialties, the masalas have to be ground to the consistency of a powder.

***Serves:** 4*

INGREDIENTS

250 g green chillies (preferably the mild large variety with a smooth, even skin)
1 cup oil
2 onions, finely sliced
½ tsp onion seeds
½ tsp mustard seeds
1 tsp cumin seeds
¼ tsp fenugreek seeds
12 curry leaves
1 tbsp ginger paste
1 tbsp garlic paste
8 tbsp sesame seeds, finely ground
1 fresh medium coconut, finely grated

4 tsp lime juice (or *karna*, a citrus fruit found in Hyderabad)

METHOD

Cut the stalks off the green chillies, make one long slit with a knife and remove the seeds while keeping the chillies whole. Wash and dry the chillies with a cloth. Heat the oil in a kadhai or a frying pan and fry the chillies on a low flame, until soft but not golden. This should only take a few minutes. You may have to cover the pan with a lid while frying as the oil tends to splutter. Remove the chillies from the pan and fry the onions in the same oil until golden brown and crisp. Remove and crush. In the same oil, throw in the cumin, onion seeds, mustard and fenugreek until they splutter. Add the ginger and garlic pastes and cook till brown. Add sesame seed powder, curry leaves and coconut. Fry for a couple of minutes. Now add the chillies, crushed onions and ½ cup of water. Simmer for 5 minutes. Add the lime juice, cover and simmer for a further 10 minutes until the oil comes to the surface. Serve immediately. This dish also keeps very well in the fridge and is even more delicious one day after it has been prepared.

***Tip:** If large chillies are not available, use capsicum and a couple of hot green chillies.*

BAMBOO SHOOT STIR FRY

BAIMBALE BHARTHAD (PRON:BAYMBLAY BHARTAAD)

Coorg, in the hills of southern India, is about 250 km from Bengaluru. It is an area with a sense of nobility and belonging, of dense forests, coffee plantations and some spectacular estates. The terrain is quite different from the rest of South India. As you take the gentle climb from the plains to Coorg or Kodagu, as it is now known, you will witness beautifully shaped mountainous rocks, areca palms which produce betel nut, palm trees and then paddy – it's a really stunning scape that looks a little bit like a nineteenth-century English painting of India. The capital, Madikeri or Mercara as it was called before, looks like any town in India, but as you dig a little deeper, go and visit the vast estates and eat with locals, you find a generosity of spirit, an unbelievably high education level and a joy of preserving traditions, which includes food.

Coorg is known for 'spicy' food. There is an abundance of spices – pepper, cardamom, cloves and the tiny bird's eye chilli known as *parangi* – all locally grown. Spices are roasted and ground which lends complexity and density of flavour to their dishes, both vegetarian and non-vegetarian. Although Coorg is known for the famous pork dish, *pandi* curry which is a great specialty, there are a host of vegetable dishes which use local vegetables like bamboo shoot, wild mushrooms and a kind of red-leafed spinach, that are all quite delicious and different. Most of their cooking involves roasting and dry grinding different spice combinations which are then thrown into a quick stir-fry or a slow-cooked meat.

We stayed at the rather splendid Coorg Wilderness Resort in a stratosphere of its own which was quite a different experience when compared to the little homestays with British bungalows which Coorg is known for. They have a very talented chef who recreated sumptious dishes from painstakingly researched local recipes resulting in a traditional Coorgi lunch – complete with the perfect Chicken 65 and velvety fish *moilee*. Chef Ranjan even makes his own Coorg vinegar extracted from the dry *kachampuli*, a mangosteen-like fruit which when dried produces a distinctive black vinegar that is intensely sour, so you literally need a teaspoon of that in any dish to have that particular 'Coorg flavour'.

This is a vegetarian recipe from Chef Ranjan's kitchen. I think it showcases extraordinary use of local ingredients, mixed together in a roasted spice blend. He uses local bamboo shoot, but you could also use tinned bamboo shoot.

Serves: 4

INGREDIENTS

500 g tender bamboo shoot, fresh or canned

For the spice blend

1 tbsp coriander seeds
1 tsp cumin seeds

METHOD

If the bamboo shoots are fresh, wash and soak in water for 2 days. Drain, slice or chop finely and boil in water with a little salt and a pinch of turmeric powder till the shoots turn tender. If canned, just drain and slice. Put all the dry spices in a small pan and roast them, stirring constantly, until they change colour and darken slightly. Do not allow the spices to turn dark brown. Grind the roasted spices to a fine powder. Add the spice powder

1 tsp peppercorns
¼ tsp fenugreek seeds

½ tsp *kachampuli* vinegar
2 tbsp sunflower oil
5 dry red chillies
1 tsp mustard seeds
5 cloves of garlic, crushed
4–5 curry leaves
1 onion, chopped

to the bamboo shoot with 1 cup of hot water. Bring to a boil and simmer for 5–7 minutes. Add the vinegar. Heat the oil in a pan and add red chilli, mustard seeds, garlic, chopped onion and curry leaves. When the mustard splutters, pour it over the tender bamboo shoot dish and stir through. Serve hot with rice.

PUMPKIN CURRY

KUMBALA CURRY (PRON:KOOMBALA)

I met Kaveri Ponnapa one day over lunch at a Coorg festival she curated at the palatial Leela Palace in Bengaluru. It was like stepping back in time. Kaveri is a food writer who looks and writes like she has stepped out of a nineteenth-century romantic novel. She is dedicated and devoted to the Coorg Table – preserving traditions, flavours, aromas and life in Coorg, where she comes from and which forms a part of so many of her childhood memories. Her blog 'The Coorg Table' will soon be a book with her evocative photographs and almost lyrical prose. Here's an unusual everyday recipe for pumpkin (butternut squash) which I now make often and adore. It also puts to bed the myth that the food of Coorg is meat-centric. Pumpkin curry, eaten for breakfast in Coorg, is a star vegetarian dish – warm, earthy cubes of tender pumpkin with a distinct touch of garlic, this is usually eaten with rice or rotis and a splash of ghee.

***Serves:* 2–3**

INGREDIENTS

For the curry

300 g pumpkin, with skin (choose one with tender, green skin)
1 tsp red chilli powder
½ tsp turmeric powder
1 tsp coriander powder
1 green chilli, slit vertically
Salt to taste
¼ cup coconut, freshly grated and ground to a smooth paste
1 tsp cumin, toasted and finely powdered

For the tempering

2 tsp oil
½ tsp mustard seeds
5-6 curry leaves
1 dried red chilli, broken in half
3-4 pods of garlic with skin, lightly crushed

METHOD

Remove all the seeds and filament clinging to the inside of the pumpkin and cut into approximately 1-inch cubes. Leave the skin on. Place in a saucepan or vessel, add water to just cover and bring to a boil. Reduce the heat to a simmer, add red chilli powder, turmeric powder, coriander powder, green chilli and salt to taste, and cook uncovered until the cubes of pumpkin are very tender, but not mushy. Add the ground coconut and the toasted and ground cumin powder, and simmer gently until all the ingredients are well blended. If the curry seems too thick, add just enough hot water to give you enough gravy that can be mopped up. Remove from the heat.

Heat the oil in a small pan, and, when hot, toss in the mustard seeds. When they begin to sputter, add the curry leaves, dried red chilli and crushed garlic. Stir once or twice and pour the contents of the pan over the pumpkin curry.

Tip: *Toasted/roasted and ground spices give a distinctive taste to many Coorg dishes. Dry roast the cumin in a pan until quite dark and aromatic. Cool, before grinding to a fine powder in a mortar and pestle.*

SINDHI DAL WITH FLAKY BREAD

DAL PAKWAN (PRON: DAAHL PUCK-WAAN)

Dal and flaky *pakwan* or *poori* is served usually for Sunday breakfast in Sindhi homes. Hindus from the province of Sindh (now in Pakistan) fled to India during Partition. They were primarily a trading and business community with ties all over the world and have been compared to the Jews of Europe. I have been to a Sindhi lunch in Casablanca where the most amazing satay (made by a family member from Jakarta) was served in addition to traditional Sindhi food and Moroccan couscous! Wherever they are – from South America to Singapore – a Sindhi is guaranteed to not miss breakfast – *seyal dabal* roti (bread and green chutney cooked together), *koki* (crispy roti made with ghee) and, of course, dal pakwan. This is a recipe shared by my neighbours, the Shewanis, whose dal pakwan I adore.

Serves: 6

INGREDIENTS

For the dal

500 g chana dal
4 green chillies, whole
1 tsp salt
1 tsp turmeric

For the tempering

5 tbsp ghee
1 tbsp cumin seeds
1 full head of garlic (about 12 small cloves), finely chopped
1 tbsp red chilli powder
8 curry leaves, finely chopped
A pinch of asafoetida

For the garnish

3 tbsp coriander leaves, chopped
1 onion chopped
¼ tsp chaat masala
½ tsp raw mango powder

For the pakwan

500 g all-purpose flour
½ tsp salt
1 tsp cumin seeds
Oil to deep fry

METHOD

Dal

Soak the dal in water to cover for a minimum of 2 hours. Drain the water and wash several times. Boil in a pressure cooker or in a pot with the salt, turmeric, green chillies and one litre of water. Cook till the dal is soft. This will take about 10 minutes in a pressure cooker and 40 minutes in a pot. Mash and stir a little. Heat ghee in a small pan and add the garlic and cumin seeds, then the curry leaves and red chilli powder. Pour over the dal and garnish with coriander leaves, chopped onion, chaat masala and raw mango powder.

Pakwan

Knead all the ingredients into a firm dough with water. Rest for 30 mins. Roll into a round shape about 7-inch diameter and ⅛-inch thick. Punch multiple holes in the rolled dough to avoid puffing of the *pakwan*. Heat oil in a deep fat fryer or kadhai till very hot. Immerse one *pakwan* at a time and fry till they are golden and crispy. Drain on absorbent paper. Serve alongside the dal with date and tamarind chutney.

FISH TIKKA WITH DILL

I'm not sure where this recipe came from (I have a sneaking suspicion it may have been from Jiggs Kalra) but I have been using it for donkey's years with great success every time. What I like the most is that it doesn't have that awful red masala they slather on everything in the tandoori section of the menu in many Indian restaurants. The spices are gentle so you can taste the flavour of the fish and the addition of dill gives it an international feel. The recipe uses Norwegian or Atlantic salmon which is divine. This is a signature item at Colonel Saab.

Serves: 3–4

INGREDIENTS

For the first marination

600 g fish fillet, preferably salmon with skin, cut into 3 or 4 pieces
2 tsp ginger paste
3 tsp garlic paste
Salt to taste
3 tsp lemon juice

For the second marination

½ cup thick yoghurt (Greek yoghurt is perfect)
½ cup cheddar cheese, grated
4 tbsp cream
1 egg
1 tbsp chickpea flour
A pinch each of cumin powder, green cardamom powder, black pepper powder, cinnamon powder, clove powder

½ tsp carom seeds
A pinch of turmeric powder
2 tbsp fresh dill, chopped

METHOD

Mix all the ingredients for the first marination with the fish and keep aside for 20 minutes. Then drain off all juices. For the second marination, whisk the yoghurt and cheese in a bowl, add the remaining ingredients. Whisk and rub the fish with this marinade. Keep aside for 30 minutes. Place the fish on a baking tray on foil paper and roast in a preheated oven on 220°C for 5–7 minutes. Baste with a little butter, turn once and roast again for 3–4 minutes.

ASSAMESE FISH WITH TOMATO

MASOR BILAHI TENGA (PRON: MAASOAR BILLAHEE TAYNGA)

I discovered this utterly simple, utterly delicious Assamese fish curry at the home of my son's in-laws in Guwahati, during what turned into an 'engagement' dinner. Meeting the in-laws for the first time must be a daunting task, I expect. All barriers were eventually broken over a bottle of Scotch and a dinner table laid for a king. Of all the marvellous dishes that were prepared in our honour, mother-in-law Anju Deka was, I think, mildy horrified to hear that the homestyle fish tenga or sour fish was my favourite amongst the many more elaborate dishes she produced that evening. This is traditionally made with bony river fish whose soft flesh has a particularly flavourful sweetness in that part of the world.

Serves: 6

INGREDIENTS

1 kg river fish – rohu/katla, cut into 10 pieces or slices of sea fish, if you can't manage the bones
1 tsp turmeric powder
Salt to taste
8 medium-sized tomatoes, finely chopped
2 cups coriander leaves, chopped
5 tbsp mustard oil
1 tsp yellow mustard seeds
2–3 green chillies (optional), sliced vertically

METHOD

Rub turmeric and salt on the pieces of fish. Keep aside for 10–15 minutes. Heat 4 tbsp of oil in a pan and fry the fish for no more than a minute on each side. Take another pan and heat 1 tbsp of oil in it. Add mustard seeds and, once they start to crackle, add tomatoes. Add the turmeric powder and salt. Turn heat to a simmer and cook the tomatoes till they turn soft and pulpy. Add a cup and a half of hot water. Bring to the boil and add the green chillies and the fried fish pieces. Cook for about 5–7 minutes only. Garnish with the chopped coriander leaves and serve with steamed rice.

FISH STEAMED IN BANANA LEAVES

PATRA NI MACHCHI (PRON: PAATRAA NEE MUCHCHEE)

Brilliant, cliquish, funny and, most of all, lovers of good food – Parsis are Zoroastrians who fled Persia in the eighth century and landed in Gujarat. Today they are a much smaller but very significant community who have many top industrialists, artists, musicians and writers amongst them and their amazing cuisine lives on, especially at functions like marriages where everybody is served on long tables and the five- or seven-course feast is still served on banana leaves.

Parsi cooking is a delicious mix of western influences – Gujarati and Persian. You'll find almost no vegetarian dishes at all at a Parsi dinner. Vegetables are almost always cooked with meat, fish or eggs. The great Parsi banquet begins with a luminous coloured soft drink; then comes the sweet and sour chutney and wafers (crisps). The first course is almost always fish – typically pomfret in a piquant white sauce spiked with green chillies, vinegar and baby tomatoes – *saas ni machchi* or pomfret coated with a thick coriander coconut chutney and steamed in a banana leaf – *patra ni machchi*. Then a chicken followed by the meat and rice and lastly custard (pronounced 'custar') which is a bit like a crème caramel without the caramel. Although the Parsi kitchen is known for *dhansakh* – a mammoth concoction of rice, lentils, vegetables and meat – it is not usually part of the wedding feast dinner. This is made for Sunday lunch. Parsi condiments, chutneys and pickles are often sold at little shops near an *agiary*. This is the famous fish cooked in banana leaves. It's easy to do at home and, if you don't have banana leaves, fear not, it's very much doable using foil.

Serves: 4–6

INGREDIENTS

For the fish

3 full banana leaves
6 slices pomfret or any white fish, cut into thick slices
2 tbsp sugarcane vinegar

For the coconut chutney

1 heaped cup of coconut, grated
6 green chillies, deseeded
1 cup coriander leaves
½ cup mint leaves
12 cloves of garlic, peeled
½-inch piece of ginger
1 tsp cumin, roasted
4 tbsp lime juice
1 tsp sugar
1 tsp salt

METHOD

Combine all ingredients for the coconut chutney in a mixer/grinder/blender and grind to a smooth paste.

Cut the banana leaves into 6 large pieces, removing the centre stem. Pass the banana leaves quickly over a gas flame to soften them. Layer the coconut chutney on each slice of fish and place on a piece of banana leaf. Fold the leaves over to completely cover the fish and form a parcel. You may need to use two pieces of leaf per slice of fish in order to cover the fish properly. Tie the parcels with thread and set aside. Heat water and vinegar together in the bottom part of a steamer or a large pan. Place the banana leaf parcels two at a time, in the steamer or in a colander over the pan. Steam for approximately 15–20 minutes, depending on the size of your fish. Unwrap the parcels at the time of serving only.

FISH IN FRESH FENUGREEK SAUCE

METHI MACHCHI (PRON: MAYTHEE MUCHCHEE)

Fenugreek or *methi* is an acquired taste. You either love or hate these tiny bitter leaves. For those who are new to its flavour, this recipe is perfect because it blends spinach and tomatoes with the fenugreek, thereby, toning down the bitterness. As far as I know, it is only the Sindhis who combine fenugreek with fish in India. This is a Sindhi family recipe which works every time.

Serves: 4

INGREDIENTS

500 g fish, cut into slices (pomfret, *rawas* or any firm-fleshed white fish)
1 tsp salt
2 tbsp lime juice

3 tbsp oil
2 onions, chopped
10–12 small cloves of garlic, peeled but left whole
3 green chillies, chopped
1 tsp coriander powder
1 tsp cumin powder
¼ tsp turmeric
½ tsp red chilli powder
1 cup spinach, chopped
2 cups fresh fenugreek leaves, chopped roughly
2–3 medium-sized tomatoes, peeled and chopped

METHOD

Wash the fish and marinate with salt and lime juice. Keep aside for 30 minutes. Heat the oil in a frying pan and fry the onions and garlic till golden. Add the coriander, cumin, turmeric and red chilli powder and continue frying on a slow heat for a couple of minutes. Add the fenugreek, spinach, tomatoes and ½ cup of water. Swirl around, cover and cook on a low heat till the tomatoes are cooked to a pulp. Check and adjust seasoning. Drain the fish and pat dry and then slide it into the sauce in the pan. Stir once and cook covered on a low heat until the gravy thickens and sticks to the fish (this should take about 10–12 minutes). Serve hot with rice or chapati.

PRAWN GHEE ROAST

Here's another recipe with the very deceptive 'roast' in its name. An Indian'roast' basically means a dry dish with roasted and fried spices rather than one with a gravy. I have had 'roasts' mainly in the south – in Kerala and Bengaluru but I haven't been to Mangalore where this dish is said to have originated. In Kerala, they 'roast' by frying onions and then the spices in coconut oil. In Mangalore, a roast is made with ghee and usually contains chicken. The popular recipe 'chicken ghee roast' is said to have originated in a small town called Kundapur just outside Mangalore. The chicken is cut into bite-sized pieces and marinated in yoghurt, ginger and dry spices. The ghee is used to fry garlic and a whole bunch of other spices. This mixture is cooked with water and made into a paste, added to the chicken and the whole lot is cooked together until the masala is quite dry. In Chettinad chicken ghee roast, the marinated chicken pieces with bone and skin are fried in ghee first to render the chicken skin crispy.

I tasted the most wondrous prawn ghee roast a couple of years ago in a restaurant in Pune called Mr Rabbits. Nanda Shetty and her two sons owned the popular restaurant and bar. The place was packed every night with regulars. It looked like an Indian version of the sitcom *Cheers*. People drove miles for Nanda's Kerala mutton pepper fry, the fried fish and her amazing prawn ghee roast. I spoke to the rather shy Nanda who explained that they were on a family holiday in Mangalore and had amazing dishes of prawn and chicken ghee roast at a small restaurant called Anupama. Of course, nobody would divulge the recipe and so, being an accomplished cook herself, she set about to discover the secret. After much trial and error, she recreated the recipe, which is a much simpler version of the many 'original' ones and frankly it's the best I have ever had. She cooked it right in front of me in a matter of minutes! So here it is.

Serves: 4–6

INGREDIENTS

1 kg prawns, peeled and deveined (with tail on)

For the marinade
1 cup yoghurt
½ tsp turmeric
Pinch of salt

For the roast
15 *byadgi* chillies
2 tbsp coriander seeds
1 tsp cumin
5 cloves

6 tbsp ghee
6–8 onions, finely chopped
A handful of curry leaves, fried

METHOD

Marinate the prawns in the yoghurt, salt and turmeric for about half an hour. Dry roast the spices individually in a frying pan or under a grill and grind to a powder together – this will be your base roast masala powder. Heat ghee in a pan and fry the onions first on a low flame to cook and then on a high flame till they brown. Add the roasted spice powder and fry for a few seconds. Add the marinated prawns and stir on a high flame till the masala dries up and the prawns are cooked. Season with salt. Garnish with the fried curry leaves.

HOT, SWEET AND SOUR PRAWNS OR FISH

PRAWN OR FISH PATIA

Every Parsi family has its own recipe for *patia*. The word originated from the vessel in which it was cooked. This was a large flat-bottomed utensil with curved sides, usually made of copper or brass and tinned on the inside. The one thing that all *patias* have in common is the masala of chillies, cumin and garlic that is ground in vinegar. Some people add drumsticks while others, ladyfingers. This is Parvana Boga Noorani's recipe.

Serves: 4–6

INGREDIENTS

For the *patia*

1 cup sesame or groundnut oil to fry
1½ kg (10–12 large) onions, finely sliced
3 x 3-inch sticks of cinnamon
8–10 cloves
8–10 black peppercorns
2 bay leaves
2 sprigs of curry leaves
½ cup spinach leaves (optional)
1 kg fresh prawns, shelled and deveined or sliced pomfret
1 cup sugarcane vinegar
A walnut-sized lump of jaggery, chopped
Salt to taste

For the masala paste

15–20 Kashmiri chillies
2½ tbsp cumin seeds
½-inch piece ginger (optional)
1 whole head of garlic

For garnish

¼ cup coriander leaves, finely chopped

METHOD

Heat the oil in a heavy-bottomed vessel until hot. Make sure it does not reach the smoking point. Add sliced onions and fry until they just start to turn colour. Add the cinnamon, cloves, peppercorns and bay leaves and continue frying until the onions are a rich golden brown but not burnt. Add the curry leaves and the ground masala paste (made by combining the spices with ½ cup of sugarcane or malt vinegar and grinding to a fine paste), and fry on a low heat, stirring constantly, until the masala releases a rich aroma and the oil rises to the top. Take care not to let the masala burn. If the masala sticks to the pan, add a tablespoon of water. Add the chopped spinach leaves, if using, and the prawns or fish and cook for 2 minutes on high heat. Add the remaining vinegar and the jaggery and stir well. Cover and cook on a low flame until the jaggery has melted and the flavours blended. Serve with chopped coriander leaves sprinkled on top.

CHICKEN FINGERS

CHICKEN KAINCHI KEBABS (PRON: KAYCHEE)

The problem with great chefs is that they are forced to constantly 'create' new dishes, come up with new twists to old themes and, for want of a better expression, reinvent the wheel. Such is the case of the old charmer, the inimitable maestro of masala, whose forefathers cooked for the Nawabs of Awadh (Lucknow), Imtiaz Quereshi.

What can I say, the man had me speechless (and for those who know me well, that's saying something!) with his deft hand, his amazing accuracy and the way he cleverly manoeuvred the conversation to something else, every time I asked him for his recipe for garam masala (undoubtedly one of his real secret weapons). He was already in his early seventies when I first met him, presiding over a Lucknow food festival at the ITC Grand Maratha in Mumbai and smiling for the ever-present cameras. For all his apparent shyness, I think he secretly loved the glitz.

Was he still capable of cooking a simple recipe though? One that didn't involve a thousand ingredients and a trek across India? Alone in the kitchen (with a half a dozen or so young disciples), he asked for some breast of chicken and a pair of scissors. 'I am going to show you *kainchi kebab* (scissor kebab). This was invented when there was leftover raw chicken or mutton, intended for *pasanda*. You cut the flattened meat or chicken with scissors since this was easier than using a knife.' He sprinkled a bit of this and that, asked me to mix the lot and watched carefully out of the corner of his eye, as if to test my skills. Within a minute, the kebabs were dusted with chickpea flour and deep-fried to crisp perfection – definitely a much superior version of KFC – and walloped by us all. The true test of a great chef is impromptu cooking. Imtiaz Quereshi proved to me that afternoon that he really is one.

***Serves:* 4**

INGREDIENTS

For the chicken kebabs

500 g boneless chicken, cut into finger-sized pieces
1 cup chickpea flour (to dust)
Oil for deep frying

For the marinade

2 tsp salt
2 tbsp green chillies, finely chopped
2 tsp great garam masala
2 tsp black pepper
2 tbsp ginger-garlic paste
1 tsp red chilli powder
Juice of 1 lime

METHOD

Mix chicken with all the marinade ingredients and keep aside for 10 minutes. Dust with the chickpea flour and deep fry in hot oil. When golden, remove, drain and eat as is.

Great Garam Masala (don't ask me the exact proportions, I took this down on the back of a paper napkin as Imtiaz was speaking!) I use about a teaspoon of everything powdered and mixed together, except nutmeg, which is so strong that a quarter of a teaspoon, when powdered, is more than enough.

Green cardamom, cumin, bay leaf, whole coriander, cloves, cinnamon nutmeg, mace, fennel seed, star anise

CHICKEN 65

Nobody has been able to give me an adequate explanation of why this delicious dish of fried chicken is called Chicken 65. Stories abound: the chicken is marinated for 65 days; it is made from 65-day-old chickens; a chef once added 65 chillies to the recipe to make it super spicy and so on. A couple of the more plausible explanations: that it was the 65th item on a menu and that it was invented in 1965 by Buhari's hotel in Chennai. The latter is likely because the same eatery also featured a Chicken 78, 82 and 90 on their menu.

Stories aside, it is one of the most delicious fried chicken dishes I have ever tasted. This recipe from Chef Ranjan at the Coorg Wellness Resort had us almost licking the plate after we proclaimed we weren't hungry in the first place. In the original recipe, you marinate and deep-fry the chicken. It is then tossed in a pan on high heat with curry leaves and a bit of yoghurt. In this recipe, everything is added to the marinade and the chicken is deep-fried and not tossed again. The chicken pieces remain succulent on the inside and crispy on the outside.

I once made this in Venice for friends. Instead of the 500 g of chicken, I bought 1.5 kg by mistake. Back home, I thought it looked like quite a lot but a few glasses of Prosecco down, I carried on regardless. So all the spices were proportionately much less. I fried and fried in that tiny kitchen and the plates kept coming back empty. Neighbours kept joining and staying for longer than the traditional '*aperitivo*'. And the bubbly kept popping. The moral of the story – when abroad in the company of those not used to chilli and spices, halve (at least) the amount of spices you would normally use if you want people to have a great time without gasping for glasses of water ... or Prosecco!

Serves: 2–4

INGREDIENTS

500 g boneless chicken
1 egg
2 tbsp ginger-garlic paste (1:1)
½ cup thick yoghurt
Juice of 2 limes
2 tbsp Kashmiri chilli powder
1 tsp turmeric powder
1 tsp garam masala powder
½ tbsp cumin powder
½ tbsp black pepper, crushed
½ tsp dry fenugreek powder
2 tbsp rice flour
2 tbsp cornflour
Salt as required
Oil to deep fry
20 curry leaves
4 green chillies

METHOD

In a bowl, mix together all the ingredients except oil, curry leaves and green chillies. Marinate the chicken pieces with this spice batter and let it rest for 30 minutes.

Heat plenty of oil in a wok or kadhai. When the oil is hot, add the chicken pieces, and make sure not to overcrowd them. You may need to do this in 2–3 batches. Fry for 3–4 minutes, turning the pieces occasionally till golden. Remove and drain on paper towels. When all the pieces are fried, add the curry leaves and green chillies to the oil for 30 seconds. Remove and toss with the hot chicken in a bowl. Serve hot with lime wedges and onion rings.

CHICKEN CHETTINAD

MILAGU MASALA KOZHI (PRON: MILAGA MASALA KOREE)

The journey to Chettinad from the nearest airport, Madurai in South India, is an hour and a half's ride through sleepy villages and arid farmlands of Tamil Nadu. The Chettiyar community began as merchants trading salt and rice in Southeast Asia for the Chola kings between the tenth and twelfth centuries. They then traded gems and finally functioned as the middlemen between imperial bankers and local farmers and traders. Their trade routes stretched to Burma, Ceylon, Malaysia, Sumatra and South Africa which had its heyday from the eighteenth century to Independence in 1947. During this time, they amassed substantial souvenirs from overseas which they brought back to decorate their lavish mansions – solid Burma teak columns, marble from Italy and ivory. They still hold an important place in the present-day world of business and finance. Pious by nature, they also donated considerable amounts to build temples in Chettinad and all over Southeast Asia. They collected spices on their travels and adopted the habit of eating meat, fish and fowl which gave their cuisine a particularity in the otherwise orthodox (vegetarian) Hindu South.

A traditional Chettinad lunch is served on a banana leaf. It consists of *rasam*, *parappu* (dal with ghee), rice, *kozhambu* (thick vegetable curry), *kootu* (vegetables with lentils), *poriyal* (vegetable with grated coconut), something crispy, *pachadi* (chutney made with jaggery) and *mandi* (a vegetable made with water from washed rice often flavoured with green chilli, shallots and tamarind). Even at lunch, a fried fish or chicken is always served. You may even be lucky enough to have *milagu masala kozhi* ('zh' is pronounced 'l' locally) or Chicken Chettinad as it is commonly known. It will be surprisingly flavourful with the heat coming from the round, red dry *goondu milagai* chilli and black pepper – light years away from the stomach-wrenching dishes labelled 'Chettinad Chicken' in many restaurants.

The one place for amazing food in the area is an oasis called Bangala. Meenakshi Meyyappan has single-handedly been promoting Chettinad, its food and its culture for many years now. She has been described by the *New York Times* writer and frequent visitor to India, Guy Trebay, as 'a chatelaine . . . an elegant and disarmingly urbane Chettiar woman habitually dressed in saris of muted colour, a pair of discreet diamond sun bursts in her ears . . . '

I found a friend and kindred spirit in Meenakshi. Aware of the latest international trends in food and fashion (she also has a fabulous store on the premises of her boutique hotel in Kairakudi), she disarms you with her frankness, her sense of humour, business and entrepreneurial skills and her up-to-date knowledge on a range of subjects. We discussed food, of course, but so much more too. Her book, *The Bangala Table*, will give you a delicious glimpse of the food.

Chicken Chettinad is easily the most requested dish at The Bangala. Its unique wet spice paste blend, dominated by black pepper, gives it the Chettinad credentials. This recipe is the real deal. It has balanced flavours with the mildly numbing but subtle heat of black pepper as the underlying essence that continues to linger on the palate, all wonderfully soaked up by the chicken. At The Bangala, chicken is often substituted with local farmed quail. This recipe is from the book *The Bangala Table* by Meenakshi Meyyappan.

Serves: 2

INGREDIENTS

For the wet paste

1 tsp fennel seeds
2 tsp black peppercorns
1 tsp cumin seeds
4 dried red chillies, mild preferably *goondu milagai*, whole
1 tsp coriander seeds
½ tsp turmeric powder
1 tsp garlic, peeled and grated
½ tsp ginger, peeled and grated

For the chicken

½ cup vegetable oil
2-inch piece of cinnamon
2 pods of green cardamom
1½ onions, finely chopped
2 tomatoes, puréed
1 tsp sea salt
600 g chicken cut into 8 pieces

METHOD

Place a heavy *tava* or flat pan on low heat and dry roast the fennel seeds, peppercorns, cumin seeds, dried red chillies and coriander seeds until fragrant and slightly darkened. Grind them on an *ammi* or mortar-pestle adding a little water or run them in a wet grinder/blender to make a paste. Add turmeric, garlic and ginger to the wet paste and mix well. Set this aside.

Place a large kadhai or wok over high heat and add oil. When hot, add cinnamon, cardamom and onion and stir. Reduce heat to medium and sauté for about 4 minutes or until the onion is lightly coloured before adding the tomato purée. Sauté for an additional minute. Add the wet masala paste to the kadhai, breaking it apart with a spoon and stirring well to incorporate. Continue to cook for 10–12 minutes, scraping the bottom of the kadhai, till the oil separates from the masala. The mixture should look well cooked and should have darkened. Sprinkle in the sea salt and stir. Then add the chicken, stirring continuously to coat well with the mixture. Continue cooking for 1–2 minutes before adding 1½ cups of water. Scrape the bottom of the kadhai to deglaze and bring to a boil on high heat. Boil for 3–4 minutes then turn heat down to low and cook covered for 15–20 minutes. Stir occasionally. Uncover and reduce till the sauce thickens to coat the chicken well. Remove from heat and serve immediately.

Tip: *Substitute an equal weight of quail (around 6 quails) for the chicken to make Quail Chettinad pepper masala. Cut the quails into two pieces each, separating the breasts from the legs and follow the recipe above. Also try this masala with potatoes or mushrooms for a vegetarian Chettinad pepper masala.*

CHICKEN WITH DRIED APRICOTS

JARDALOO MA MURGHI (PRON:J'RDALOO MAA MOORGHEE)

This is a classic Parsi recipe which combines the Parsis' ancestry with flavours of their Indian home and a bit of local British influence thrown in. My dear friend and once catering partner, Parvana Boga Noorani, made this on a show I did for the *Good Food Guide* on Star TV. She made it with lamb which is the traditional recipe and the meat went off while we were sitting around doing take after take. We eventually patched it up for the sake of photography and TV. She then made another one with chicken for all of us to enjoy and we decided that this was a safer and easier bet. Cherry on top – we had singer Gary Lawyer serenade us on and off camera. The chicken was predictably perfect.

Serves: 4

INGREDIENTS

1 kg chicken legs and thighs, with skin
1 cup oil
1 kg onions, thinly sliced
2 x 1-inch sticks of cinnamon
2 pods of cardamoms
10 cloves
2 bay leaves
1 tbsp ginger paste
1 tbsp garlic paste
2 tsp red chilli powder, roasted
1 tsp cumin seeds, roasted and powdered
250 g dried apricots soaked in hot water with a little sugar (stone removed)
3–4 tbsp Worcestershire sauce
1 tbsp vinegar
2 tsp salt
250 g *salli* potato straws

METHOD

Heat oil in a large heavy-bottomed pot and fry the sliced onions until they just start to brown. Add cinnamon, cardamom, cloves and bay leaves and continue to cook until the onions are well browned. Add a splash of hot water and scrape up all the browned bits in the pan. Add the ginger, garlic, chilli powder and cumin. Fry for 1 minute and add the chicken. Brown well and then add 2 cups of hot water. Cover and cook on a low heat until the chicken is almost done. Add salt and continue to cook until the chicken is tender. Add the apricots along with the water they have been soaked in, Worcestershire sauce and vinegar, and heat through to blend the flavours. Stir and serve hot with deep fried potato straws on top, known locally as *salli*.

PORK WITH BAMBOO SHOOT

BAANHGAJOR LAGOT GAHORI (PRON: BAAHGAAZOR LAAGOAT GAAHOREE)

Once upon a time, in Shillong, I had a dish of pork with bamboo shoot which was so delicious that I decided I must replicate it. Driving upto Shillong on winding mountain roads from Guwahati, I noticed some makeshift food stands with rosy-cheeked local women selling brined bamboo shoot, gigantic pineapples, pickles and deadly looking tiny red chillies. I was told we would stop on the way back, and so we did. We had already found some extraordinarily exquisite orange blossom honey from a farm shop in Shillong and some interesting varieties of local chillies made into a pickle-like condiment. It had been raining and, as I leapt from the car in excitement towards one of the shacks to explore, I fell through the makeshift floor covered with wet bamboo matting. This is the kind of moment where you call to the universe very quickly for help and wish you had gone on that diet. I managed to save myself by sheer instinct, a bit of muscle and chunky elbows. Of course, husband and son came to the rescue very quickly and they managed to pull me out. What they didn't see was that below the non-existent floor was a 100-metre drop and a river running beneath. There is a moral to this story. Support local but watch your step!

Of course, the incident didn't stop me from buying a huge jar of bamboo shoot in brine. Before Imaleen shared her mother's recipe, I decided to give it a go myself. Based on instinct and a bit of laziness, I put all the ingredients below into a big Creuset pot (I didn't add the chilli powder or tomatoes) with no oil. I crushed the pods of garlic, skin on and roughly chopped the onions and newly acquired bamboo shoot with cubes of pork. I slow-cooked it with a bit of water and a tight lid for an hour. The result was quite divine. Not as elegant as the recipe below, but pretty delicious, nonetheless.

Serves: 6

INGREDIENTS

1 kg pork, boneless with a small amount of fat only
1 cup bamboo shoot, chopped roughly
4–5 whole dried red chillies
2 whole pods of garlic, peeled and chopped
2 big onions cut into cubes
4 medium-sized tomatoes, cut into small pieces
1 tsp turmeric powder
3 tsp mild red chilli powder
5 tbsp mustard oil
Salt to taste

METHOD

Cut the pork in 1½-inch pieces. Boil in a pressure cooker with a cup of water and 1 tsp salt for 10 minutes. Alternatively, slow cook for an hour with 2 cups of water and cover with a tight lid. Heat oil in a pan and add the dry chillies and chopped garlic. Fry until the garlic turns golden brown. Then add the onions and fry on low heat till translucent. Add the tomatoes and cook until pulpy. Now add turmeric powder, red chilli powder and salt and fry for a little while to cook the spices. Then add the bamboo shoot and cook for another 4–5 minutes. Finally, add the pork from the pan with its water and cook on a low heat for about 10–15 minutes to render the fat. Once the oil rises to the surface, your dish is done. Serve hot with steamed rice.

COORG PORK CURRY

PANDI CURRY

Here's an excerpt from Kaveri Ponappa's recipe for Pandi Curry on her blog, *The Coorg Table*, 'We smoke, dry, preserve, curry, braise, fry and roast pork, extracting every ounce of flavour, varying the texture as much as we can, sometimes scooping a spoonful of preserved pork fat from a ceramic jar into a dish, intensifying flavours. At the big village feasts and celebrations, besides the barbecued pork, there is always a deep, rich, pandi curry ... There are probably as many versions of this ancient dish, born out of our hunting past, as there are kitchens ...'

One of my favourite Pandi curries is by my cousin Nina (née Uthappa) Agtey. Her recipe is similar to Kaveri's and the result is the same smoky sensation in a vibrant, peppery roasted masala with a hint of curry leaves.

Kaveri wins me over with her prose on the subject, '... food changes with the ingredients available at hand; but sometimes one comes across a dish that has evolved so perfectly in its own time and place that it is best left alone ... The cubed chunks of tender pork in a dense, molten gravy, releasing the slow heat of black peppercorns, grown in the hills of Coorg since the times when wild vines could be seen looping across trees, sketching great arcs and webs across the dense jungles. Red chillies were latecomers: even the violent little bird's eyes, referred to locally as *parangi*, betray their foreign origins. Hidden notes from dark roasted spices that have survived a pounding in a mortar and pestle, and have begun to release their flavours into the pork should follow the heat of the roasted peppercorns. A sharp burst of *kachampuli* – that's all you need – to slice through the gleam of melted fat.'

It is as perfect a dish that ever came out of an extraordinary place.

Serves: 4–5

INGREDIENTS

For the spice mix

1 tbsp black peppercorns
1 tbsp cumin seeds
1½ tbsp coriander seeds
1 tbsp mustard seeds
A pinch of fenugreek seeds

For the curry

1 kg pork, cut into approximately 1-inch cubes
1 tsp turmeric powder
Red chilli powder to taste (optional)
3 large onions
3-inch piece of root ginger
1½ bulbs of garlic, peeled

METHOD

Dry roast the ingredients for the spice mix separately. Cool and grind to a fine powder in a mortar and pestle or spice grinder.

Wash the pork and pat dry. Sprinkle and rub the pork cubes with turmeric and red chilli powder and set aside to marinate. Finely chop the onions. Scrape the ginger, peel the garlic, and grind together to a smooth paste in a food processor. Slit the green chillies and set aside.

Heat the sesame oil in a pressure cooker, and when hot, add the chopped onions. Stir and fry over medium heat until translucent. Add the ginger-garlic paste, and fry until the raw smell disappears. Add the marinated pork cubes, raise the heat and fry until the meat changes colour. Now reduce the heat, add the dry-roasted spices, and mix until the cubes of pork are well coated with the spice mixture. Add salt to taste, about 2 cups of hot water and bring to a boil over medium heat. Cover, reduce the heat to low-

2-3 fresh green chillies
3-4 tbsp sesame oil
Salt to taste
1 tbsp *kachampuli* (Coorg vinegar)

medium, and pressure cook for about 20 minutes. Remove from the heat and allow the pressure to drop. Test the meat for doneness – the pork should be tender but firm. Place the cooker back on the heat, toss in the slit green chillies, add the *kachampuli*, and simmer for about 5–7 minutes over low heat. Serve with an extra squeeze of lime and *kadambuttus* (steamed rice dumplings).

Tip: *A few days' old Pandi curry tastes even better!*

MINCED MUTTON KEBABS

SHIKAMPUR KEBABS (PRON: SHIKAAMPOOR)

Many years ago, I had the fortune of being invited to the ancestral home of ad film maker Zafar Hai in Hyderabad. The detailing was perfect – from the silver slippers in the bathroom to the intricacy of the table setting and, of course, the rich, painstakingly prepared food. Zafar's mother confessed she never went into the kitchen herself, but she clearly knew about food and laid a superb table. All the dishes came out together with the biryani or the *safed pullao*, as I recall, coming out last and you were advised on the food pairings and their order, the *lukhmi* first, then the kebabs and *sheermal* or *kulcha*, the vegetables and '*kut*', meats and, lastly, the biryani. There was a raita somewhere in the middle and two desserts at the end. This elaborate menu and method of laying everything down together is also the case at a traditional *dastarkhan* dinner and a wedding. The crockery was bone china and the dishes in which the food was served, pure silver. It was a feast for the senses and made me realize that Hyderabadi food was both complex and difficult to replicate without a serious amount of help. However, in terms of 'gourmet' ingredients, it was sublime – rose petals, saffron, fragrant cardamoms. What was interesting was also the inclusion of the tart and pungent flavourings of the South – mustard seeds, curry leaves, hot chillies, peanuts, tamarind and tomatoes. A sauce of roasted and ground sesame seeds, which in the Middle East might appear under the guise of mild-flavoured *tahini*, is mixed with fiery green chillies and the tart tamarind paste to become the mouth-watering *gudtil ki chutney*. Dried beans and lamb, which are often stewed together in Persian cuisine, are perked up with tamarind, cumin seeds, red chillies and curry leaves to become the delectable *dalcha* of Hyderabad. The biryanis are distinct with aromatic *potlis* (spices tied in muslin pouches), and lamb added raw, so that it cooks along with the rice.

The royal family and the landed gentry of Hyderabad were, for many generations, great gourmets and patronized fine cuisine, fine-dining and elaborate menus (whether for breakfast, for a hunt, for great banquets or *dastarkhan* dinners). These traditions live on through some of the families – the only problem being the number of staff required to prepare the painstaking recipes since tradition demands that many of them must be done by hand, without the use of mixers and grinders. Much has been documented about Hyderabadi royal food in books about the Nizam and his entourage. Because genuine Hyderabadi dishes are painstaking to prepare, they are rarely found on restaurant menus. Mrs Mumtaz Khan, Zafar's aunt, invited me into her home thereafter, and shared with me this recipe for traditional Shikhampur kebab, a minced lamb kebab with a stuffing of yoghurt chutney which melts as you bite into it. I have made this several times. The result is a melt-in-the-mouth piece of ecstasy every time.

Serves:* 5 *(or 15 kebabs)

INGREDIENTS

1 egg white
200 g chutney for stuffing
½ cup oil

For the chutney
100 g fresh hung curd (cream cheese is a worthy substitute)
½ onion, finely chopped
2 green chillies, finely chopped
2 tbsp coriander
½ tsp salt

For the kebabs
500 g boneless mutton, cut into small cubes
2 onions, sliced
1 tsp ginger paste
1 tsp garlic paste
1 tsp red chilli powder
½ tsp turmeric powder
A handful fresh coriander, chopped finely
Salt to taste
2 tbsp Bengal gram dal

For the ground masala
2 tsp *charoli*
1 tbsp white poppy seeds
2 tbsp almonds or cashew nuts
5 pods of green cardamom, skin removed
5 cloves

METHOD

Mix together all the items for the kebabs in a pan. Cover and cook on a medium flame for 25 minutes. Do not add any water or oil. Remove the lid and stir occasionally until all the water dries up. Continue to stir until the meat turns a little brown in colour. Remove from the heat, cool and grind to a fine paste using a grinder/blender.

Add the ground masala mixture to this paste. The masala can be prepared in advance and kept aside or refrigerated till required. Add the beaten egg white to the meat mixture.

For the chutney, mix all the ingredients together in a bowl. This chutney should be of a very thick consistency.

Apply some oil to your palms and take a little of the meat mixture in the palm of the hand (slightly smaller than the size of a ping-pong ball). Flatten it between your palms and put a little chutney (approx 1 tsp) into the centre of the meat mixture. Cover the chutney stuffing with the meat on all sides, form a round shape and flatten again. Refrigerate for an hour to firm up the uncooked kebabs. Shallow fry on both sides until dark brown. Drain oil on kitchen towels and serve hot.

Note: *Shammi kebabs are made in exactly the same way but without the chutney. This quantity will make 20 shammi kebabs.*

COMING SOON
THE METROPOLITAN BOROUGH OF HOLBORN
COLONEL SAAB

MUTTON WITH GLASS NOODLES

PHING-SHA (PRON: PING SHA)

I was fortunate enough to experience the stunning scenery of Ladakh in 2019. I honestly wasn't expecting much in terms of food and thought for once we could have a holiday that didn't revolve around produce and recipes and incessant chats with chefs. Was that possible? Of course not. I ended up cooking trout from the Indus River for a group of friends; found time to ferret out dried apricots for a jam and sought out the most delicious yak cheese made in nearby Zanskar (which is a great substitute for Parmesan).

Ladakh, because of its severe climate, high altitude and remoteness, has always been cut off from the rest of India. Until recently, the staple carb was barley or buckwheat. Lamb and chicken are wild, take ages to cook, given the altitude, and are served quite dry and chewy which the Ladakhi palate has grown accustomed to. There's fish from the Indus River, which is certainly fresh but has neither the sweetness of the West Bengal *bhetki* nor the salty savouriness of the west-coast pomfret. In terms of vegetables, there is an abundance of green leaves, sweet new white and purple potatoes from the valleys and herbs. Most noodle-stews and *thukpas* in Ladakhi cuisine do not use garlic. Instead, they use fresh onion and garlic chives, scallions and celery greens and fresh coriander. In winter, they use dried *kotstay* or wild garlic which is reconstituted in a tempering or *chhong* and added to soups for extra flavour. Fruit is pretty amazing – orchards of apricots, peaches, dozens of varieties of sweet and crisp apples, mulberries and cherries. Many of these are dried and sold in local markets all year round. Tiny apricot kernels (bitter almonds) and walnuts are some of the best I have ever had. A golden oil is extracted from the bitter almond which is used on the skin and hair to combat dryness at that altitude.

I came across two young women, Tsezin and Kunzes Angmo, who are doing marvellous things with breakfast. It's called the Artisanal Alchemy Breakfast experience and starts with a local bread, salad and cheese platter served with local white butter, seasoned with fresh thyme leaves, borage blossoms and organic local veggies. *Khambir* is a Ladakhi sourdough flat bread which is traditionally baked over a wood fire on a flat stone. They have converted part of their parents' house down a 'secret' lane in Leh, into an exquisite little B&B. The four-course feast, that could take up to three hours to get through, is made entirely by them. Some of the dishes are a little 'vernacular', like the butter tea with barley flour *kholak* – an acquired taste, but the interactive kneading is quite therapeutic. I would fly back to Leh for their walnut chutney and their in-house hummus made from Ladakhi *karzae dal*. Everything comes from farms not more than a couple of kilometres away and from their own orchard. A couple of dishes later (still breakfast), came *phing-sha* (mutton and glass noodles). Here's the recipe which clearly proves Ladakh has more to offer than just *thukpa* soup and *mokmok* dumplings.

Serves: 3–4

INGREDIENTS

1 medium-sized onion, chopped
2 medium-sized tomatoes, chopped
½ tsp red chilli powder
½-inch piece of ginger, peeled
Freshly ground pepper
250–300 g boneless meat (preferably leg of mutton), cut into thin slivers or small chunks
1 packet of rice glass noodles (*phing*)
2 tbsp cooking oil
Fresh coriander for garnish

METHOD

Heat oil in a pressure cooker. Add chopped onions to the oil and sauté till brown. Add the meat and sauté till the water evaporates and the meat browns. Add the chopped tomatoes, red chilli powder and salt and cook till the tomatoes are pulpy and the oil separates. Add the whole piece of ginger, some freshly ground pepper to taste, two cups water and pressure cook till the meat is done. Could be a while if you live in Ladakh!

Meanwhile, in a separate pan, boil 2 cups of water and add the *phing* (noodles) without trying to break them. Keep it for a minute and then turn off the heat. Let the *phing* soak in the hot water for a few minutes. Drain the noodles and roughly cut them into about 2-inch lengths on a board or with a pair of scissors. When the meat is cooked, add the cooked *phing* to it and let it boil for just 2–3 minutes. Garnish with fresh coriander.

Note: *At 11,000+ feet altitude, it takes very long to cook meat, so a pressure cooker is essential. At a lower altitude, the cooking time will greatly reduce so you may not even need a pressure cooker.*

In winter, this dish is made with dried onions that are stored in cellars and sun-dried tomatoes that are powdered. A teaspoon of the dried tomato powder is substituted for the fresh.

CARDAMOM MUTTON STEW

FOTO BHUNO GOSHT (PRON: PHOTO BOONO GOASHT)

Sindhis are an ethnic group who speak the Sindhi language and are native to the Sindh region, which is in modern-day Pakistan. After the Partition in 1947, most Sindhi Hindus and Sindhi Sikhs migrated to the newly independent India and other parts of the world. Many started small businesses and others became formidable international traders. They are all over the world and integrated into the local communities through marriage and education. Many speak several languages but continue to speak Sindhi. Having been part of a Sindhi family for many years through marriage, I noticed food was an integral binding factor, whether in Casablanca or Caracas, and there are some dishes like the famous Sindhi spinach mish mash, *sai bhaji* or the delicious bread and green chutney mish mash, *seyal dabal roti*, which I adore, which remain the same in any Sindhi home anywhere in the world. I also love Sindhi mutton. It's an easy, satisfying dish, often given to convalescents – a sort of Sindhi chicken soup for the soul – that is also recommended for nursing mothers.

Serves: 2

INGREDIENTS

½ kg mutton chops
6–8 pods of green cardamoms, ground with skin
2-inch piece of ginger, finely chopped
1 tsp black pepper, coarsely ground
3 tsp coriander powder
1 tbsp all-purpose flour
4 tbsp coriander leaves, finely chopped
4 tbsp oil or ghee
Sufficient water to cook the mutton
Salt to taste

METHOD

Heat oil or ghee in a degchi and fry the cardamom pods and finely chopped ginger till golden brown. Add the mutton chops and salt and continue frying. When the water from the mutton dries up, add the pepper and coriander powders and the flour. Stir and cook for a few more minutes and then add water to cover. Bring to the boil and then simmer till soft. The mutton should take around 30 minutes to cook in an open pot, less in a pressure cooker. It should have a stew-like consistency. Sprinkle the chopped coriander leaves on top before serving.

RAJASTHANI LAMB

LAAL MAANS (PRON: LAAL MAAS)

I am reliably informed by my chef friends that the best mutton (goat) in India comes from Rajasthan. Not surprising then that two of the most flavourful mutton dishes in the country come from this state – *Laal maans* and *junglee maans*. The Royal Rajputs from Jaipur and Mewar, led an action-packed life; when they were not at war, they spent months pursuing their favourite pastime – *shikaar* or hunting. Rather like golf today, *shikaar* camps were also an exercise in diplomacy and networking and somewhere the Maharajas could meet their counterparts from neighbouring states informally. Many dishes were invented and perfected on these hunts – *khad khargosh* (hare cooked in a sandpit), *sooar ki saanth* (curried wild boar), laal maans (red meat masala) which was often smoked and *junglee maans*. *Junglee maans* contains four basic ingredients – ghee, dried red *Mathania* chillies, salt and the meat, any meat. The game was cleaned and rubbed with salt. Then the ghee and hot red chillies were thrown into an earthenware pot along with the game and allowed to cook on a slow fire till soft. The problem is that without those specific chillies and really good quality ghee, the dish just doesn't taste the same. So here is *Laal Maans* or Red Meat which is easier to get right. This recipe was shared by Chef Simran Singh Thapar, Executive Chef at the Leela Palace Udaipur, who produces the best laal maans I have ever had – amazingly tender meat in a pool of spicy sauce enriched with a paste of *Mathania* chillies. *Mathania* chillies have a natural smoky flavour. If you can't get hold of them, substitute with any hot dried red chilli and smoke the dish as I have described below.

Serves: 2–3

INGREDIENTS

500 g mutton, cut into 2-inch pieces with bone
2 tbsp garlic paste
2 tbsp ginger paste
1 tbsp *Mathania* chilli paste (whole chillies stem removed, soaked for an hour in water and ground to a smooth paste)
1 tbsp coriander powder
1 tsp salt
¼ cup ghee
2 *Mathania* chillies dry (whole)
2-inch piece cinnamon
2 bay leaves
6-8 cloves
2 tbsp garlic chopped
4 black cardamoms
1 cup onion chopped
1 cup tomato, fresh purée

METHOD

Marinate mutton with ginger and garlic pastes, red chilli paste, coriander powder and salt for 2 hours at room temperature. Heat ghee, add the whole dry *Mathania* chillies, cinnamon stick, bay leaves, half the cloves, garlic and black cardamom and stir to allow the ghee to absorb the flavour of the spices. Add chopped onion and fry till golden brown. Add the marinated mutton. Leave the extra marination in the bowl. Cook well for 10 minutes on high heat then add the extra marinade and lower the heat. Cook for 5–7 minutes. Add hot water to cover, bring to a boil and simmer till the mutton pieces are soft. Remove the pieces from the gravy, strain the gravy. Cook the tomato puree till it reduces by half and add to the gravy. Cook over low heat till the gravy turns smooth. Add the pieces of mutton and cook for 5 more minutes.

To finish the dish, take a piece of burning charcoal and place in a bowl using tongs (!). Put this into the pot of laal maas. Add remaining cloves and a teaspoon of ghee to the hot charcoal in the bowl. Cover the pot and allow the smoke to be absorbed by the meat. Leave it covered for at least 5 minutes. Remove the bowl of charcoal before serving. Eat with paratha or millet rotis.

KASHMIRI LAMB IN A RICH RED SAUCE

ROGAN JOSH (PRON: ROWGUN JOE-SH)

I have never been to Kashmir. Every time I plan a trip, there's some political unrest which keeps me away. But I have been fortunate enough to try Kashmiri food in homes and at that marvellous restaurant in Delhi, Chor Bizarre, which specializes in the Kashmiri thirty-six-course *wazwan* and the Kashmiri *tarami* or thali. Kashmir to me spells India at its exotic best – the weather, stunning shawls, lakes, mountains, history and – of course – food. Kashmiri cooking traces its history to the fifteenth century when Timur (a Turco–Mongol from what is modern-day Uzbekistan, where he is known as Amir Timur) invaded India, resulting in the migration of accomplished woodcarvers, painters, weavers, architects, calligraphers and cooks from Samarkand to the Kashmir valley. His direct descendant was Babur, founder of the Mughal Empire, who ruled over most of the Indian subcontinent. *Wazas* are Kashmiri cooks with a lineage that traces its origins to Uzbekistan. The descendants of these cooks are the master chefs of Kashmir. So the elaborate feast prepared on special occasions came to be called *wazwan*. Kashmiri food is complex and beautiful and, like its culture and crafts, an alloy welded by some of the world's greatest warriors and civilizations.

Nestled in the Himalayas, Kashmir, with its almost legendary beauty of crystal-clear lakes and snow-clad mountains, depends largely on the valley of Srinagar for agricultural produce. Fruits and nuts are the only real crops of Kashmir. Kashmiri food is characterized by its subtle blending of fragrant spices (especially the world's most expensive spice – saffron), by its richness (often the results of nuts and poppy seeds) and by the use of asafoetida.

A Kashmiri pandit or Hindu feast will always have a red meat dish, a yellow curry or *kalia*, a white meat or vegetable preparation called *yakhni*, a *khatti* sabzi, a slow-cooked vegetable, fish, something crispy like *churma*, a green leafy vegetable and *kabargah* or koftas or fried lake fish. An old favourite which is hardly ever made anymore is *mutanjan pullao*, rice cooked with bone marrow, flavoured with saffron, *kewra* and green cardamom. Pandit dishes do not use *praan*, a small shallot onion with a garlicky flavour, nor do they use any garlic or onion but they eat meat and fish at every meal and give body to their gravies with yoghurt. Muslim Kashmiris also eat a large variety of meats, cooked with garlic, onion and whole spices. Both use Kashmiri red chilli, which has a bright red colour and a mild flavour. Everyday cooking often combines vegetable and meat in the same dish. Mutton and turnips, chicken and spinach, fish and lotus root. Pure vegetarian dishes include dum aloo – deep fried potatoes in a yoghurt-based gravy, and *chaman* – fried paneer (cottage cheese) and turnips with greens. Non-vegetarian dishes are considered in Kashmir to be a sign of lavish hospitality and, at a *wazwan* or banquet, not more than one or two vegetarian dishes are generally served. Sweets do not play an important role in Kashmiri cuisine. Instead *kahwa*, a fragrant saffron tea, is used to wash down a meal.

The aromatic Kashmiri *rogan josh* must be one of India's most famous curries. Like '*vindaloo*', that has so many hotchpotch versions, the *rogan josh* has a similar story. And as many people don't know that *vindalho* is a Goan dish with Portuguese origins, they are also clueless about the *rogan josh*, which is a Kashmiri dish of Mughal origin. *Roughan* means oil or ghee in Persian, while josh means to boil, braise or stew. There are two versions of this dish – a Hindu Pandit one and a Muslim one. Of the two versions, the Hindu Pandit version below, from my dear friend Sudha Raina, is the one I prefer. I have eaten it at her home and I loved the simplicity of the flavours. The Pandit version uses dry ginger powder, fennel seeds and yoghurt while the Muslim version uses Kashmiri pearl garlic and *praan* and no yoghurt whatsoever. They both use Kashmiri saffron and the bright red, mild Kashmiri chilli. The ideal meat is mutton (goat) and, if unavailable, lamb. The best and traditional cut is the shoulder for the Kashmiri Pandit version. In Kashmir, several natural colouring agents are used which give the curry that bright red colour; *mawal* or red cockscomb flower in the *Wazwaan* version, and *rattan jot*, a kind of wood shaving known as alkanet root or *alkanna tinctoria*, in the Pandit preparation. No authentic version of *rogan josh* has tomatoes and it is never stomach-wrenchingly spicy.

Serves: 4

INGREDIENTS

1 kg mutton (*adla* and *golboti*, shank and boneless goat meat), cut into 1½-inch chunks
750 g natural yoghurt, whisked till smooth
1 tbsp ginger powder
Salt to taste
¼ tsp asafoetida
1 tsp garam masala
¼ cup mustard oil
1 tbsp red Kashmiri chilli powder
2 tbsp fennel seeds made into a powder
4 cloves, crushed
8–10 small pods of green cardamom, powdered with skin
¼ tsp *kewra* extract
½ tsp strands of saffron

METHOD

Wash and marinate meat in a third of the yoghurt, ginger powder, salt, asafoetida and half the garam masala for at least 2 hours. Heat oil and slide the mutton into it. First cook on a slow fire and then on a high fire until the meat looks caramelized. Sprinkle some water to avoid burning. When the meat is brown, add red chilli powder, fennel powder, salt, the rest of the garam masala, crushed cloves, powdered cardamom, the remaining yoghurt and *kewra* extract. Cover and cook on a low heat until the meat is soft (around an hour). Remove the lid, add the saffron diluted in a little water. Stir through and serve with rice.

LUCKNOWI LAMB SHANKS

NIHARI (PRON: NEEHAREE)

Nihari is something very special in the history and repertoire of Mughlai food in India. I remember going to Hyderabad many years ago in the winter, waking up at the crack of dawn and taking a rickshaw to the Old City around the Charminar to try a breakfast specialty from a large cauldron called *Nalli Nihari*. This thin, slow-cooked soup of trotters and tongue, I was told, had been simmering away all night and was a Hyderabadi breakfast dish I had to try. *Nihari* involves the slow cooking of meat with stock in a large vessel. Though it can be made of mutton and chicken, *Nihari* is traditionally made with beef shanks.

Nihari comes from the Arabic *Nahaar*, which means 'early in the morning'. Nihari could include trotters, koftas and even goat head (*siri nihari*)!

In Delhi, Mughlai or Muslim food can still be found all over the old, and what is called the 'Walled City', areas of Turkman Gate and Jama Masjid. Dishes like *Siri Nihari* are mopped up with *baquerkhanis* (large Afghan style bread baked in a tandoor) or *khameeri* roti. I discovered a tiny hole in the wall eatery opposite Kali Masjid where this delicious roti, soft on the inside and crispy on the outside is still made. Nihari, though traditionally cooked all night, is available all day long and way into the night in the walled city. According to the late Sadia Dehlvi, a writer and food historian, who could trace her ancestry back to the bylanes of the walled city, a unique aspect of *nihari* is that a few kilos from each day's leftover is added to the next day's cooking. Called '*taar*', it is believed to be responsible for the unique flavour. There are some Nihari shops in Delhi who boast of unbroken taar going back more than a century.

The first time I ventured into the walled city, I took along a couple of hefty chefs for protection since nobody I knew in Delhi had ever been to Turkman Gate (incidentally the original gate is still there and is believed to have been constructed in the twelfth century, named after the Sufi saint Shah Turkman Bayabani). Everyone in the eatery stared as I walked in but they soon forgot about me as they tucked into their soupy meat or rushed away with their parcels. When we went to pay the bill, the owner refused to take any money. He said I was the first woman to sit in his eatery since his grandmother and so out of respect couldn't charge me. I was touched. As I looked around, I saw only men.

I am proud to say that I have been associated with the popular and very successful Bombay-themed café in London, Dishoom. I helped create the menu and concept and recruited the chefs in the cafe's initial stages. Relatively new to the menu is *Nihari*, which is only available at the Kings Cross branch. This is Corporate Chef Naved's recipe, which I have slightly tweaked. It combines a traditional and very refined 'curry' with a superlative (and quite large) shank of lamb. It is both flavourful, authentic and yet doesn't have that familiar layer of oil on top which you often find in Indian restaurants. I could eat Dishoom's *Nihari* every day (well if I was a size zero!). The lamb just falls off the bone and the spice is effective but not alarming. The gravy or *salan* is velvety with the grainy masalas having been strained out. It's not an easy dish and has several stages. Oh but it's so worth the attempt for that special dinner!

Serves: 4–6

INGREDIENTS

For the nihari
170 ml mustard oil
700 g onions, sliced
2 lamb shanks
4–6 lamb shoulder chops
500 g boneless lamb legs, cut into
4 cm chunks
60 g garlic paste
30 g ginger paste
4 tsp *deghi mirch* chilli powder
4 tsp turmeric, ground
10 g fine sea salt
200 g full-fat Greek yoghurt
1.2 l lamb stock
A large pinch of saffron strands
1 tbsp lime juice
1½ tsp rose water
1 tsp *kewra* water
2 tsp garam masala
¼ tsp ground cardamom
A large pinch of ground mace
1 tbsp chickpea (gram) flour

For the potli
1 tsp dried rose petals
1 tsp black peppercorns
4 cloves
2 bay leaves
5 pods of green cardamom
1 cinnamon stick, cut into pieces
1 tsp fennel seeds

To serve
Mint leaves
Coriander leaves
Ginger matchsticks
Lime wedges
Green chilli, finely sliced
Crispy fried onions
Crispy sesame and onion seed naan

METHOD

Place a large, wide saucepan over medium-high heat and add the mustard oil. Add a quarter of the onions and sauté for 15–20 minutes or until dark golden brown, while stirring regularly. Add a splash of water if they start to stick to the pan. For the *potli* (spice bundle), put the ingredients in a piece of muslin and tie with a kitchen string.

Add all the lamb meat to the onions and sauté until lightly seared – about 3–4 minutes. Turn the heat down to medium. Combine the garlic and ginger pastes and dilute the combined paste with 100 ml water, then add to the mix. Stir well and sauté for 5 minutes. Now add the potli. Scatter the remaining onions over the meat to form a layer, then sprinkle the chilli powder, turmeric and salt over the surface; do not stir. Lower the heat to a simmer, put the lid on and let the onions start to steam. After 5 minutes, stir and replace the lid. Let the onions cook covered for 45 minutes or until the lamb is soft; keep stirring regularly. The steam from the onions should be enough to prevent burning though you can add a little stock (from the quantity listed) if needed. When the onions have disintegrated, add the yoghurt and cook until the oil separates. Then add the lamb stock. Simmer gently for an hour, stirring occasionally. The lamb should be completely tender.

Turn off the heat and transfer the lamb to a plate with a slotted spoon, leaving most of the onions behind. Remove and discard the *potli*. Pass the sauce through a sieve into a large bowl or jug, pressing down firmly on the solids in the sieve to extract as much flavour as possible; discard the residue. Allow the sauce to settle for about 15 minutes, then skim off the fat and place it in a small bowl; reserve this. Pour the sauce back into the pan and bring to the boil over a high heat. Simmer rapidly for 10 minutes, skimming off any impurities from the surface. Add the saffron water, lime juice, rose water, *kewra* water, garam masala, ground cardamom and mace, and stir well. Now turn the heat right down.

Warm a small saucepan over medium high heat and add 2 tbsp of the reserved fat. Sprinkle in the chickpea flour and cook, stir for 2 minutes to make a thin roux. Allow to cool for a minute, then whisk into the stock over the heat and cook. Let it slightly thicken by whisking for a few minutes (be careful as it can splash). Return the lamb to the gravy and heat through gently, then transfer to a warmed serving dish. Serve with the plate of garnishes on the side and some warm sesame and onion seed naan.

OLD DELHI-STYLE LAMB AND LENTILS

DAL GOSHT (PRON: DAAHL GOASHT)

Sadia Dehlvi was my 'go-to' girl for anything to do with the food of Old Delhi. A rare combination of deep knowledge of the history and food of *Dilli* and ever ready to share! This is her sublime recipe for dal gosht from her book *Jasmin and Jinns*. The original recipe comes from the book *Razia ka Shahi Dastarkhwan*.

Here's an excerpt from her essay, 'Dilli Ka Dastarkhwan, Traditions of Food in Delhi', which she shared with me some ten years ago when I was working on a restaurant for the Hilton in Delhi which centerred around the food of Old *Dilli*:

'It was in the late fifties that my grandfather, Abba moved from our ancestral home in the *galikuchas* of the walled city to a sprawling bungalow in the plush area of Diplomatic Enclave in New Delhi. The house was designed by Kanvinde, a leading architect of the times who did a splendid job. The house with its large lawns and fountains came to be known as the *Shama Kothi*. Abba had by then made a tremendous success of *Shama*, the literary and film magazine in Urdu which he edited and published. To his first name Yusuf, he added Dehlvi, meaning "from Delhi" which stuck as a family name. As was the tradition with the Dilli nobility, Abba hosted *mushairas*, qawaalis, dance and music *mehfils* at the *kothi*. *Mahmannawaasi* (hospitality) was almost a religious virtue with *Dilliwalas* and Abba was known to have the finest cuisines of *Dilli* on his *dastarkhwan*.'

Serves: 4

INGREDIENTS

For the main dish

300 g chana dal
½ kg mutton *quorma* or plain *salan*

For the dal

300 g chana dal
½ tsp turmeric powder
1 tsp red chilli powder
½ tsp garlic paste
Salt to taste

For the quorma

1 kg mutton or chicken
1–1½ cups oil
2 tsp garlic paste
1½ tsp ginger paste
10 pods of green cardamoms
1 tsp red chilli powder
1 tsp *deghi mirch* powder

METHOD

Dal

Ideally, chana dal should be soaked in water for a few hours before cooking. Boil the dal with turmeric, red chilli, garlic paste and salt. Add just enough water for the dal to cook while remaining whole. If using a pressure cooker, one whistle is enough.

Quorma

Heat oil and fry meat along with garlic and ginger paste for 5–10 minutes till oil bubbles rise. Now add 5 pods of green cardamom, chilli powders, coriander powder, almond paste, cloves, nutmeg and mace, peppercorns, salt and curd to the meat. The *deghi mirch* adds a deep red colouring. Continue to fry the meat for 5–10 minutes till the oil rises. Now add 2–3 cups of water for the gravy. Cover and leave on low flame till almost done. Hand-crush the golden fried onions into tiny pieces. Do not use a blender as crushing by hand ensures the *danedar* or coarse, thick texture of the gravy. Lastly, add crushed onions, remaining pods of cardamom (crushed), and *kewra* to the meat. Cover and leave on low flame for another 5–10 minutes till

4 tsp coriander powder
Paste of 10–12 almonds
6 cloves
6 peppercorns
400 g yoghurt
¼ tsp nutmeg, crushed
¼ tsp mace, crushed
5–6 medium-sized onions, golden fried
1 tsp *kewra* water (optional)
Salt to taste

For the garnish
Dried mint or fresh mint leaves
Garam masala

the meat is tender. When the meat is soft and cooked, remove the oil layer and set aside. If it is left in the utensil, the chana dal will later absorb it all up.

When the dal is ready, add it to the mutton quorma. Take the oil that you set aside before and pour over the serving dish. Garnish with *sookha pudina* or dried mint or fresh mint leaves and a sprinkling of garam masala.

Tip: *If you want a really smooth gravy, blend the fried onions and curd together for a few seconds in a mixer. Another method is to add all these ingredients with the curd, mix well and then add to the meat.*

DATE AND TAMARIND CHUTNEY

This is a chutney made all over India. Some versions of it are quite simple with just tamarind and jaggery boiled together and strained, while others are quite complex with additional spices and dates. This one comes somewhere in between – it has enough complexity of flavours to make it interesting but not too many ingredients to make it a pain to prepare. It is also the base of most chaats – our beloved savoury street snack.

In India, we are fortunate enough to find fresh and dry tamarind very easily. We make tamarind pulp by soaking this for a few hours in boiling hot water, making a wet paste by hand, and then straining the pulp. You can buy readymade pulp abroad, but it is often dark and concentrated. In that case, please reduce the quantity of pulp in the recipe by half.

INGREDIENTS

½ tsp red chilli powder
1 cup light brown tamarind pulp
½ cup jaggery
3 cups water
1 tsp finely chopped ginger
¼ tsp cumin
½ cup dates, deseeded and cut into 4, lengthwise
½ tsp cloves
2-inch stick of cinnamon
1 tsp Himalaya salt

METHOD

Put all ingredients together in a pan on a medium flame and bring to the boil. Simmer for about 10–15 minutes or until the ingredients turn soft. Sieve through a fine strainer. Put back in a pan and cook on a low flame until it reaches the consistency of a thick, pouring sauce. You should have two cups of chutney. Adjust the seasoning as per your taste. Cool and serve with any chaat, salad or raita. The chutney will keep in the fridge for weeks.

LIME AND CHILLI CHUTNEY

Pickles and chutneys are things our grandmothers used to make in summer – labour-intensive tasks which involved much cutting and drying and too many hours in the sun. This is a quick and simple recipe shared with me by my old friend Padu Hingorani. I kind of half-expected it not to work. Chutney in a pressure cooker? But, surprisingly and brilliantly, it did! I recently shared the recipe with a cousin of mine who lives in California. Unable to find green chillies and limes where she lives, she substituted them with habaneros and lemons and reported that the result was fantastic.

INGREDIENTS

30 limes, quartered and deseeded
4 tbsp sea salt
100 g green chillies, cut into ½-inch pieces
750 g sugar (preferably brown or organic)
2 tsp yellow split mustard seeds
2 tsp fenugreek seeds, finely ground
A pinch of turmeric powder
½ cup sugarcane or malt vinegar

METHOD

Mix the quartered limes with the salt and ensure there's no water.
Place in a glass or steel bowl and place the bowl in a pressure cooker.
Pour water in the pressure cooker, enough to come halfway up the bowl and cook for 15 minutes or until the limes become soft. Open the pressure cooker and add the green chillies to the bowl. Mix thoroughly. Close the pressure cooker again and cook for a further 5 minutes. Remove and transfer everything to a fresh glass bowl. Add the sugar while the mixture is very hot and stir well until the sugar melts. Stir in the spices. When the mixture cools down, add the vinegar. Mix well and store in airtight glass jars.
Eat after 3–4 days.

Tip: *So what do you do if you don't have a pressure cooker? In the old days, this chutney would have been 'cooked' in the sun in a big glass jar. If you don't have a pressure cooker, you can boil the limes with water to cover till soft and then add the rest of the ingredients.*

RAITAS

(PRON: R-EYE-THA)

Raita is basically anything with natural yoghurt to which you add fruit, vegetables and spices. In India, they accompany a meal, especially when there is rice on the table. In South India, a popular main course is *curd rice* where natural yoghurt is mixed with soft rice and a hot tempering to create a one-pot meal of sorts. I often have a big bowl of raita for lunch. Nothing else! Best to use fresh yoghurt or Greek yoghurt. These are some of my favourite raitas.

SPINACH WITH YOGHURT AND WALNUTS

Serves: 4

INGREDIENTS

3½ cups natural yoghurt, whipped lightly
½ tsp garlic paste
Salt to taste
1 tsp honey
1 big bunch or 500 g fresh spinach
1 tsp black pepper, coarsely ground
½ cup walnuts, finely chopped and some larger pieces for garnish

METHOD

Mix the garlic, salt and honey into the yoghurt. Blanch the spinach in boiling water in batches until it just wilts. Cool, drain and squeeze out all the excess water. Chop roughly. Add the blanched spinach and the fresh ground pepper to the yoghurt mixture and mix well. Stir in the chopped walnuts. Garnish with larger pieces of walnuts before serving.

Chill and serve as a salad or as a raita. You can also serve this as a dip. Buy a round, crusty loaf of bread. Carefully scoop out the centre, taking care not to touch the bottom and fill it with the dip. After all the dip is over, you can eat the bread which has by then soaked up some of the dip!

LADYFINGER AND MUSTARD RAITA

Serves: 4

INGREDIENTS

½ kg ladyfingers (okra)
½ cup fresh coconut, grated
2 tbsp mustard seeds, roasted
½ cup fresh coriander, chopped
4–6 green chillies, chopped
2 tbsp oil
3 cups yoghurt, whisked yoghurt
Salt to taste
A pinch of asafoetida
1 tbsp whole cumin, roasted
8–10 curry leaves, roasted

METHOD

Blend the grated coconut, 1 tbsp mustard seeds, chopped coriander and chopped green chilli to a fine paste with a little water. Cut the ladyfingers into very small pieces and stir-fry in half the oil till they turn nonsticky. Allow to cool. Add yoghurt to the coconut masala and puree in a blender. Season with salt. Add the chopped ladyfingers to the masala mixture in a bowl by hand. Heat the remaining oil and add the remaining mustard, asafoetida, cumin and curry leaves until the aroma changes and the mustard seeds begin to crackle. Pour the tempering onto the ladyfinger mixture. Mix well. Serve chilled. This can be served as a salad, dip or as an accompaniment to South Indian dishes.

RED PUMPKIN RAITA

Serves: 4

INGREDIENTS

¼ kg red pumpkin, peeled and cut into 1-inch cubes
2 cups yoghurt, whisked until smooth
½ tsp salt
½ tsp sugar
2 green chillies, chopped
1 tbsp peanut powder (made by grinding non-oily peanuts in a grinder)
2 tbsp fresh coriander, chopped
½ tsp cumin, roasted and coarsely crushed

METHOD

Steam the pumpkin in a colander over boiling water until soft (approximately 7–9 minutes). Cool and mash the steamed pumpkin roughly. Add the yoghurt, salt, sugar and green chillies to it and mix thoroughly. Garnish with peanut powder, fresh coriander and roasted cumin. Serve at room temperature.

PRASANNA GOKHALE'S TOMATO RAITA

Serves: 2

INGREDIENTS

3 medium-sized tomatoes
1½ cups yoghurt
3 green chillies
1½ tsp mustard seeds
1 tsp salt to taste
2 tsp sugar to taste

METHOD

Plunge the tomatoes into boiling water and blanch for 5–7 minutes. Remove, cool and peel the skins off. Put the yoghurt into a muslin cloth and drain for 2–3 hours. You will be left with a little less than one cup. Grind the green chillies and mustard together. Cut the peeled tomatoes in half, scoop out as many seeds as possible and throw away. Blend the tomatoes, the ground chilli-mustard, salt and sugar. Add to this the hung yoghurt. Whisk until well blended. Check and adjust the seasoning. Serve chilled.

MISHTI DOI CHEESECAKE

(PRON: MISHTEE DOI)

I created this dish for an Indian festival in Hong Kong (India by the Bay) which successfully ended a dinner titled 'Flavours of India'. While Indian food is such a hit internationally, people often find Indian sweets and desserts far too sweet and a bit vernacular. It is a safer bet to go for familiar desserts like cheesecake, chocolate mousse or bread & butter pudding and give them an Indian twist with the addition of Indian fruit or spices. This is my old New York cheesecake recipe. I substitute Bengali ingredients for the American ones. We also serve this at Colonel Saab in London.

Serves: 6–8

INGREDIENTS

750 g *mishti doi* (or cream cheese)
¾ cup *nolen gud* (palm jaggery), grated
1 tbsp cornflour
4 eggs
2 tbsp *gondhoraj* lemon juice, freshly squeezed (or the juice of kaffir lime)
1 tbsp *gondhoraj* lemon rind (or rind of kaffir lime – *magrut*)
1½ tsp vanilla extract
¼ tsp salt
1 cup thick cream
1½ cups digestive biscuits or Tiger glucose biscuits in India, crushed with 50 g melted butter

METHOD

Preheat the oven to 180°C. Grease an 8 x 2½-inch or higher spring form tin. Crumble the biscuits using a rolling pin or food processor. Pour in the melted butter and mix well. Press this butter-biscuit mix firmly into the base of the tin. Refrigerate for at least 1 hour till the base is firm. Remove and wrap the outside of the tin with a double layer of heavy-duty foil to prevent seepage. If you are using *mishti doi*, hang around a kilo in a muslin cloth for 4–6 hours to drain off the excess water so you are left with 750 g hung *mishti doi* (drained weight). In a large mixing bowl, beat the *doi* or cream cheese and palm jaggery until very smooth, preferably with an electric whisk. Now beat in the cornflour. Add the eggs, one at a time, beating the batter after the addition of each egg. Keep beating the mix until smooth and scrape down the sides. Add the lemon juice, vanilla and salt and beat until incorporated. Add in the thick cream and beat just until blended. Add the lime/lemon rind by hand.

Pour the mix into the prepared tin with the biscuit base. Set this tin with your cheesecake mix in a larger tin and pour in 1-inch of very hot water into the larger tin. This gives the cheesecake a lighter texture. Bake in an oven for 45 minutes, covered loosely with foil. Turn off the oven without opening the door and let the cake cool for an hour in the oven. Remove and cover with a plastic wrap (cling film) and refrigerate.

To unmould: Keep the cheesecake at room temperature for 10 minutes or dip into hot water for a few seconds. Wipe the sides of the tin with a hot, damp towel. Run a thin metal spatula around the sides of the cake and release the sides of the spring from tin. Garnish with a little lime rind.

Tip: *If you can't get your hands on mishti doi, substitute with half hung yoghurt and half cream cheese and increase the quantity of jaggery to one cup.*

ANDRAAB'S KEHWA - KASHMIRI TEA

(PRON: KAYVA)

I love the handwoven pashmina shawls that twin brothers Mubashir and Muzakir create under their brand Andraab. When you enter their store in Jaipur, you are first greeted by the shy and charming Muba, whom we all call Mubashir. He then serves you their famous Kashmiri tea. *Kahwa* or *Kehwa* can be made with green tea but, at Andraab, they make it with cinnamon, cardamom and Kashmiri saffron only (which they incidentally sell as well) so it's a sort of infusion. Served with a spot of Kashmiri honey, it is so delicious that it's hard to resist another cup and often buying another pashmina!

Serves: 1

INGREDIENTS

1-inch stick of cinnamon
2 pods of green cardamom
2–3 strands of Kashmiri saffron
1 cup hot water

METHOD

For every 1 cup of hot water, add 2–3 strands of saffron, 1-inch stick of cinnamon and 2 pods of green cardamom. Bring all the ingredients to a boil and let it simmer for a few minutes till the tea turns a golden-yellow colour and the fragrance of cardamom and cinnamon fills the air. Multiply the ingredients according to how many cups you require. Add honey if you need it.

And that brings us to the end of our journey of feasting through India! Bon appetit!

SUHANA SPICE MIXES

As much as I have tried to make regional Indian recipes accessible and easy to follow, there are days when you simply don't have the energy to cook but still want the luxury of a home-cooked meal. The idea of sifting through drawers for a whole bunch of spices or going through any lengthy cooking process is simply not welcoming. I came across Suhana spice blends over ten years ago when they asked me to help them with recipes on the back of their boxes, destined for the UK market. They have grown enormously as a company, from a small family business producing homestyle ground spices in 1962 (all made by their granny, the late Mrs Kamalbai Hukmichand Chordia) to the present-day state-of-the-art production facilities across India. They produce a range of products, including pickles, papads, a variety of ground spices, spice mixes and ayurvedic products. Vishal Chordia asked me to try some of the new range of masalas they had created for a possible launch in the UK last year. I received three boxes and I was quite sceptical at first. Could authenticity really be so convenient and come out of a packet? But, after trying them out, I must say I was amazed both at the quality of the taste and the ease of use. These spice mixes come in dry powder form and contain no artificial colours, flavours or additives and no MSG. And because they are powders that are sealed and preserved in hygienic foil pouches, they remain fresh for a long time. Most of them require you to only add water to make a paste. You can then fry the paste, add your cooked dal, vegetables or meat, heat through and serve. They offer nearly fifty amazing spice blends, based on recipes from all over India. I have included images of five of the most popular (and the most gobble-worthy) masalas here – butter chicken (*chicken makhani*), black dal (*dal makhani*), mutter paneer, prawns curry mix, and chicken biryani mix. So, you don't have to feel guilty if you use a packet every now and then to create an amazing curry. Trust me, no one will notice the difference!

INDIAN GRAVY
Suhana
TASTEMAKERS OF INDIA SINCE 1962
बटर चिकन मिक्स
BUTTER CHICKEN MIX
An unique spice blend for world famous Indian style Butter
COMPLETE SPICE MIX
JUST ADD
Tomato,
Chicken

Suhana
TASTEMAKERS OF INDIA SINCE 1962
चिकन बिरयानी मिक्स
CHICKEN BIRYANI MIX
COMPLETE SPICE MIX
JUST ADD
Chicken,
Rice

Suhana
मटर पनीर मिक्स
MUTTER PANEER MIX
COMPLETE SPICE MIX
JUST ADD
Tomato, Peas & Paneer

GLOSSARY

A

AAMRAS – mango puree, typically part of a Gujarati meal or thali
see 56

AMARKHAND – shrikhand (yoghurt dessert) with mango
see 82

AMCHUR – raw mango powder
see 60

APPAM – a round fermented rice pancake, crispy on the underbelly
see 88, 95, 96, 99, 100, 111

B

BAFAT MASALA – a mix of dry spices which includes a variety of dry red chillies, coriander, cumin, pepper and turmeric. It is also the name of a dish made by the Christian communities along the west coast from Mumbai to Mangalore
see 120, 121

BAINGAN KA BHARTA – a Punjabi dish of roasted and mashed aubergine, a spicy version of the Middle Eastern Moutabel
see 4

BARFI – a popular milk-based sweetmeat found in shops all over India. It is derivative of the Urdu word *barf*, which means snow
see 3

BATATA VADA – eaten almost like a vegetarian hamburger, potatoes coated in a chickpea batter and deep fried. Can be eaten as is or in bun known as pau
see 3

BHAJI – a vegetable dish in India
see 131, 218

BHAJIYA – crisp fritters made with vegetables, coated in a chickpea flour batter and deep fried till crisp
see 54, 57, 60, 121, 123

BHEL – in Bombay, bhel refers to bhel puri which is a savoury street snack of puffed or beaten rice and spices seasoned with tamarind and green chutneys
see 3, 123

BHUZNA – stone-ground masala made specifically by the Pathare Prabhu community and is also the name of a dish
see 140

BIRYANI – traditionally a Mughlai dish of rice cooked with spices and meat, it is said to have been invented in in the royal kitchens of the Mughal Empire in sixteenth-century northern India. The origin of biryani is probably from the Persian *pullao/pilaf*. It is said to have originated from *birinj* – the Persian word for rice
see 148, 89, 91,114, 148, 214

BUN CHOP – a beef cutlet in a white bread roll
see 3

C

CAFREAL – fried chicken in thick green masala
see 19, 31

CALDIN – a lightly spiced Portuguese – Goan curry made with coconut milk
see 3

CHAAT MASALA – very rarely made at home since there are many good commercial brands that make this available, chaat masala contains cumin seeds, black pepper, dry mango powder, asafoetida and black salt. Everything should be dry roasted for a minute and then ground to a fine powder. Used to zing to Indian street food and to sprinkle on kebabs and many North Indian specialities
see 60, 192, 197

CHAROLI /CHIRONJI – calumpang nuts which are often ground and added to kebabs to bind
see 215

CHEVDO/CHIVDA – called 'Bombay Mix' in the UK. A savoury snack made with flattened rice flakes, chickpea flour bits, nuts and spices
see 3, 54

CHHENCHKI – a stir-fried Bengali vegetable dish
see 154, 165

CHILLA – a pancake made with chickpea flour
see 57

CHOWNK – a tempering of spices in oil
see 54

CHUM CHUM – a Bengali sweetmeat
see 3

CHILLIES
Bedige or byadgi chilli – a relatively mild dry red chilli from Karnataka
see 40, 203

Boriya mirch – small round dry red chillies slightly bigger than a marble. Available all over India and have a lovely rounded (pardon the pun) flavour and a medium spice level. Not to be confused

with the roundish Scotch bonnet chilli which has a lethal spice level
see 67

Bhavnagari chilli – a large green chilli pepper, about 6-inches long, and cooked as a vegetable or stuffed and deep fried for *pakodas*. Mild flavour and spice level
see 68

Deggi mirch – a mild red chilli powder used in North India
see 227, 230

Kashmiri chilli – a mildly spicy, highly flavourful, bright red dry chilli grown now in Karnataka
see 15, 32, 40, 43, 44, 49, 104, 108, 204, 206, 225

Gavthi (Gavran) chilli – any local Indian dry red chilli, usually quite hot
see 141, 181

Mathania chilli – another lethally hot, bright red dry chilli from Rajasthan
see 221

Sankeshwar chilli – a slightly crinkly dry red chilli from the town of the same name near Kolhapur, used in Konkan and Malwani food
see 141

CHOURIÇO OR CHORIZ – Goa sausages or *chouriço* (pron: choriz) is a spicy cousin of the Portuguese and Spanish chorizo sausage. Made with chopped pork, salt and spices, the mixture is stuffed into a sausage casing, cured, dried and smoked over dried coconut husks. *Choriz* is native to the Iberian Peninsula, but the Goans have added red chilli and toddy vinegar to produce this indispensible item to the Goan kitchen. Goa sausages, as they are commonly called, are fried, casing removed and eaten in a bread roll, like a sandwich (*choriz – pao*), boiled with potatoes and onions like a spicy stew or added to *pullao* for added flavour. They should never be eaten raw
see 20, 30, 46

D

DALS
Chana dal – biggish yellow lentils
see 75, 129, 130, 171, 197, 230, 231

Tuvar dal – bright yellow lentils
see 67, 75, 76

Urad dal – small off-white lentils
see 75

Masoor dal – orange lentils
see 137, 163, 168

Whole masoor dal – brown lentils
see 137

Whole moong dal – green lentils
see 75

Moong dal – yellow lentils
see 75, 131

Matar dal – off-white round dried peas
see 164

DASTARKHAN – literally means 'tablecloth', but more generally refers to the lavish style of eating and entire meal setting of the Mughals, Nawabs and Muslim rulers of India
see 214

DRY PRAWNS – dry prawns or shrimp have been sun-dried and are used in Southeast Asian, Chinese and South Asian cuisines. They give a unique 'umami' flavour to *balchao* and *kismoor*. In Goa and along India's west coast, they are called *sungta*, *sookhem* or *galmo* and are available with the shell or without
see 143

DUM – to steam and slow cook
see 224

F

FLOURS
Atta – whole wheat flour
see 79

Bajra – pearl millet, ground into a flour
see 73

Besan – chickpea flour
see 83

Maida – refined flour
see 50, 51

FISH
Bhetki – barramundi
see 18, 104, 154, 157, 175, 178, 180, 218

Ilish – hilsa
see 154, 157

Katla – lake perch
see 157, 175, 177, 199

Karimeen – pearl spot
see 86, 89, 103, 104

Podimeen – anchovies
see 86, 90, 95

Rawas – threadfin or Indian salmon
see 104, 177, 202

Rohu/rui – river carp
see 175, 157

FARSAN – fried snacks usually made with chickpea flour and often tossed to make a snack mix that is popular in Gujarati

and Rajasthani cuisine
see 54

FRITHAD MASALA – a dry spice mix which is also the name of a dish associated with the East Indian community from Bombay. The masala consists of Kashmiri chillies, coriander, cumin, poppy seeds, sesame seeds, cinnamon, cardamom, peppercorns and cloves
see 121

G

GHEE – nutty tasting clarified butter popular all over India for cooking and in religious rituals. It is also used in Ayurvedic medicine
see 51, 55, 66, 67, 74, 76, 82, 83, 99, 110, 115, 118, 128, 136, 150, 158, 159, 164, 171, 172, 183, 196, 197, 203, 208, 220, 221, 224

GONDHORAJ – a heady fragrant lemon found in West Bengal which is similar to the Thai magrut
see 155, 175, 180, 238

GUISADO – a mild fish stew popular in Goa and of Portuguese origin
see 120

GULAB JAMUN – a very sweet Indian sweetmeat with its origins in Persia. It consists of deep-fried milk-based balls of dough which are then immersed in a sweet syrup
see 3

I

IDDIAPPAM – a rice vermicelli-like steamed cake
see 91

IDLI – steamed rice cakes
see 91

IMLI – tamarind
see 3

INDIAN BREADS
Bhaakri – millet flatbread
see 118, 121, 129, 135, 136, 137, 144, 145, 147

Brun – a type of white, crusty, round bread which is mainly found in Irani (Persian) bakeries in Bombay and Pune
see 3

Chapati – freshly made unleavened bread that most people eat in India
see 78, 131, 135, 202

Luchi – *puri* in West Bengal, made from refined all-purpose flour and deep fried
see 164, 171

Naan – a North Indian flatbread usually baked in a tandoor oven made with white flour
see 227

Paratha – A flaky, layered, unleavened bread cooked on the griddle usually made with whole- wheat flour. In Kerala, it is often made with refined flour
see 3, 57, 111, 165, 183, 221

Puri – can be made from whole- wheat or refined flour and deep fried. Eaten mainly in North India
see 3, 73, 80, 165

Roti – could be a *chapati*, rolled and cooked on a *tawa* or griddle or a *phulka* – a puffed roti made on a griddle on the gas and puffed over a flame
see 3, 54, 57, 67, 73, 78, 118, 129, 135, 136, 137, 143, 144, 147, 196, 197, 220, 221, 226

Sheermal – a saffron-flavoured traditional bread found in Moghlai dishes from Lucknow and Hyderabad
see 214

J

JALEBI – an orange coloured sweet, popular all over India, made from a flour and yoghurt batter which is deep-fried and then dipped in sugar syrup. The distinctive orange colour used to come from saffron but commercially artificial colour is used
see 57

K

KABARGAH – Kashimiri fried lamb ribs
see 224

KACHUMBER – a finely chopped salad of onion, tomato, cucumber and fresh green chilli, usually seasoned with salt and lime juice
see 67

KALVAN – a curry or gravy dish from coastal Maharashtra
see 140, 141

KHEEMA PAU – spiced mince served with a white roll
see 120

KHEEMA GUTLI – another word for *kheema pau*
see 3

KHOYA – reduced full fat milk
see 158

KOLAMBI – prawns in Marathi
see 140, 141, 143

KOOTU – a vegetable curry from Kerala and Tamil Nadu
see 208

KOSHIMBIR – a Marathi word for Kachumber
see 118

KADHI – a thin curry made with yoghurt and chickpea flour
see 54, 56, 57, 66, 128, 136

KACHAMPULI – a sour dense black vinegar made from the fermented juice of the dried Kodampuli fruit, which is found in Kerala and Coorg. The fruit is used to sour fish curries and the vinegar, only made in Coorg to my knowledge, is used specifically in Pandi Curry and other Coorg specialities. It looks a bit like Italian balsamic vinegar but has no hint of sweetness although the older ones can be a bit fruity
see 194-195, 212-213

KEWRA WATER – extract of the screwpine and a floral water used like rose water to flavour mainly Moghlai dishes
see 231

KHICHIDI – a mix of rice and dal, mixed with spices and sometimes ghee. A sort of wet savoury porridge
see 76

KISHMISH – yellow or brown raisins
see 171

KOFTA – an Indian meatball, can also be vegetarian
see 4, 224, 226

KOKUM – the sundried rind of a red/purple fruit which looks likes the Asian Mangosteen. It has a tangy sour flavour and is used much like lemon for its sour notes. It imparts a pinkish purple colour to drinks and curries. In Ayurveda, kokum is considered a 'cooling agent'. Made into a summer squash with jaggery, it reduces inflammation and the effects of a heat stroke. Along India's Konkan coast, it is also made into a sour spicy digestive drink with salt, green chilli and coconut milk known as *sol kadi*
see 13, 15, 18, 21, 27, 39, 40, 41, 44, 67, 118, 136, 137, 141, 157

L

LADDOO – a round sweet found in all sweetmeat shops in India. Usually made of flour (usually chickpea flour or semolina), fat
and sugar
see 83

LUKHMI – a crispy parcel stuffed with minced meat from Hyderabad
see 214

M

MISCUT – Goan mango pickle
see 15

MOKMOK – a steamed dumpling from Northeast India and Ladakh, (popularly called momo in India) stuffed with minced pork, chicken or vegetables
see 218

MALAI – cream collected from the top of the milk after boiling
see 3, 108, 154, 157, 172

METHI BHAJI – fresh fenugreek
see 28

MEWA – dried fruit
see 158

MITHAI – Indian sweetmeats
see 3, 83, 158

MISHTI DOI – yoghurt from Bangladesh, West Bengal and Assam, sweetened with palm jaggery, fermented and set in a terracotta pot
see 158, 236

MASALAS

Bengali garam masala – equal amounts of cinnamon, cloves and cardamom ground to a powder
see 157, 172, 183

Bhaja moshla/masala – a Bengali staple spice blend made from coriander, cumin, cardamom, bay leaf, dry red chillies and black pepper. Some people add fenugreek and fennel seeds which add a depth of flavour. All the spices are lightly roasted together and then ground into a fine powder
see 164, 174

Garam masala – basic garam masala contains black and green cardamom, black pepper, cloves, cassia bark, nutmeg and mace, roasted and ground together to a fine powder. In addition, it can also contain star anise, fennel seeds and bay leaf. Commercial garam masala often contains coriander and cumin powder too
see 71, 99, 109, 110, 111, 114, 137, 145, 157, 172, 183, 192, 205, 206, 225, 227, 231

Goda masala – used in many Maharashtrian dishes, all spices are individually roasted in a frying pan with a little sesame oil and then ground together. Traditionally, there are about 6 more spices in this recipe which are almost impossible to find outside Maharashtra or South India
see 135, 137, 145, 148

4 tbsp coriander seeds
4 tbsp cumin seeds
1 tsp sesame seeds
A pinch of asafoetida
¼ tsp turmeric
4 cloves
2 bay leaves
1 tsp black pepper
2-inch stick of cinnamon
1 cardamom (skin removed)
1 black cardamom pod (skin removed)
A pinch of grated nutmeg
1 piece mace
2 dried red chillies
½ tsp salt

Kanda lasun masala – usually store bought in Maharashtra since it is used in many dishes. It is a wettish mix of onion, garlic, red chilli and salt
see 145

Kashmiri masala – a readymade spice mix made by Pathak's UK which contains Kashmiri chillies, garlic, ginger and cumin
see 3, 4

Kolhapuri masala – roast and grind the following to a powder
see 4, 147

2-inch stick of cinnamon
½ tsp black pepper
1 piece of mace
1 tsp coriander seeds
1 bay leaf
2 tsp poppy seeds
¼ tsp cumin seeds
½ tsp fennel seeds
1 piece of star anise
1 green cardamom, skin removed
7–8 hot dry red chillies

Malabar masala – a simple recipe for Malvani masala. I call it Malabar masala but technically it isn't from that part of the coastline at all. All you need is a teaspoon or so of it, a little lemon juice and salt to liven up any seafood. Try it as a marinade for crab, clams, prawns and fish and even in a curry
see 144

Ingredients
10 dry red chillies (preferably Bedige or Kashmiri)
1 tsp coriander seeds
1 tsp black pepper
½ tsp black mustard seeds
Pinch of nutmeg
6 cloves
2-inch stick of cinnamon
A pinch of asafoetida
½ tsp turmeric

Paanch phoran – an aromatic Bengali spice mix similar to Chinese five spice. Used for vegetables as well as fish. It is made with equal amounts of fenugreek seeds, nigella, cumin, black mustard (or a tiny black mustard called *radhuni* which is more authentic) and fennel which are roasted and then ground to a powder
see 177

Sambhariyu masala – a Gujarati spice mix with the almost overpowering aroma of fenugreek seeds and asafoetida. Used with raw mango to make a fresh seasonal pickle. It also adds a wonderful Indian umami kick to a dish of rice in much the same way as Sichuan chilli oil does in Chinese food and furikake in Japanese
see 76

Podi – South Indian spice sprinkles usually made with either, curry leaf, peanuts or roasted channa. In addition to the main ingredient, there will be dry red chillies, urad dal, asafoetida, occasionally garlic and sometimes spices such as mustard seeds and pepper. They always contain salt. They are either sprinkled directly on rice but in the case of dosai milagai podi (gun powder chutney), it is mixed with a little sesame oil or ghee and eaten with dosa
see 60

MUTTON
Difference between mutton and lamb
What we call mutton in India is actually goat. We slow cook most meats in India. There is no concept of 'pink'. We also barbecue over coals but the meats and kebabs are well marinated first. If you are going to use English/Welsh/NZ lamb, the cooking time will be much less to the recipes in this book.

P

PACHADI – a South Indian chutney or raita
see 208

PANI PURI (also called phuchka and gol gappa) – a street snack made with an intensely savoury and spicy chilled water which is filled into a crisp roundel and eaten whole
see 123

PARA – fish pickle from Goa made from dried fish
see 15

PARAPPU – a yellow dal which is part of a traditional *Sadya* (banana leaf meal in Kerala)
see 208

PAU BHAJI – a spicy dish of mashed mixed vegetables served with soft buttered rolls
see 123

PERADA – guava cheese
see 15

PLOV – a Central Asian pullao or pilaf
see 114

PASANDA – a variation on the Urdu word *pasande*, meaning favourite, which refers to the prime cut of meat traditionally used for a dish. It was originally made with leg of lamb or goat flattened into strips, marinated and fried slowly till tender
see 205

PAYASAM – called *kheer* or *phirni* in North India, Payasam is another version

of a rice pudding. It is sometimes made with green moong and coconut milk
see 115

PHING – glass noodles that come packaged in different sizes of 30–40 g, depending on which one is used. In Leh, rice glass noodles are used. In some areas, where this is not available, mung bean glass noodles (vermicelli) are also used
see 218, 219

PORIYAL – Tamil word for a sautéed vegetable dish usually with grated coconut and spices
see 208

POTLI – a bunch of herbs or spices tied in a muslin cloth. An Indian bouquet garni
see 3, 132, 214, 227

PULLAO (or Pilaf) – a dish of rice cooked with stock and spices of Persian origin. In medieval Delhi, it was considered superior to the biryani
see 148, 154, 214, 224

Q

QUORMA – comes from the Urdu word 'to braise'. Korma or quorma is a dish of meat or vegetables braised with yoghurt or cream, water or stock, and spices to produce a thick white/light yellow sauce or gravy. Quorma has its roots in Moghlai cuisine and can be traced back to sixteenth-century India. Quormas were often prepared in the Moghal court kitchens, such as the famous white quorma, perhaps garnished with *vark*, said to have been served to Shah Jahan and his guests at the inauguration of the Taj Mahal
see 230, 231

R

RASAM – a thin sour and spicy water served hot and eaten along with rice in South India
see 208

RAITA – savoury yoghurt accompaniment to an Indian meal
see 129, 148, 166, 214, 232, 234, 235

RAVA – semolina
see 150

RICE
Ambemohr – Mango blossom short grain rice grown in Maharashtra
see 118, 136, 148

Basmati rice – long grain white rice grown in North India
see 3, 46

Kaima rice – Jeerakasala or Wayanadan Kaima rice is a short grained aromatic rice used especially for Calicut biryani (Kerala)
see 114

Red rice – usually unpolished rice available in Goa and Kerala
see 40, 41, 46

S

SAAG – a cooked Indian vegetable made usually with spinach or any green leafy vegetable
see 154

SALLI – thin fried potato straws
see 164, 210

SAMBHAR – a South Indian thin dal with vegetables and is usually served at breakfast with dosa, etc., and on a traditional banana leaf *sadya*
see 91

SEYAL DABAL ROTI – chapatis or bread layered with green chutney and cooked covered, eaten warm
see 197, 220

SHAAK – a Gujarati word for a vegetable dish
see 54, 57, 64, 68

SHENGDAANYA – peanut
see 136

SONDESH – a Bengali sweetmeat made from cottage cheese
see 154, 158

SALAN – a curried or gravy dish in Mughlai cuisine
see 193, 226, 230

SADYA – a traditional vegetarian meal served on a banana leaf in Kerala. It means banquet in Malayalam
see 94

SEV – a popular Indian snack food, consisting of small pieces of crunchy noodles made from chickpea flour paste, which are seasoned with turmeric, chilli and carom before being deep-fried
see 71, 123

SALT
Himalaya salt – natural pink mineral salt
see 232

Sea salt – non iodized white/grey salt mainly found in markets in India
see 15, 28, 39, 208, 227, 233

SUGARS
Jaggery – unrefined cane sugar blocks or powder. Ranges from golden to brown in colour, depending on how old it is
see 15, 50, 51, 66, 67, 76, 91, 95, 115, 118, 121, 128, 129, 132, 135, 136, 137, 148, 164, 184, 204, 208, 232, 236

Palm jaggery – unrefined, unprocessed sugar from the palm sap. It is sold in triangular blocks in Goa. Black jaggery can be found all along India's west coast from Goa down to Kerala
see 15, 154, 158, 236

Nolen gud – Palm jaggery or nolen gud as it is called in West Bengal is delicious and comes in semicircle blocks or a syrup like maple syrup. You can substitute with dark muscovado sugar but it doesn't give you the same candle wax texture of jaggery
see 154, 236

T

TARAMI – a Kashmiri silver thali or plate
see 224

TENGA – an Assamese thin fish curry
see 208

THUKPA – a noodle soup from the North East and Ladakh
see 218

TAMARIND PASTE – Tamarind paste is a tricky one because there are several varieties of tamarind and several pastes ranging from light brown in colour and sweet and sour in flavour to an almost black block which is intensely sour. In my recipes, I use the light brown one which I extract myself by soaking a ball of tamarind the size of a lime or *nimboo* in a cup of hot water for 20 minutes, mixing the pulp with my fingers and then straining it through a sieve
see 43, 103, 214

THECHA – a spicy Maharashtrian relish made with chilli, salt and garlic
see 121, 129, 125, 138

THORAN – a vegetable dish from Kerala cooked with grated coconut and always part of a *sadya*
see 94

TODDY – Toddy is the sap of the coconut palm. Unfermented toddy (called *neera*) is a harmless, inexpensive drink sold on the roadside along India's west coast. It is completely non-commercial and unbranded. Slightly fermented and with a very low alcohol content, toddy is used instead of yeast for the Goan bread *poiee* and for vinegar. This is sometimes called coconut vinegar
see 13, 20, 31, 32, 40, 45, 86, 103

U

UTENSILS
Degchi – a traditional utensil with a wider bottom and a smaller neck which is often made of brass, copper or steel
see 89, 147, 220

Handi – an everyday cooking utensil with straight sides made of brass, steel or aluminium
see 3, 64, 136, 145, 147, 150

Kadhai – an indian equivalent of a wok with two heavy round handles, made from brass, cast iron and nowadays often aluminium or nonstick
see 60, 68, 73, 75, 96, 103, 109, 110, 121, 132, 135, 136, 137, 138, 143, 145, 147, 165, 168, 174, 177, 181, 193, 197, 206, 209

Thali – a round plate usually with a raised edge used for everyday eating in most of India. Can be made of steel, bell metal or silver
see 54, 56, 63, 67, 79, 118, 138, 224

Urli – a South Indian wide, shallow utensil made of brass or bell metal
see 104, 112, 115

V

VADI – small lentil cake
see 130, 168

VARQ – silver leaf
see 150

VEGETABLES
Aubergine, brinjal, eggplant, baingan – all the same thing but in india a myriad of varieties
see 28, 36, 43, 49, 70, 71, 118, 135, 157, 166, 168

Bhendi – okra
see 40, 43, 192

Doodhi – long white pumpkin
see 36

Rajali banana – a long (not particularly pretty) banana used mainly in savoury dishes
see 70

Red pumpkin – butternut squash
see 28, 165, 168, 235

Shepu – dill
see 131

Surti papdi – a bit like edamame. If they are tender, you can eat the pods too
see 70

Sambhar onions – shallots
see 103, 107

Y

YAKHNI – a light thin curry made with yoghurt and saffron from Kashmir
see 224

RECIPE INDEX

ACKNOWLEDGEMENTS

There are several people without whose support and generosity *Masala Memsahib* would not have been possible. This book has had a relatively long and contorted history which began in 2020 as the pandemic got underway and India was locked down. A dear friend (yes, you, Atul Khanna) shouted one evening in the middle of helping us to strategize our food business, 'Time to do another book. Indian food this time!' He proceeded to introduce me to a bunch of people who could help, including Anuj Bahri, from the famous Delhi bookshop Bahrisons, who was to act as my agent. Unfortunately, Covid-19 hit everyone, including the publishing world. I trooped on relentlessly, writing, cooking, rummaging through photo albums and calling old friends to verify old stories. What began to emerge in the process was more than a cookbook. It became a culinary memoir of sorts. I finished the book that year itself and then became obsessively involved with a new project, an Indian restaurant in central London called Colonel Saab. It took and still takes my breath away. Thanks to Sohan Bhandari, the calmest, coolest executive chef I have ever met, for recreating some of the recipes for the restaurant. And, of course, Roop Partap Choudhary for giving me the opportunity to show off my skills and share my vision. Thanks also to Cath Lowe for capturing images of our early days.

Then Gavin Morris came into my life. He is responsible for the brilliant cover and an introduction to Hemali Sodhi, founder of A Suitable Agency, who acted as my de facto agent and found a home for the book with Pan Macmillan India, under Teesta Guha Sarkar. Finding the right publisher is, for an author, almost like finding the right partner – either it works or it doesn't. If it works, it's magic. If it doesn't, it's a disaster. Thank you, Teesta, for a joyful ride. And thank you to Shreya Gupta for persevering over the editing. Haitenlo Semy, you are a godsend, stepping in to design the pages of the book when Gavin couldn't. I would also like to thank Rabia Gupta (of RGD design), who did a fabulous job designing the initial twenty-page draft on which my pitch to publishers was based, and Pooja Vir, who diligently edited the same. The recipe images in the book were taken by Madhushree and Anindya Basu of Pikturenama Studios in Kolkata, who came to my rescue when no travel was possible. She cooked and styled, he did the photography and I did the art direction via Whatsapp – every evening after their young children had gone to bed (you might remember that schools in India were closed for almost two years!). Madhushree is also a great cook and was always at the other end of the line when I needed help cooking the Bengali recipes. Thanks also to my sponsor, Vishal Chordia of Suhana Masala (a brand of ready-to-cook spices I often use when I am pushed for time), who listened and said simply, 'I'll do it.' The standard of design and photography integral to a book like this was achieved thanks to his support.

Let's do the rest by chapter. A cookbook is as much about photography as recipes. A big thank you to Shantanu and Siddhanth Sheorey and the students of The One School Goa (Rahul Borge, Anuj Pratap Singh, Prithvi Patil, Surabhi J., Ganesh Mahajan) for capturing 'my' Goa so vividly in the Introduction. To Pedro Figuereido for sharing images of his grandmother, Maria de Lourdes, and their stunning south Goan mansion. To Sanjay Ramachandran, for the image from O Pedro and to the off-beat tour company in Goa, Soul Travelling. By the way, many of the vintage images in Goa are my personal ones taken over thirty years and many trips when we had a second home in Goa.

For the Gujarat chapter, a big thanks to Abhay Mangaldas for many of the images in the Introduction.

He also sent me numerous Gujarati cookery videos from the House of Mangaldas just in case I lost my way between the dhokla and the dhebra. In Kolkata, thanks to Mathures Paul who I hear gets up every morning at five to shoot the city as it awakens, for his captivating images of it. In Maharashtra, Pawan Manglani for his image of Kolhapuri mutton, Jayesh Paranjpe who specializes in off-beat tours of Pune and Maharashtra, for his contribution to the intro images, Nandita Khaire, family and friend, whom I would ring whenever I had doubts about Maharashtrian recipes and Sagar Deshmukh for his Prawn Thecha image. For Kerala, Asa Abraham, thank you for images from Kumarakom Lake Resort and Fort Kochi. And a big thank you to my old friend and Indophile Karen Levi Borley who kept all those old pictures of our first visit there in the mid-eighties and took some more gorgeous ones for the intro. There are many people to thank for the chapter titled 'Memorable Meals' and most of them are mentioned in the recipes themselves. Kaveri Ponnapa for her beautiful prose and her image of Pandi Curry, Vinayak Grover for the image from Kappa Chakka Kandhari; Sadat Sathak, thank you for the wonderful images from Old Kent estates and Coorg, and Giovanni Meghigian for that captivating picture of me and Petu Cariappa on his coffee estate. Bharath Ramamrutham, thank you for the brilliant photography of Chettinad mansions and Jigmet and Padma of Namza in Ladakh. It is difficult to take a bad picture of Ladakh but there are no words truly to describe your photography (I know they are destined for a fashion site) and your terrific food in Leh. To Krithika Subrahmanian whom I had the privilege of working with on her stunning heritage boutique hotel Svatma in Thanjavur.
The opening image of 'Memorable Meals' says it all. To Shamil Thakrar, founder-walla of Dishoom London (his words, not mine) for the opportunity to be a part of your pre-opening team and for the constant support and to Haarala Hamilton for the beautiful Nihari photograph from the *Dishoom* book.

Lastly, a big thanks to my own team – my family Yadu, Pogo and Sasha. Always there. Yadu for his indulgence, Pogo for this patience and Sasha for his energy. And, of course, Ms Devotion, Afra Fonceca, who has the memory of an elephant, tidies up all my scribbles and gets the job done. If there is anyone I've forgotten, please forgive me. You'll get a big hug and a book!